Iron Shipbuilding on the Thames

HMS *Albion*, from the Thames Ironwork Yard, 1896. Tower Hamlets Local History Library and Archives, London.

Iron Shipbuilding on the Thames, 1832–1915

An economic and business history

A J Arnold

LONDON AND NEW YORK

First published 2000 by Ashgate Publishing

Reissued 2018 by Routledge
2 Park Square, Milton Park, Abingdon, Oxon OX14 4RN
711 Third Avenue, New York, NY 10017, USA

Routledge is an imprint of the Taylor & Francis Group, an informa business

A Library of Congress record exists under LC control number: 00107107

ISBN 13: 978-1-138-72818-9 (hbk)
ISBN 13: 978-1-138-72816-5 (pbk)
ISBN 13: 978-1-315-19060-0 (ebk)

Typeset in *Times New Roman* by Password Publishing Services, Herefordshire, UK

Contents

Tables

Acknowledgements

I would particularly like to thank Chris Lloyd and David Rich of the Bancroft Local History Library, Tower Hamlets for their considerable help and patience with numerous obscure enquiries, Jenny Wraight of the Navy Historical Branch of the Admiralty Library and also staff at the Bishopsgate Institute Library, the National Maritime Museum, the library of the London School of Economics and the Guildhall Library for help with source material, David Lyons for supplying his listing of shipbuilders and ships built in the period 1825–60 as a check on published sources and John Armstrong, Bob Greenhill for his advice on shipping sources, and John and Mary Hoggard for their help concerning HMS *Warrior*.

In memory of C. J. Mare (shipbuilder), 1815–98

CHAPTER ONE

Introduction

Prior to the First World War, shipbuilding was one of the great capital goods industries and British shipbuilders 'enjoyed a supremacy such as few other industries are ever likely to rival' (Pollard 1952, p. 98; see also Lyon 1980, p. 8). British shipbuilders, 'year upon year launched around 60 per cent of world output' (Slaven 1992, p. 4), helped by the fact that the British merchant marine, representing 40 per cent of the world fleet even in 1914, was largely constructed in British yards. The pre-eminence of British shipbuilding provided strong support for the nation's political power and naval supremacy and the importance of shipbuilding during the nineteenth century was reinforced by the contribution that 'invisible earnings', based upon British domination of world trade, made to the balance of payments (McClelland and Reid 1985, p. 152).

While ships were built from wood, shipbuilding was a highly skilled craft and the Thames was the leading area in Britain, establishing an enviable reputation for the quality of its workmanship, expressed in such phrases as 'river built' and 'Blackwall fashion'. As iron began to replace wood, however, as the main material for the construction of large commercial and naval vessels, the British shipbuilding industry was transformed. Trade boomed and small, skilled craft-based firms were at first overtaken and then eliminated by large, technologically innovative businesses. During the period 1830–75, the shipbuilding trade expanded enormously, employment within the UK trebled, and a trade which was in 1830 still a craft, soon became a branch of the heavy engineering industry (Slaven 1980, p. 107).

Numerous books and articles have been written about the extraordinary growth of the iron shipbuilding trade on the Clyde, Tyne, Tees and Mersey and its impact on those areas,[1] particularly during the latter part of this period but they usually make little reference to the fact that London did not simply decline as the dominant technology changed; instead, with the 'introduction of iron as a shipbuilding material and of steam as the propelling power that supremacy became still more pronounced' (Pollard 1950, p. 72).

Having established itself as the pre-eminent area for the construction of both iron and wooden-hulled ships, shipbuilding on the Thames did then suffer a marked and rapid decline but the reasons for this have never been

1. See, for example, Walker (1984), Dougan (1968) and Keys and Smith (1996).

fully explored; only one article, Pollard (1950), specifically considers the reasons for the decline of shipbuilding on the Thames, although two more recent publications, by Banbury (1971) and Palmer (1993), do provide useful information thereon.

The most obvious factors do not provide a proper explanation for either the growth or the decline of iron shipbuilding; the distance of the London area from the major coal and iron deposits, for example, certainly represented a cost disadvantage which gradually weakened London's competitive position (Pollard 1950, p. 72), yet the region had never been close to the sources of raw materials relevant to ship construction.

The Thames did enjoy some geographically based advantages – its proximity to assured, locally based demand, to sources of capital, to suitable ship construction sites and to skilled labour – but these did not prevent its decline. Some commentators have blamed this on labour problems and costs, as the London shipbuilding unions were unusually well-organised and labour costs were higher than in some other shipbuilding areas. This must have been a contributory factor, as wages make up 30 to 50 per cent of the cost of a ship, but it is all too easy to exaggerate its importance. Pollard concluded instead that 'the Thames managed to hold its own in the first half of the century, when wage differences were just as great, and became increasingly unable to do so after 1850. The main reason for the geographical redistribution must lie elsewhere' (1950, p. 81). Moreover, as Palmer and others have emphasised, 'London's decline was not a consequence of a failure to recognise or act on the opportunities offered by new technology' (Palmer 1993, p. 60; see also Slaven 1980, pp. 110–14).

In the opinion of one historian of shipbuilding on the Clyde, the conditions on the Thames were in fact 'not so dramatically different from the Clyde – wages were higher in the London area, steel had to be transported further and ship repairing had a sapping effect – but none of these alone or collectively explains the demise of Thames shipbuilding during the period of expansion of the industry on Clydeside'. Instead he saw the fact that, within a comparatively short space of time, the country's leading shipbuilding area ceased to build ships at all,[2] as being due to 'mysterious reasons which continue to attract historians and economists to this day' (Walker 1984, p. 43).

The purpose of this book is to examine both the initial domination of the iron shipbuilding trade by firms located on the Thames and what Pollard has called 'the eclipse of one of the major London industries' (1950, p. 72), the factors that were causal and the effects the industry had on its

2. Although repair work did continue at a relatively modest level.

locality.

The dates which best define the rise and fall of the new trade are 1832 and 1915. On 28 August 1832, Maudslay, Sons and Field launched an iron steamboat they had made for the East India Company, the first iron vessel built on the Thames; in 1915 'serious shipbuilding ceased on the Thames' when J. & G. Rennie moved their business to Wivenhoe (Banbury 1971, p. 17).[3]

The chapters are arranged in a chronological sequence but it is the broad themes that were important in successive periods of time that have determined the precise periods of time applicable to each chapter. It will also be seen that the themes that were important to the trade themselves changed considerably over time.

Iron shipbuilding was highly specific to particular localities. The parish of Poplar, which includes the districts of Blackwall, Millwall, the Isle of Dogs and Cubitt Town was central, although some iron shipbuilding was carried out at Limehouse and on the south side of the river, between Deptford Dockyard and Greenwich College, neither of which are very far from Poplar and also at Chiswick, well inland of the City of London.

The explanations of events provided in this book rest essentially on two perspectives and on the provision of improved data series closely related thereto.

Firstly, the London shipbuilding trade has been seen as much in business as in industrial or economic terms. Clearly, the two perspectives are related, but there are important differences of scale. Economic or industry-level data is sufficiently broadly based to be representative and reliable and to avoid the risks of conclusions based upon relatively anecdotal sources; data at this level has therefore been provided across the period 1832–1915 to provide a consistent framework for analysis. On the other hand, where trades are dominated by small numbers of individual business units, success can depend as much on personal or micro-scale reasons as on broader economic factors and it is therefore equally important to examine the progress of at least the more important businesses and businessmen.

Secondly, existing explanations (and data series) have tended to emphasise the trade between shipbuilders and their customers in the private sector, despite the fact that the new technologies themselves transformed the nature of naval provision and the relationship between the Admiralty

3. After the First World War there were 'only three of the famous Thames yards left, all of them engaged in [building] small craft only; Edwards of Millwall, Fletcher Son and Fearnall of Limehouse and the Lea Shipping Company of Canning Town were the last survivors, apart from Pipers and Shrubsalls of Greenwich and some war efforts to build concrete ships' (Bowen 1938, p. 53).

and private sector shipbuilders. Pollard and Palmer, for example, have explained the decline in the London trade largely by reference to shifts in private sector demand, perhaps because no series were available on warship construction by firms in the private sector although, as Slaven has said 'it was the development of the naval market that had the most dramatic effect on the structure of the [British shipbuilding] industry' (1992, p. 8). Private sector firms constructed 10 per cent of the vessels built for the Navy in 1866–67 and 58 per cent in 1913 (Singleton 1992, p. 231), partly because naval contracts generally provided better profits than commercial work, although they could also go badly wrong.[4] Moreover, changes in the demands of the state (and of foreign navies) had specific and very important effects on the trade on the Thames.

In order to provide a better basis for these analyses, the existing data series have been extended at both the macro and regional levels. Firstly, at an aggregate national level, the UK tonnage figures of Mitchell and Deane, which are used as the starting point for almost all analyses of the industry, have been extended beyond their existing base of 'ships built in the UK for British Citizens or Companies' (Mitchell and Deane 1962, p. 220). Foreign citizens and companies, foreign navies and the British Admiralty were all important customers of British shipbuilders and new series have accordingly been constructed from primary sources in order to at least approximate the overall annual demand for British private sector shipbuilding tonnage. The result is a relatively comprehensive series of annual shipbuilding tonnages and numbers of vessels constructed across the period concerned. Secondly, the very useful series on aggregate London shipbuilding tonnage from 1866, produced by Palmer (1993),[5] and based upon the Mitchell and Deane series, has also been extended so as to include the tonnage built for foreign citizens, companies and navies and for the British Admiralty.

The book focuses on the iron shipbuilding trade. Inevitably there are definitional problems, because some ships were of composite construction (wood and iron), because all iron shipbuilders made wooden vessels as well and because firms that did concentrate on iron shipbuilding also built other products, such as bridges and dock gates, that could successfully utilise their facilities and expertise. Other firms that did not concentrate

4. See, in particular, Peebles (1987, pp. 38–40, 57–9, 79–81), Campbell (1980, pp. 66–9) and More (1982, pp. 176, 181).

5. Palmer's tonnage figures, based on Board of Trade data exclude (UK) Admiralty ships but include 'vessels built in various ports for sale overseas, both for military and mercantile use' (Palmer 1993, pp. 45, 50). Board of Trade returns, on which the regional analysis is based, were not available until 1866.

on the construction of iron-hulled boats, nonetheless made them very occasionally or only made small vessels. The ownership and identity of the firms concerned also varied over time.

Nonetheless, from examining the available sources, two things became clear. Firstly, there were eight private sector yards that produced iron-hulled ships on an appreciable scale during the overall period concerned and were used by the following firms:

1. Millwall Shipyard; William Fairbairn, John Scott Russell and Co., Millwall Ironworks and Shipbuilding Co. Ltd.
2. Orchard Shipyard, Bow Creek, Canning Town; Ditchburn and Mare (previously at Deptford), C. J. Mare and Co., Thames Ironworks and Shipbuilding Ltd.
3. Blackwall Yard; Money Wigram, R. & H. Green.
4. Samuda's Yard, Poplar; Samuda Bros. (previously at Orchard Place).
5. Norman Road, Greenwich; J. & G. Rennie .
6. Dudgeon Wharf, Cubitt Town; J. & W. Dudgeon.
7. Chiswick; John I. Thorneycroft and Co. Ltd.
8. Folly Shipyard, Poplar; Yarrow and Co. Ltd.

Secondly, the Orchard shipyard was by far the most innovative, successful and enduring iron shipbuilding site on the river. Accordingly, the appendices include annual tonnage figures (also subdivided by main type of customer) for the successive owners of that yard and, to the extent that data sources permit, also include the names, tonnages and brief descriptions of individual ships constructed in the main yards.

These improved data series provide the basis for a proper analysis of the iron shipbuilding trade on the river, although considerable use has also been made of less systematic and more anecdotal sources, including surviving memorabilia and the business records of the firms concerned, particularly those which occupied the eight main shipyards.

Three leading shipbuilding historians recently described the 'near total disappearance of the archives of the numerous enterprises which built on the River Thames' as 'the great misfortune in British shipbuilding history' and saw Thames shipbuilding as 'little better documented than King Arthur or Robin Hood' (Murphy et al. 1998, p. 163). It is hoped that this book will cast some light on at least the more important causes of the rise and fall of this fascinating and important trade, and thus ease this misfortune somewhat, and also help in some small way to commemorate the extraordinary efforts of those who struggled, and for a time succeeded, in establishing iron shipbuilding on the Thames.

CHAPTER TWO

Iron shipbuilding comes to rural London, 1832–46

For centuries, shipping and shipbuilding had been particularly important to the British economy and to its government, although this was not surprising; an island with highly-developed trading networks across the globe was bound to attach peculiar importance to the operation and construction of the major form of travel, transportation and communication.

While wood was the main material used in their construction, ships were quite small; in 1832, at the start of our period the UK was making about 750 boats a year of some importance, of an average weight of 125 net tons. It took a great deal of skill to ensure that the vessels were seaworthy and there were no particularly pronounced economies of scale, so that the trade was well distributed to a large number of towns and to many yards within those towns, given of course the availability of suitable riverside sites.

Although shipbuilding could take place successfully in small towns or even in villages, it was an activity which brought business to a number of related, ancillary trades, and thus tended to stimulate local trade and employment. The trade also benefited from being close to existing centres of trade and population, which provided a local demand for transportation services in general and, it was hoped, the construction of ships in particular. This was important because, throughout the period that ships were made largely from wood, shipbuilders satisfied a predominantly local market, rather than a national one.

Although the trade was dispersed, for centuries the Thames had been the leading area for shipbuilding in Britain and, at the start of the nineteenth century, there were fourteen shipbuilding firms of importance on the Thames, five at Rotherhithe, three at Limehouse,[1] two at Deptford and the others at Northfleet, Wapping, Blackwall and Shadwell, capable of building large ships for the East and West Indies or for the Navy. After London, the chief shipbuilding ports were Newcastle, Sunderland, Plymouth, Yarmouth and Rochester but few shipbuilders were in operation on the Clyde or Mersey.

1. Limehouse was apparently so called because of the numerous lime kilns on the banks of that part of the Thames, used primarily in connection with chalk excavation from the cliffs near Gravesend (Thames Ironwork Quarterly Gazette [TIQG] Vol. 1, p. 35).

London's dominance rested on the quantity of ships it built and on the widely attested quality of its work; the phrases 'river built' and 'Blackwall fashion' had by now passed into general usage as indicators of high-quality workmanship. The reasons for London's dominance are not hard to identify.

The London shipbuilders, at least until the middle of the nineteenth century, were 'essentially responsive to the demands of local ship-owners' (Palmer 1993, p. 57) and thus benefited from their proximity to assured, locally based demand, to sources of capital, to suitable ship construction sites and to concentrations of skilled labour.

The presence of the Admiralty in London helped the development of the local shipbuilding trade, although often in a rather fitful manner. Until 1689, the Royal Dockyards, including those at Woolwich and Deptford, met nearly all the needs of the state for warships and only occasionally did the Admiralty need to look to the private yards for help. In times of crisis, however, things were liable to be different and the facilities available in the Blackwall yard in particular were then greatly sought after as a supplement to the Royal Dockyards' construction of warships.

More generally, the private sector obtained a good deal of business during the great wars of the eighteenth century, when at least thirty private yards were working to full capacity in a two-mile stretch of the river from Globe Pier to Deptford Creek (Banbury 1971, p. 20) but, during the Napoleonic Wars, the effects on the trade were less beneficial; in 1802 for example, trade throughout the UK was at a very low level and there were very few contracts to be obtained anywhere (*Engineering* 21 April 1893, Editorial).

In more settled times, and while wood continued to be the preferred building material of the Admiralty, the Royal Dockyards could cope so that, during the thirty years after the end of the Napoleonic wars, the private yards received virtually no such orders. From 1832 until 1846, for example, less than twenty ships were built in private yards and many of these were small steam vessels and packets (Pool 1968, p. 213; see also Appendix 1) although, when the government did place contracts in the private sector, most of them went to firms on the Thames, who were experienced and conveniently local.

A government report, analysing expenditures on four categories of shipping work over the ten calendar years to 1847, for example, showed that:

- out of £419,000 spent on building ships, £247,000 (59 per cent) went to the Thames (Glasgow 11 per cent, Birkenhead 10 per cent, Liverpool 9 per cent and Greenock 6 per cent)
- out of £1,654,000 spent on marine machinery, £1,186,000 (72 per cent) went to the Thames (Birmingham 9 per cent, Liverpool and Glasgow each 7 per cent)
- out of £108,000 for repairing ships, £69,000 (64 per cent) went to the Thames

(Cowes 18 per cent, Liverpool 16 per cent) and finally, out of £274,000 on repairs to steam machinery, £147,000 (54 per cent) went to London (Birmingham 22 per cent, Liverpool 18 per cent).[2]

The economic importance of London itself was at this time more important than naval orders and depended on several closely related factors: it was by far the largest single consumer market in England, it was the centre of government and the royal court and thus operated as the focal point of conspicuous consumption and its attendant luxury trades, it was a pre-eminent manufacturing centre (although largely consisting of a diverse and unspectacular range of small businesses)[3] and, finally, it had long been the major port of the English import and transhipment trade (Jones 1976, p. 19).

Although it provided several, largely market-based advantages, London was distant from the major sources of raw materials, including fuel (which was expensive) and this meant that the capital encouraged certain types of business more than others. Trade was effectively promoted in such lines of business as high-value finished consumer goods and luxury products but, partly because this helped to raise the level of demand for scarce urban land and led to higher rents, large-scale factory-type production could be 'almost prohibitively expensive unless counterbalanced by very strong compensating advantages' (Jones 1976, pp. 20–21).

From the point of view of shipbuilding, the importance of the Port of London, as a means of commercial entry into and from the capital, was undoubtedly the most beneficial aspect, although it had not always functioned as helpfully as it might have done.

From 1588, it had been obligatory for Port of London merchandise to pass through one of twenty legal quays, all on the north bank of the river between the Tower and London Bridge, which were licensed by the Customs authorities to handle specified categories of imported materials. This was a logical but highly restrictive arrangement and the legal quays became very congested, particularly in the eighteenth century, when London was the world's busiest port (Elmers and Werner 1989, p. 4; *Port of London Monthly* July 1939, pp. 223–4).[4] Despite these inconveniences, London was pre-eminent; in 1700, 'the Port of London handled seventy-seven per cent by

---

2. P.P. UK Navy Appropriations and Expenditures, Return on Shipping, Cmd. XLI 1847–48.
3. As late as 1861, 14.9 per cent of all manufacturing workers in England and Wales were employed in London; Sheppard 1971, pp. 158–9).
4. Some sufferance wharves were, however, established 'mostly on the south side of the river, with limited rights for the discharge of certain goods brought there in barges' (Sheppard 1971, p. 110).

value of all Britain's foreign trade' (Wheatley, 1990, pp. 80–81) and in 1790, imports through the Port were still 70 per cent of the national total, although exports (themselves enhanced by transhipments of foreign goods) had fallen below 60 per cent and were to decline further in relative importance during the nineteenth century (Sheppard 1971, pp. 159–60).

The restrictions on the landing of such a large volume of goods often meant the mooring in mid-river of ocean-going ships, with their cargoes taken by hoy or lighter up the river to the legal quays, but an 'incredible piece of archaism, with all the pilfering it had permitted, came abruptly to an end' with the building of the docks (Rose 1951, pp. 125–6). The Howland Great Wet Dock was built at Rotherhithe in 1697–1700 as a safe place for light (empty) ships to lie up (Ritchie-Noakes 1987, p. 6) and other docks were then suggested. Several proposals found favour in the early years of the nineteenth century and led to a London dock boom; by 1815, despite the effects of the French wars, construction had been completed or at least begun on a series of new docks, the West India (1902), the East India (1906) and the London, Commercial and East Country, involving a total investment of around £5,000,000 (Stern 1952, pp. 70–71; Rose 1973, p. 51) which greatly improved seaborne access to London. This in turn provided its own considerable stimulus to the local seagoing trade, to the building of the vessels which carried it and also to economic activity in the immediate locality, particularly on the Isle of Dogs.

The beginnings of shipbuilding in iron

The early part of the nineteenth century was a period of considerable innovation. The use of a steam engine (then called a fire-engine) to move the paddle-wheels of a wooden-hulled boat had first been tried in 1788 and was taken further in 1803 when an engineer called Symington fitted engines into the *Charlotte Dundas* on the Forth of Clyde Canal, leading to the development of the first steamer (Henry Bell's *Comet*) for regular passenger traffic in 1812. By 1820, such vessels were more effective in their use of the power source and, therefore, far more common; a further 41 steamboats had been built on the Clyde, for example, by 1820.

At this time, steam was increasingly being used to propel boats with wooden hulls, despite the associated risk of fire, but iron was coming into increased use, both as a form of reinforcement and support in the construction of ships (even though it had to be bought in, rather than made, by the shipbuilders; Lyon 1980, p. 13) and in the form of boilers, engines and machinery.

On canals, where neither the fouling of hulls by marine growths nor compass deviations were a problem, iron had been used to construct barge hulls from the latter part of the eighteenth century; in 1787, John Wilkinson had launched an iron barge and Sir Samuel Bentham had built copper boats, exhibiting one on the Thames in 1794. Some canal boats made of iron were in use on the Midlands Canal by 1813 and the passenger barge *Vulcan* was built in 1819 for use on the Forth and Clyde Canal.

It was not until 1821, however, that the first iron-hulled vessel made a sea crossing, when the *Aaron Manby* used an 80-horse power engine built by Aaron Manby at Tipton to steam from London to Paris (Clapham 1964, p. 438; Cornford 1924, p. 28; Gardiner 1992, p. 47). Manby continued to make similar boats and John Grantham of Liverpool, David Napier and William Neilson of Glasgow and John Laird of Birkenhead all launched iron boats in the 1820s (Smith, March 1924).

Laird continued with the construction of iron ships, building two in 1832 and then making a larger paddle steamer, the 148-ton *Lady Lansdowne* in November 1833 for the City of Dublin Steam Packet Company (Hollett 1992, pp. 2–3). John Vernon on the Mersey and David Napier and Tod, McGregor and Wingate began to make iron ships on the Clyde in the mid-1830s (Napier 1912, p. 21; Slaven 1980, p. 112).

In 1830, the Council of the Forth and Clyde Canal, concerned about the potential effects of railway competition, contacted William Fairbairn, an engineer from Manchester, for advice. He thought that iron steamboats would provide the most useful way forward and he therefore built three iron sternwheelers in Manchester, including the *Lord Dundas* and the *Manchester*, which he sailed down the Irwell Navigation.

Iron shipbuilding comes to the Thames

The development of iron shipbuilding relied upon an initial technological transfer: the application of a material in widespread use on land to marine purposes. Thereafter, a whole series of innovative developments were necessary before the idea could become commercially worthwhile.

The actual idea of using iron for marine construction was a relatively revolutionary one and the important innovations in its initial development were made by engineers experienced in working with iron, rather than by existing shipbuilders, who had a long tradition of working with wood. In many ways, iron shipbuilding challenged rather than adapted existing approaches to shipbuilding and the transfer in 'ownership' of the new technology was probably responsible for the series of confrontations which marked its early history.

On the other hand, there were a number of secondary factors which were more evolutionary in nature and which encouraged the commercial exploitation of the new technology to take place within existing shipbuilding areas in general and, for a time, in the London area in particular.

Few technologies advance in isolation and the development of iron as a major constructional material for ships was linked to and partially dependent upon progress in two related technologies: the use of steam as the source of power, discussed above, and the slightly later development of the screw form of propulsion. This provided its own considerable impetus to changes in hull construction, for the screw 'imposed intolerable stresses on wooden hulls' (Peebles 1990, p. 26); the relatively small sections of wood used in ship construction were too easily loosened by vibration and wood was in any case 'too flexible for long, rigid drive-shafts, which needed careful alignment, and did not readily provide water-tight glands for the shaft to pass through' (Lyon 1980, p. 20).

Moreover, the new iron ships needed engines and other marine equipment which could be most easily obtained in existing shipbuilding areas. On the Thames, there was a great deal of accumulated experience at the highest levels of competence in marine engine construction and Pollard saw the 'early growth of engineering skill' in establishments such as Maudslays, Penns and Rennies as one of the most important factors fostering the expansion of the iron shipbuilding industry on the river in the period to 1850 (1950, p. 72).

In fact, the very first iron ship constructed in the south of England was built by the noted marine engineers and engine-makers, Maudslay Sons and Field of Lambeth (who had just changed their name from 'Henry Maudslay and Co., Engineers', the original name of the firm when it was formed in 1813). The East India Company in 1831 had invited tenders for four iron steamboats and four 'accommodation vessels' (Smith, March 1924) and the *Lord William Bentinck* was launched at Lambeth on 28 August 1832, to become the first iron vessel to be built on the Thames (Petree 1934–35, p. 42). Although Maudslay built one or two similar steamers in the next few years, they then stopped shipbuilding until 1865 (Petree 1934–35, p. 48).

Henry Maudslay had started the business in 1797, had moved to larger premises on Westminster Bridge Road, Lambeth in 1810, and began to build marine engines in 1814. The firm developed an admirable reputation, becoming the leading firm in marine engineering and engine-making and the training centre for a whole generation of mechanical engineers. When Henry retired, his family continued the business which, until 1835, was the only Thames firm to receive Admiralty contracts for engines.

In that year, the Admiralty widened their list to include other firms, including John Penn and Co., who had been building marine engines since 1825, but who were to really make their name in 1844, when the substitution of their own oscillating engines for the original beam engines on HMS *Black Eagle* produced the most successful results. The other leading firms were

Rennie of Norman Road, Greenwich, Seaward and Capel (of Canal Ironworks, Millwall) and Miller and Barnes who started at Glasshouse Fields, Ratcliff in 1822 and were later to be known as Miller and Ravenhill or Ravenhill and Salkeld. Predictably, given their location and technical expertise, it was the London engine-makers that dominated the naval demand for engines; in 1840, the engines of fifty out of seventy steamships in the Royal Navy had been built on the Thames (Banbury 1971, p. 199).

Improvements in marine engine performance were closely linked to the formation of the overseas mail companies and the London engine companies had close links with several of these companies, including Royal Mail, P&O, and Union Steam Ship, although others, such as Cunard, never had their ships built or engined on the Thames.

Royal Mail's first fleet of fourteen ships was one of the largest in the world and 'considerable difficulties were experienced in finding shipyards capable of undertaking the work'. In the end, and partly in order to ensure early delivery, the orders were spread over seven builders. The largest order was for the four ships built by Pitchers of Northfleet, who often used engines supplied by Maudslay.[5] At first, Royal Mail tried to have their major hull repair work carried out by the Royal Navy in their dry docks at Portsmouth but the delays consequent upon naval priorities proved too inconvenient and a contract was instead entered into in 1844 with Pitchers. Even this, however, was far from ideal, as it took a long time to send the ships from Southampton and the limited time that the caulking of wooden ships lasted, meant that the journeys were necessarily frequent (Bushell 1939, p. 38). The contacts established in connection with the construction of early wooden steamships tended to persist as ship design and methods of propulsion improved and helped to bring, but of course did not guarantee, further trade when iron-hulled boats were in demand.

London was also a good place for people who wanted to attract the attention of those in government or the Admiralty. When Fairbairn, who was encouraged by the success of the iron boats he had built in Manchester, decided to move to London in 1835 to build more iron ships, it was in the hope that it would not only enable him to carry out his 'entirely new and important principle of construction but to prove that his previous researches were entitled to consideration, both on the part of the government and those connected with the commercial enterprise of the country'. Instead, in his early years of building iron ships at Millwall, he experienced mostly the considerable opposition of the 'great builders and shipwrights of the capital' (Clapham 1964, p. 440), before facing active, local competition from other entrepreneurs who had been quickly attracted to the new technology and its possibilities.

---

5. W. H. Pitcher was also Royal Mail's first accountant (Bushell 1939, p. 12).

In the 1830s, the Peninsular Steam Navigation Company sailed from the Thames, and this was of considerable benefit to local shipbuilders and engine-makers. In 1836, Miller and Ravenhill were chosen to engine the *Iberia*, the first ship specifically built for the company, who also placed the construction orders for three of their first eight wooden paddle-steamers with firms on the Thames (four orders went to Scotland and one to Liverpool), one with Curling and Young of Limehouse (the *Iberia*) and two with Fletcher Son and Fearnall of Poplar (the *Braganza* and the *Don Juan*).

In 1841, however, Peninsular sold their wharf at Blackwall and began to sail from Southampton, where they were better able to expand their business. During the 1840s, they bought 24 ships direct from shipbuilders, of which seven were from Scotland, five from Merseyside and nine from the Thames. After three small Nile steamers of 40–60 tons, all built in London, Peninsular's first iron-hulled vessel of any size, *Pacha*, was built in 1842 by a favoured supplier, Tod and McGregor of Partick but, from 1845 until 1847, six contracts were placed on the Thames for iron paddle-steamers of reasonable size, two of which went to Money Wigram of Blackwall, two to Ditchburn and Mare and one each to Fairbairn and Miller and Ravenhill.[6] The tonnage increased from under 500 tons for the first to more than 1350 tons for the last three. Clapham has argued that it was P&O's 'success with the iron ship [that] did perhaps more than anything to establish it' (Clapham 1964, p. 440) and it was a source of considerable revenue to the shipbuilders concerned as P&O were prepared to pay over £40 a (gross) ton for their boats.[7]

Another source of local, passenger-based trade for local shipbuilders was the river service from London to Gravesend, the original down-river terminus for passenger traffic on the Thames. In January 1815, a 70-ton wooden paddler, the *Margery*, was put into service (although it was said never to work for more than three weeks at a time and thus to spend as much time under repair as in work).[8] Later the same year, a service was also provided to Margate. The introduction of steam as a form of ship propulsion brought keen competition to excursion traffic on the Thames, although the boats built in the 1820s and 1830s for the two main companies, the London and Gravesend and the London and Margate, were still rather primitive and

6. Money Wigram (*Ripon* 1508 g.t. and *Indus* 1386 g.t.); Ditchburn and Mare (*Ariel* 709 d.t. and *Erin* 1065 d.t.); Fairbairn (*Pottinger* 1401 g.t.); Miller and Ravenhill (*Madrid* 479 g.t.).
7. Calculations based upon listings in Rabson and O'Donoghue (1988).
8. The *Margery* had been built at Dumbarton for a Glasgow merchant but was instead bought by the London company and brought south via the Clyde, the Forth Canal and then the east coast (Smith, February 1924).

often consisted merely of the addition of engine power to the hulls of old sailing ships.

In 1816, another Clyde-built steamer, the *Argyle* (later renamed the *Thames*) steamed to London round Land's End and took over from the *Margery* in 1816. The *Regent*, the first steamboat built (by Courthorpe of Rotherhithe) and engined (by Maudslay of Lambeth) on the Thames, 112 tons, with side paddle-wheels, was soon in use, at least until its destruction by fire in July 1817 (Smith, February 1924). Between 1815 and 1822, twenty-one steam packets were put to work on the river, of which thirteen were built locally, four of them by Evans of Rotherhithe (who built HMS *Monkey* in 1820, the first steamboat used in the Royal Navy; Smith, February 1924) and the others by Searle of Westminster, Brent of Rotherhithe, Lafort of Blackfriars, Wallis of Blackwall and Brocklebank of Deptford, the last-named being one of the founders of the General Steam Navigation Company.

By 1825, 50,000 people were being taken to Margate by water each year (Howe 1966, pp. 216–17) and pleasure trips on river steamers on the Thames and Medway, particularly to Margate, became so popular that in some years the annual number of passengers exceeded a million (Cornford 1924, p. 28). Even in 1830, however, speed was very important in attracting trade and thus to the struggle for supremacy between the London and Margate and the London and Gravesend companies. Thomas Ditchburn, manager of Fletcher and Fearnall's shipyard at Limehouse, was one of the first designers to realise how modifications to the shape of a sailing boat's (wooden) hull could suit steam propulsion and his success in reshaping the Margate company's *Magnet*, and thereby increasing its speed, helped to bring business to his employers and also to establish his own personal reputation (Jordan 1925, p. 27).

By now, Ditchburn was convinced that 'iron was the material of the future' (Bowen 1944, p. 500) and he went into business with Charles Mare. In 1838, they designed and built the *Daylight*, *Moonlight*, *Starlight* and *Twilight* for the Iron Steamboat Company, that went on to establish a fleet of 16 boats. At this time, many of Ditchburn's professional brethren regarded him as 'out of his mind' but the ships, complete with oscillating engines made by John Penn, confounded their critics and helped the river companies to compete, even against the new railways which were opening, including the first line out of London, the London and Greenwich, opened in December 1838 and the Blackwall railway, opened in August 1841.

Fifteen steamboat companies eventually put 'craft in commission on the London river' (Burtt 1949, p. 29) and the largest of these, General Steam Navigation, formed in October 1824, also established important trade and mail contract business with the nearer parts of the continent (Palmer 1982, pp. 1–3). In 1837, before Ditchburn and Mare started building for the Iron

Steamboat Company, McGregor Laird had sought an interview with the directors of General Steam to persuade them to invest in an iron ship, the Rainbow, built in Liverpool on 'very stringent terms which allowed for a decrease in price if the vessel did not come up to expectations' (Palmer 1982, p. 16). The directors were apparently 'well pleased with the experiment' but Laird's special initiative did not establish a new trade with GSN, who did not build any more iron ships until 1845, when four were ordered in five years, all from Ditchburn and Mare on the Thames (Palmer 1982, pp. 14–16).[9]

The London trade in relative terms

London was a leading shipbuilding centre throughout the late eighteenth and early nineteenth century. At that time, shipbuilding output was relatively dispersed, geographically, although the tonnage statistics in Slaven (1993, pp. 153–4) and Palmer (1993, p. 47) indicate that the Thames made 13 per cent of the UK output in 1791 and 11 per cent in 1820. The Mersey and Wear were of similar importance, each with an output approximately double that of each of the next most important shipbuilding centres, the Bristol Channel, the South West, the Humber, the Clyde and the Tees. Similarly, in 1831 the Thames was providing work for the order of 15 per cent of the shipbuilding workers in the UK (Slaven 1980, p. 107) and remained 'the heart of both the old and the new industry' (Slaven 1992, p. 3), although the picture thereafter is less clear as detailed annual statistics on tonnage built are lacking for the important period from 1833 to 1865 (see Neal 1993, p. 112; also Palmer 1993).

The early innovations in shipbuilding did not always enable the firms concerned to take over large sections of the market. The availability of steam as a marine power source, for example, made an early initial impact but it was thirty years before its annual output approached that of sail (Slaven 1980, p. 115). Similarly, Slaven shows, from an analysis of a 20 per cent sample of all tonnage registered, that iron was taken up relatively slowly and was 'only used seriously in the 1840s' (eight times as many ships being built from iron in that decade as in the 1830s) and still represented only 9.5 per cent of UK construction in 1850 (Slaven 1980, p. 113).

Where innovations were adopted by shipbuilders in one particular area, however, the new technologies could be important to their market position. Recent analysis (cited by Slaven 1993, p. 157) indicates that the adoption of steam power helped the market position of firms on the Clyde from 1810–

9. The *Briton* in 1845 (204 registered tons), *Albion* 1848 (236), *Seine* and *Rhine* 1849 (262 and 378 tons respectively).

19 and the Thames from 1810 onwards. Between 1810 and 1819, London firms were building 14.5 per cent and, in the 1820s, 37 per cent of the UK's steam tonnage (Slaven 1993, pp. 157–8), a lead maintained into the 1840s. Sample-based data also shows that, in periods up to 1849, the Thames, Mersey and Clyde were the pioneers in iron construction, with the Thames having a 21 per cent share of the total market (Slaven 1980, p. 113; Slaven 1993, p. 159).

Liverpool was one of the earliest centres for iron shipbuilding, which grew to 26 per cent of its total output in the 1850s and 55 per cent in the following decade (Neal 1993, pp. 117–8) but, in the 1830s, only a handful of iron vessels were constructed.

The Clyde was a pioneering area for the building of steamships and produced slightly more than 20 per cent of UK steamship capacity in the 1820s and 1830s (Moss 1997, pp. 13–14). Iron shipbuilding on the Clyde was helped by the state of iron construction in the area, which had itself been advanced by the presence of rich deposits of coal in the Govan and Gorbals areas and by the financial support of the tobacco merchants in the eighteenth century (Devine 1990, pp. 37–42), and the first iron shipbuilding yard on the river was that of Tod and McGregor, established in 1837 opposite the Lancefield Foundry where they had previously worked. They laid out a larger yard in 1844 and other yards soon followed, particularly at Govan and Scotstoun.

Napier had moved his marine engineering business to the Clyde in 1821 and established the Lancefield Foundry, but in 1835 he leased the foundry to his cousin Robert and moved to London, where he believed the prospects for shipbuilding were better. Over the next twenty years, the Lancefield works, which Robert bought outright in 1841, became almost a 'kindergarten to the Clyde shipbuilding industry' and the place where many important shipbuilders learned their trade (Moss 1997, p. 14). Certainly, the area had local deposits of coal and ironstone and was thus better placed than any other river to develop iron shipbuilding, although in large part 'it was the business acumen of Robert Napier that was to make the Clyde's reputation for iron shipbuilding'. His practices included building deliberate 'loss leaders' to generate further business and investing as a shareholder in several shipping lines, notably Cunard, in order to secure shipbuilding orders (Moss 1997, p. 14).

Table 1: UK Shipbuilding statistics, 1832–46

	(1) UK (no.)	*(2)* UK (000) (n.t.)	*(3)* UK tonnage per cent Admiralty	*(4)* UK tonnage per cent London Admiralty
1832	747	92.2	2.1	1.0
1833	715	89.5	0.4	0.0
1834	786	101.0	0.7	0.0
1835	870	118.2	2.1	1.4
1836	686	87.2	0.7	0.0
1837	939	131.5	0.2	0.0
1838	1,094	157.6	0.3	0.0
1839	1,217	181.3	0.0	0.0
1840	1,373	212.0	0.3	0.0
1841	1,112	161.3	1.1	1.1
1842	915	130.0	0.1	0.1
1843	699	83.5	0.5	0.5
1844	689	95.0	0.0	0.0
1845	864	138.5	9.3	3.3
1846	813	127.3	1.5	1.1
Average p.a.	901	126.9	1.3	0.6

Notes: no. = number of vessels
n.t. = net tons
Displacement tons have been multiplied by 1.125 to convert them to net tons.

Sources: Mitchell and Deane (1962), pp. 220–22; Banbury (1971); Lyon (1993); Brassey (1883) private listings kindly made available by David Lyon.

The London trade generally gained from the proximity of the Admiralty, but in the period 1832–46 the benefit was quite modest. In part this was because the Admiralty had very little use for steamships, prior to the development of screw propulsion; the earliest method of using steam propulsion, involving the use of paddle-wheels, took up far too much of the broadside area normally devoted to guns and also presented an easy and damaging target to enemy guns (Lambert 1987, p. 103).

Table 1 shows, in column 1 the total number of ships built in the UK and in column 2 their aggregate tonnage for each year in the period 1832–46. The percentage of tonnage due to Admiralty contracts placed in private yards in the UK and in private yards in the London area are then shown in columns 3 and 4, respectively. Shipbuilding grew during this period and achieved an average annual tonnage of 126,900, well above the levels in the early 1830s and of those in the eighteenth century, when total UK tonnage never exceeded 100,000 tons a year. Equally it is clear that Admiralty contracts were of very little importance, averaging less than one and a half per cent of total tonnage, although it is worth noting that London did build half the modest amount of naval tonnage that was available (see also Appendix 1 for details of the ships concerned).

The effects of the iron shipbuilding trade

The iron shipbuilding trade had profound effects upon the organisational forms prevalent in the shipbuilding industry, on its labour force and on the areas in which shipbuilding took place.

There were some large yards on the Thames for building wooden ships, but most were smaller and employed only 20–30 men. Shipbuilding businesses at this time did not need large amounts of capital; the land was often rented, the men owned their own tools, the timber was bought on commercial bills and customers generally paid in instalments, which helped to fund the next round of materials and wage payments, as the work proceeded. The coming of steam brought some changes to but did not completely overturn these arrangements, as engines and boilers were specialist parts and were usually bought-in and assembled on site.

The new applications of iron-working techniques to marine vessels offered numerous advantages. Iron hulls could be considerably lighter, more rigid and far less vulnerable than wood to serious damage from, for example, accidental contact with submerged obstacles but there were also potential disadvantages, stemming from the fact that a single defective bolt or faulty plate could endanger the whole structure (*Working Man* 10 February 1866, p. 82).

The constructional tightness necessary for successful iron shipbuilding was recognised by its practitioners from the outset and appeared to provoke an ardent if not excessive use of force and hammering. The visual aspects of the new working arrangements were clearly both startling and impressive to contemporary observers.

The new techniques and skills transformed the shipbuilding trade from one which was largely craft-based to a specialised branch of heavy engineering industry (Slaven 1980, pp. 107–8). To use the facilities economically, business operations had to be conducted on a much greater scale than previously, and this soon raised the employment levels in some yards to more than 500 men. The new scale of operations also required far greater amounts of capital to be committed to the business, of the order of £5–25,000 (McClelland and Reid 1985, pp. 152–4). The various inputs were highly inflexible and meant that successful businessmen in the industry would also need the abilities and contacts to be able to raise sufficient capital and to attract sufficiently regular business to make good use of the more expensive, and extensive, facilities.

The traditional, wooden shipbuilding trade on the Thames had established its own, distinctive labour relations and working practices. In particular, there were considerable differences between the position and status of the most skilled workers, the shipwrights, and other shipyard workers. The shipwrights' union, the 'Shipwrights Provident Union of the Port of London', had been formed in 1824 and, after a successful strike in 1825, focused largely on wage-related issues, had become very powerful and was able to achieve good rates of pay for its members. Under agreed working arrangements, only union members could function as shipwrights in the Port of London and new entrants into the trade were required to undergo a seven-year apprenticeship. There were also other unions for those who worked in other trades within the industry, including joiners, blacksmiths and sawyers.

The amounts to be paid on the Thames for labour had been established in 1825, specified in a rate book, and did not change until the 1850s. Formally, however, the book applied to particular types of repair work on wooden ships carried out by shipwrights and did not apply to shipbuilding, or to other categories of work. Moreover, the rates specified the local norms and did not actually fix the cost of the work produced, which was based upon a 'job and task', not wage rate system.

The working practices in the traditional shipyards were both distinctive and well established. Shipwrights typically worked in groups and their 'leading hand' would agree the price for a particular piece of construction or repair work with the master. The men were then paid weekly wages at the agreed book rates (usually 6s 6d a day) as, effectively, an advance on the agreed sub-contract sum. The arrangement was clearly asymmetrical; if the weekly wages advanced were below the agreed sum, then the men would receive the balance but when the wages had absorbed the specified sum, the men were not willing or expected, under established practices, to continue without further wages.

The 'leading hand' and his fellow shipwrights would receive the same amounts of pay, although there were some variations to recognise the gradations in skill levels, these being largely determined by the union rather than by the master. The shipwrights were expected to maintain appropriate discipline over their own membership, as a form of quality control, and would also employ less skilled workers, including labourers, at much lower fixed rates of pay, of the order of 3s 4d to 3s 8d a day (Royal Commission on Trade Unions 1867–68, Minutes of Evidence, pp. 7–8).

The position adopted by the shipbuilder was fairly consistent and predictable; he would expect to charge a price for the work to be done which would amount in effect to the addition of a percentage to the payments he would make to the shipwrights and the materials that were likely to be used. The masters generally looked for a commission of 10 per cent on the sum agreed with the shipwrights, although the percentage could obviously vary according to the nature of the work concerned and in the light of current market conditions.

As a system, it clearly relied upon the predictability, experience and judgement of the main parties involved; assuming the masters generally were able to anticipate the sum that the shipwrights would expect, then the resultant pricing of jobs and their level of cost were both likely to be sensible, although the masters did not have particularly strong incentives to drive down wage rates. Obviously, the level of competition in the industry would exercise its usual discipline, although this was less effective in the case of repair work than shipbuilding, as the work was less standardised and often could not be properly costed until some initial 'opening-up' and exploratory work had been carried out. Also ship buyers tended to operate in local markets, so that well-established and widely-observed local practices would tend to persist, unless the outcome was so costly that buyers would feel the need to look elsewhere. In the London area this tended not to happen, although the prices were not particularly keen, because the shipyards concerned were known to deliver consistently high-quality work.

The new technologies for building iron-hulled vessels brought industrialisation into an area dominated by craft practices, themselves integral to the system of wage determination. The working of the new materials obviously owed far more to the power that only machinery could deliver, than to the types of skills necessary to shape wood and, therefore, greatly increased the importance of the level of investment in plant and equipment. The new arrangements also brought major changes to the working relationships between the shipbuilders and their employees; the power and influence of the shipwrights inevitably declined because their skills were no longer so important (McClelland and Reid 1985, p. 164), while the complex fragmentation of the assembly process for iron ships placed a premium on the employer's ability to co-ordinate the activities of disparate groups of employees and thus increased the control that the shipbuilders were able to exercise.

Environmental effects

Commercial and industrial pressures and opportunities in London in the twentieth century have operated so as to provide a strong impression of almost uninterrupted development, and journeys from the City have to be quite lengthy before the countryside is reached. Yet, as maps of London in the first half of the nineteenth century make clear, the patterns of development were patchy until comparatively recent times. The Thames, although the source of considerable wealth and numerous commercial opportunities, also imposed its own considerable restrictions on patterns of development in the marshy areas of its flood plain, particularly south of the river and to the east. Even on the north side, east of the Regents Canal, there were very extensive areas of land in Poplar, including parts of Bow, in the flood plain of the River Lea and on the Isle of Dogs, that were often waterlogged and accordingly difficult to develop.

The early shipyards were generally established in hamlets along the river which, even when quite small, were still of considerable importance to the early development of the city. Shipbuilding had been developed at Ratcliff, the port of Stepney, in the early sixteenth century. Wapping and Limehouse were also important and it is known that there was a shipyard at the latter in 1597 belonging to Joseph Pett (Rose 1973, pp. 10–11). Another shipbuilding centre, Rotherhithe, although built up in parts, was a low-lying, marshy area, containing 'no hedges or other kind of fence, nothing but ditches [that] formed a complete network of water all over the parish'. Until well into the nineteenth century, there were unobstructed views across most of the parish, much of which was given over to the cropping of hay. The water was clean enough that 'every ditch abounded with eels', others contained carp, and salmon and snipe was so prevalent that sportsmen considered the area a 'first-rate shooting ground' (Beck 1907, pp. 194–5).

After the East India Company was established, the focus of London shipbuilding moved towards Blackwall. As late as 1835 the shipyard there was thought to be one of the 'most considerable private [dockyard] concerns in Europe' (Green and Wigram 1881, p. 60; Elmers and Werner 1989, p. 17) although the yard's immediate locality remained rural; 'George Green himself had a house next to the shipyard, and fields where he kept his cows' (Rose 1973, p. 144). At this time, Deptford, Northfleet and Shadwell had also become important areas for shipbuilding but the nearby Isle of Dogs had not, despite the proximity of the Blackwall yard at its north-eastern extremity.

The area was originally known as Stepney Marsh and had always been tidal. In places it was as much as seven feet below high water mark and, in the seventeenth century, embankments along the river were raised so that parts of the land could be used for pasture (Hostettler 1990, p. 1; Stern 1952, p. 66). In the eighteenth century, large parts were still bog, covered with reeds and inundated during the wet season, but elsewhere the intersections of dikes and drainage channels provided good pasture for cattle, and the area began to be used quite extensively for the fattening of cattle and sheep prior to their sale on the London markets.

A few businesses were attracted by the space readily available in the area and, by the early years of the nineteenth century, some ship-breaking and mast-making businesses, a boat-builder's shop, several oil and corn mills and the Mill Wall foundry had been established on the riverside.[10] The area really began to change when the West India Docks were built in 1800–02 to the north of the 'island' and the East India Docks in 1804–06 to the east. These initiatives finally confronted the difficulties of access to and unloading at the Port of London and thus also stimulated the local shipping trade and, therefore, shipbuilding and other economic activity in the locality.

In 1811 a 'very extensive iron works' was established at Millwall by Jukes Coulson and Co. complete with a forge and rolling mills worked by two steam engines (Cowper 1853, p. 60) and the following year the relevant permissions were given for a ferry to operate between Greenwich and the Isle of Dogs and for the construction of the connecting toll roads. Despite this, much of the area remained meadow and marshland, a cattle-owner offering the West India Dock Company in 1829 '£2 a week for permission to pasture his stock on the company's grassland south of the City Canal' (Stern 1952, p. 67) but elsewhere, particularly next to the river, the pace of industrial development was quickening, with additional barge and boat yards, timber yards, wharves, oil and other warehouses, the chemical-processing works of the Imperial Gas Light and Coke Co. (dating from 1824), a tar works, a smithy and two cement works all coming to the area (Survey of London 1994, p. 386; Hostettler 1990, p. 4).

In the mid-1830s, when Fairbairn and Napier were looking for suitable sites for their new iron shipbuilding businesses, they were attracted to totally undeveloped sites at Millwall and when Ditchburn and Mare needed to relocate in 1838 they were able to move to the Orchard Shipyard in Canning Town, a largely undeveloped area a little further east, where the Lea joins the Thames. Further encouragement to develop the area came with the opening up of the Eastern Counties Railway in 1839 and of the London and Blackwall Railway in 1841, and the completion of the Thames tunnel in 1843, each of which helped to reduce the relative isolation of the district.[11]

In 1844, major changes began to take place east of the river Lea, following the passing of the Metropolitan Buildings Act, which 'severely restricted many toxic and noxious industries from operating in London and Middlesex', but did not apply to Essex, which began at the river Lea and contained the important industrial towns of West Ham, Stratford and Canning Town. Many noxious trades relocated into Essex (Pewsey 1996, p. 5) and the areas along the Thames and the Lea, which had long been used for silk-weaving, calico-printing and then distilling and gunpowder-making,

10. Although the terms are sometimes used inconsistently, it is normal to use 'Millwall' for the western half of the Isle of Dogs and 'Cubitt Town' for the east side, south of Blackwall.

11. The first railway out of London was the London and Greenwich, opened in 1838.

attracted further trades including chemical works, blacking factories, slate works, smelting works, floor-cloth works, breweries, distilleries, india-rubber works, manure, paint, printing ink, tarpaulin and ginger-beer factories, waterproofing works, creosote and coal-tar manufacturies and even factories for the rendering down of animal carcasses for tallow, soap and glue.

The by-laws concerning building and the emission of fumes and smells remained 'less stringent than in London' for quite some time (Howarth and Wilson 1907, pp. 139–45) and there were no by-laws relating to offensive trades in West Ham until 1885; some thought that the West Ham local authority was 'deliberately lax in its enforcement of slaughterhouse, building, factory and smoke regulations', in order to accelerate industrial development, even when it was offensive, which produced 'dirt, fumes and obnoxious waste' and was 'exceptionally destructive of the amenity of their surroundings'. A contemporary account of the manufacturing districts of West Ham, for example, speaks of the buildings and their surroundings as 'pleasing to none of the senses' (Jones 1976, p. 26; University of London 1966, p. 13; see also Howarth and Wilson 1907, pp. 109–45). Additional incentives to relocate were also provided by cheap cartage to the City, by the cheapness of land, some of which could be bought down to the water's edge (which saved on landing charges) and by the availability of Irish labour initially brought into the area by the docks.

The main Thames yards

During the period 1832–46, a number of entrepreneurs made iron ships on the Thames. The first iron ship was made and then launched by Maudslay, the renowned Thames marine engineers, in August 1832 but they saw greater potential in their main line of business and built only a few more ships.

Two experienced businessmen moved to London and set up their operations in Millwall, on the largely undeveloped Isle of Dogs; the engineer, William Fairbairn, who had experienced some success in pioneering work on iron ships, moved from Manchester and the shipbuilder David Napier moved from the Clyde in 1835. The experienced designer, Thomas Ditchburn, who was working as a shipyard manager, was convinced that iron was the material of the future and decided to go into business with Charles Mare in 1837 to make iron ships, initially at Dudman's Dock, Deptford and then at the Orchard Shipyard, by Bow Creek. The noted marine engineers, Miller and Barnes, in 1838 moved to Orchard Wharf and almost immediately began to build iron ships. Both Fairbairn, and Ditchburn and Mare, produced large numbers of iron ships but the output levels of Napier and of Miller and Barnes were quite low.

In the early 1840s, Money Wigram, the Samuda brothers and George

Rennie all decided to build iron ships. Wigram was an experienced shipbuilder and his decision caused a rift with Green and the subdivision of their historic Blackwall yard. The Samuda brothers had achieved some success in other branches of engineering but they decided to establish a yard for building iron ships, close to Ditchburn and Mare's new yard. Rennie was a successful marine engineer on the river who decided to diversify although, at first, his output of iron ships was small.

Sir William Fairbairn (Yard 1: Millwall Shipyard) – see also Appendix 3

In 1830, William Fairbairn (1789–1874) and his partner, James Lillie, had been in business for thirteen years and were running one of the largest engineering works in Manchester, which employed 'upwards of 300 hands' (Pole 1970, p. xii). Initially, they specialised in making waterwheels and constructing mills, typically around an iron frame. Enormous amounts of warehouse property were being lost in the Liverpool area from fires and Fairbairn paid particular attention to making mills that were 'fire-proof'. In 1841, Fairbairn was to construct a corn-mill which was thought to be the 'first all-iron building of its kind in England' (Pole 1970, p. 184).

Fairbairn and Lillie began to diversify into the manufacture of steam engines and in 1831 built two small iron-hulled canal boats, the *Lord Dundas* and the *Manchester*. Although the boats were small, they were much larger than the iron barges that had been used on canals for many years and the strength, buoyancy, lightness and speed of the vessels, which had rear paddles and a high-pressure, 40-horsepower engine, convinced Fairbairn of the more general advantages of iron construction for marine purposes.

They built several similar ships but the inconvenience of having to take boats of 100–250 tons apart in Manchester, where they had been built, and reassemble them at a seaport was considerable and did not seem to make sense. Fairbairn was convinced that iron shipbuilding would be the 'new thing' and he decided to establish an additional works for shipbuilding, either in Liverpool or London. Lillie did not favour these changes, however, and the disagreements, coming at a time when they had lost a good deal of money in a cotton-mill speculation, led to the ending of the partnership in 1832 (Bowen August 1952, p. 245; Simmons and Biddle 1997, p. 154).

Fairbairn carried on the Manchester business on his own and, after some further experimentation, formed a new partnership in early 1835 with an able engineering pupil of his, Andrew Murray (who was later to become chief engineer at Portsmouth Dockyard) and a Mr Hetherington. They bought a three-acre site in Millwall that was completely undeveloped, apart from a row of old cottages, in order to establish a new shipyard for the construction of iron ships.

Fairbairn was an experienced engineer and his choice of Millwall, which offered cheap land and premises but was remote from iron-ore deposits and other facilities, as the most suitable place for his work on iron shipbuilding is significant, although his choice of a London location may have been partly influenced by his ambitions to make his mark in public life. He had also worked in London from 1811–13, although his experience was not a happy one as he suffered from the restrictive entry conditions of the local Millwrights Society.

By 1836 they had laid out a yard suitable for building large iron ships and bridges, planned on a 'very extensive scale, comprising engineer's fittings and erecting shops, joiners and pattern makers shops, iron and brass foundries, smithies and a remarkably handsome chimney shaft' (Cowper 1853, p. 70). The outlay was heavy but Fairbairn was at least able to borrow most of the funds concerned (Pole 1970, p. 336).

The business, known as William Fairbairn and Sons, started well. Their first ship was the 175-ton paddler *Ludwig*, built for work on Lake Constance and within a year they had orders for twelve iron ships of 335 tons each for the East India Company. They also built the 14-ton *Little Dreadnought* (which they used themselves for ferrying men and materials to jobs afloat) and the *Sirius*, in 1837 the first iron ship listed by Lloyds. They gradually became well-known for their shallow-draught paddlers, many of which were built for foreign customers. As well as relatively standard ships, Fairbairn also built high-quality boats, including iron steam yachts for the Czar of Russia (the *Nevka* in 1838) and the King of Denmark, and ships to meet unusual requirements, such as a steam ferry drawing only 18 inches of water (to work in Calcutta), a bucket dredger and an iron fire-float to be driven by paddles cranked by a crew of 48 men (Bowen August 1952, p. 246). They began to make ships for the Admiralty in 1842, when they built the 93-ton steamer *Rocket*, which operated as a 'maid-of-all-work' in Woolwich Dockyards.

Fairbairn was a very able entrepreneur but was reluctant to ever turn down work and ended up taking on quite excessive commitments. The works at Manchester and Millwall were both very large businesses, together employing more than 1000 men, and also produced an enormous range of goods, including locomotives (orders for which were particularly numerous during the railway mania), all kinds of engineering work, including the construction of bridges, girders, cranes, caissons, mills (later to include Saltaire Mills) and many 'novel applications of wrought iron to structural and mechanical purposes' (later to include a floating flour-mill and bakery to improve the food supplies to troops involved in the siege of Sebastapol, government forts at Spithead and the roof of the Albert Hall – Pole 1970, pp. 329–32).

Fairbairn found the continual travelling between Manchester and London, allied to various trips abroad to arrange and oversee contracts, a considerable strain (Pole 1970, p. 157), particularly since the absence of his personal expertise could be very costly; on one occasion when he was in Turkey, his partners at Millwall agreed with the government to reduce the size of an iron frigate they were building, despite the fact that the firm had stockpiled large numbers of iron plates which then no longer fitted the ship concerned (Pole 1970, p. 339).

Fairbairn was proved correct in his view that iron would be the material of the future for shipbuilding but he had not anticipated the speed with which other entrepreneurs would also appreciate the potential of the new material, and the level of competition, much of it locally based, increased quickly with negative effects on price margins in a new, innovative but essentially high-risk trade. The yard at Millwall lost money throughout the period 1835–48, losses which cannot be readily attributed to incompetence on Fairbairn's part, as his Manchester business was highly successful and profitable, or even to his increasing periods of absence, as his son Thomas Fairbairn was able to put far more time than hitherto into the business in Millwall, throughout the period 1840–48 (Pole 1970, p. 154).

The constant losses in the shipyard were largely covered by the profits that were being made at Manchester, but the overall results were a poor return on the considerable amounts of capital that Fairbairn had invested. Most of the amounts involved in the shipyard were tied up in buildings, plant and machinery and Fairbairn's liquidity position steadily deteriorated.

By 1844 it was clear that the Millwall works would have to be sold as soon as the existing contracts had been completed, which included two of the most important they had obtained, one for the *Pottinger*, one of the first iron ships built for the P & O company and, at 1400 tons, the 'biggest iron steamer yet built on the Thames' (Bowen August 1952, p. 247; Cable 1937, p. 264; Banbury 1962, p. 198) and the other for the naval frigate, HMS *Megaera*, also 1400 tons, which later became a troop ship.

Throughout the period 1845–47, the works were also used for experimental work in connection with designing the large, tubular Conway and Britannia Bridges for the Chester and Holyhead Railway. The original intention was that the contracts would actually be carried out by Fairbairn jointly with Ditchburn and Mare but the railway board looked 'with suspicion' on a joint contract and the contracts were eventually taken over by Ditchburn and Mare (Pole 1970, p. 208).

In 1848, the works, which had cost £50,000, were sold, but only for £12,000, to a partnership of Albert and Richard Robinson (who were engineers) and John Scott Russell (b. May 1808, d. June 1882) who had been manager of a large shipyard in Greenock from 1835–39 and who had moved to an adjacent yard on the Isle of Dogs in 1845 to build iron screw-steamers and other small ships.

During his time at Millwall, Fairbairn is thought to have built over 100 vessels, most of them iron steamships of under 2000 tons, for a wide range of customers (including the Admiralty, the Tsar of Russia and the King of Denmark), to have generally employed about 400 men and to have suffered operating losses of about £100,000, as well as the substantial capital losses on the sale of the business (Pole 1970, p. 342; Bowen August 1952, p. 247).

Ditchburn and Mare (Yard 2: Orchard Shipyard) – see also Appendix 3

Charles Mare and Thomas Ditchburn were among the pioneers of iron shipbuilding on the Thames. Ditchburn (1801–70) had been an apprentice shipwright at the Royal Dockyards, Chatham during which time he attracted the attention of Sir Robert Seppings, Surveyor to the Navy. He became manager of Fletcher and Fearnall's shipyard at Limehouse at the early age of 21 and worked there from 1822 until 1837, doing much to develop their reputation for fast steam vessels (Memoir of T. J. Ditchburn, pp. 1–2).

Ditchburn was particularly able and innovative on matters of ship design and he was one of the first people to realise 'that the traditional cod's head and mackerel tail principle was admirable for sailing vessels but that a steamer required a longer hull and fine entrance' (Bowen July 1952, p. 56). Ditchburn's designs were particularly suited to the river-steamer trade from London to Gravesend and the 117-ton *Essex* and the 94-ton *Pearl*, both built in 1829, were highly successful. The 240-ton *Royal George*, built in 1834 and running to Margate, became the fastest steamboat on the Thames and led to further orders, both for new boats and for modifications to the shape of existing craft (Jordan 1925, p. 27). In 1836, Fletcher and Fearnall built a much larger boat, the 688-ton *Braganza* for Willcox and Anderson, who were then establishing the P&O line.

Ditchburn was aware that his employers intended to make only wooden boats and, convinced that iron was the material of the future, he decided to set up in business on his own and build mostly iron ships (Bowen 1944, p. 500). In fact, with help from John Penn of Greenwich, the marine engine-makers, who supplied their machinery on credit and with whom he maintained a long working relationship, he went into partnership with Charles Mare. Mare came from a well-to-do family, had started on a legal career but, on the death of his father, sold the family house, paid off his father's debts and started up in a line of business that was more to his liking (*Daily Mail* 18 February 1898).

In 1837 they established a yard for iron ships at Dudman's Dock, Deptford, once used to build East Indiamen. They began by building the *Inkerman* (365 tons) for the Russian government, a highly successful boat fast enough, despite its shallow draught, to pursue pirates in the shallow waters bordering the Crimea and along the Black Sea. They also built four 80-ton river steamers for the Thames excursion trade, the well-known *Starlight*, *Daylight*, *Moonlight* and *Twilight*, and this encouraged other companies on the river to place orders, nearly all of which were for iron-hulled boats.

Unfortunately, the already bitter competition with established wooden shipbuilders on the river took an ugly turn, and their works were completely destroyed by fire in 1838 (Bowen 1944, p. 500). They decided to move to the Orchard Shipyard, Canning Town, where they took over a riverside yard previously owned by the now bankrupt shipbuilders, William and Benjamin Wallis, not far from the East India Docks and the old Blackwall Yard (Bowen 1944, p. 500; Lammins 1961, pp. 33–7). The area was difficult of access by road, but a new railway had just been built and Ditchburn and Mare became the first business to take advantage of it and settle on the river bank next to Bow Creek.

The Orchard House estate had been a moated house and orchard as early as the sixteenth century but the house gradually degenerated into a 'drinking house'. In the third quarter of the eighteenth century, the estate was used as a cooperage and ship-breaking yard and as a blubber-boiling and whale-oil extraction site. The estate's remoteness from other houses, but good access by water, meant it was well suited to noxious trades and a tar-refining distillery was set up there in 1818, although the parts of the estate devoted to shipbuilding were not disturbed (Survey of London 1994, pp. 646–9). An earlier William Wallis had built ships there, including warships for the Navy during the Napoleonic Wars and, when he died in 1824, he left behind 'a shipbuilders yard, with slip, and excellent ways, ... a blacksmiths shop, mould lofts, large covered saw-pits, warehouses, sheds, counting-house and dwelling-house etc.' (Survey of London 1994, p. 683). The only drawback was that the yard was only just large enough for the ships that could be constructed in the late 1830s, although across Bow Creek (the river Lea) was an undeveloped, if marshy, area that might be useful if more space were needed. The locality was still rural (although this was soon to change)[12] and one employee wrote in the early 1840s of the fruit trees in the orchard of the old waterside inn being in full blossom and of the 'fresh and inviting' open country across the creek (TIQG Vol. 1, p. 3).

Ditchburn was highly energetic and technically adept and, with Mare concentrating mostly on the commercial side, they began to develop their business, although progress was slow at first. They were well aware of the benefits of good publicity to their future trade, however, and in 1841, they offered to build Lord Alfred Paget an iron racing yacht of twenty-five tons (the *Mystery*) that would beat any wooden yacht of similar tonnage. The new boat was as good as they had said and won her owner eleven first-class prizes

12. The Thames frontage in this area was extensively developed around the middle years of the century, particularly by the chemical industry.

within two years and her builders many new orders. By 1844, they were building iron vessels that could achieve eighteen miles an hour, which can be compared with average speeds of eight miles an hour when Ditchburn had started building steam vessels in 1822.

They gradually extended their range of ships, moving on from river steamers (particularly for the Iron Steamboat Company on the Thames) and yachts (iron-hulled from 1841) to paddle steamers (including two built in 1842 for the London and Blackwall Railway) and post office packets. Although they had made their name with iron-hulled ships, business volume was important and many naval men and mercantile fleet owners still preferred wooden ships, which they were more than prepared to build (TIQG Vol. 1, p. 3). Ditchburn was also successfully designed and built composite ships, where an iron frame was planked with wood.

In their first seven full years in business, 1838–44 their annual tonnage averaged only 910 tons but in 1845 and 1846 the scale of their business operation was transformed, with annual tonnages averaging more than 6200 tons. In 1845, the Admiralty placed orders for more ships to be built in the private sector than for many years and Ditchburn and Mare, who had built their first ship for the government in 1843, the packet HMS *Princess Alice*, were awarded the contracts for 3300 draught tons, 80 per of the UK total. This included HMS *Recruit*, a twelve-gun sailing brig, the first iron warship built for the Admiralty. In 1845 and even more in 1846, they produced far more commercial tonnage than they had before and were also awarded contracts by the P&O. To date the Inkerman (365 tons) had been the largest ship they had made, but in these two years they made several much larger ships, including HMS *Trident* (1130 tons) and the P&O steamers, *Ariel* and *Erin*.

They were also consulted by the Lords of the Admiralty on the best way to convey Her Majesty from Whitehall to Woolwich and, after some deliberations recommended the use of an Archimedean screw-driven vessel. This caused great concern at the Admiralty, where one senior official suggested that 'Mr. Ditchburn's proposal to screw Her Majesty from Whitehall to Woolwich was very like high treason' (Memoir T. J. Ditchburn, p. 5). The boat, the *Fairy*, the first screw-propelled vessel in the Royal Navy was, however, a great success and achieved 13 knots, 'the fastest for any vessel propelled by screw'. Moreover, the Queen herself liked the boat very much and, when she was due to visit Germany and Holland, Ditchburn was asked to refit the boat for sea service. The boat became in effect a private Royal Yacht (it was increasingly known as the 'Queen's Yacht') and this was very beneficial to the firm's reputation and to that of John Penn and Co., who supplied her machinery (*Illustrated London News* 5 April 1845; Memoir T. J. Ditchburn, p. 5).[13]

13. In connection with this, it was said that Mare, whose wife was a Court beauty and maid of honour to the Queen, was offered but refused a knighthood.

Money Wigram (Yard 3: Blackwall Yard) – see also Appendix 3

The Blackwall, sometimes known as the East India Yard was one of the important early centres of shipbuilding on the Thames. The East India Company was granted a licence to trade in 1600 and leased repair and storage facilities before building a new dockyard at Blackwall in 1614 for repair work and shipbuilding. The yard was very costly, however, and in June 1650 its owners decided that it should be sold, although this was not an easy matter; in 1656 Henry Johnson bought it, although for only £4,350 (Elmers and Werner 1989, p. 14). Johnson (later Sir Henry), an experienced shipwright, benefited from the growth in trade after the Restoration and from the increased government demand for naval ships for the Dutch Wars and started on the construction of a new Great Dock in 1659 to increase his firm's ability to build ships. Pepys tells in his diary for 22 September 1665 of how Johnson, 'in digging his late docks, he did twelve feet under ground find perfect trees over-covered with earth. Nut trees with the branches and the very nuts upon them ... their shells black with age and their kernels upon opening decayed, but their shell perfectly hard as ever' (TIQG Vol. 8, p. 69). Johnson's son, also Henry (and also later knighted), took over on his father's death in 1683 and continued to meet the needs of the East India Company and those of the government for warships until his death in 1719. Records exist of fifteen men-of-war built in the yard before the reign of Queen Anne (Dodd 1843, p. 461).

The yard was then sold for only £2,800, initially to the Earl of Strafford and then on to Philip Perry and his son John, who took over the lease of the yard in 1732. The yard had periods of decline but, after its acquisition by the younger John Perry, a professional shipbuilder, it was far more successful; many orders were received, particularly for warships, and the rapid growth and profitability of business provided sufficient funds to construct the Brunswick Dock in 1789–90, on marshland to the east of the existing yard. At this time, it was thought to be 'the most capacious private dockyard in the Kingdom and probably the World' (Elmers and Werner 1989, p. 17).

In 1782, Perry took on George Green as a 15-year-old apprentice and, fifteen years later, he became a partner in the business. Perry Sons and Green started building a number of frigates but in 1798 John Perry sold his interest in the yard to John and William Wells, who had been building ships in Deptford since 1715, the firm becoming Perry, Wells and Green. Although aptitude in matters of trade was the most important thing, personal connections could also prove useful; George Green married Perry's second daughter, Sarah in 1796, and Perry later married, as his second wife, Green's only sister (Bowen 1932, p. 1).

In 1805, on the death of Perry, his sons sold their interest in the yard to the successful East Indiamen owner, Robert Wigram, (later to become Chairman of the East India Docks and to be knighted). On his retirement in 1819, the business passed into the ownership of George Green and Money and Henry Loftus Wigram. For some years the firm had retained financial interests in many of the East Indiamen they built, as part of the contract for their construction, and under new ownership the business was extended considerably into the building of new types of ship, into ship ownership and related trades such as brokerage. In 1821 they built their first steamer, the 400-ton paddler the *City of Edinboro'* and followed this by building several more, including the earliest of those used by the General Steam Navigation Company.

The Blackwall yard was also the focus of one of the earliest large strikes in East End history, the shipwrights' dispute, the success of which established the union but lost the yard much business (Rose 1973, p. 144). Despite this, they produced the very successful Blackwall frigates in the early 1830s and several opium clippers from 1836. The cessation of the trading charter of the East India Company meant greater competition for the trade to the east, however, and this changed the position of the yard, although they continued to build ships for the East India Company and paddle-steamers for Hudson's Bay Company (including the famous 187-ton *Beaver*) and for several shipping lines, including the Edinburgh Steam Packet Company. Most were of 500 tons or more but in 1837, in a 'great advance in size and form on previous vessels' they built the 818-ton *Seringapatam*. The *Trident*, produced for General Steam in 1840–41, was also a successful ship and was thought to be the best and fastest steamer on the coast, on one notable occasion being preferred by Queen Victoria to any of the Navy's vessels for a trip home from Scotland (Bowen 1932, p. 3).

In 1838, when George Green was 71, he retired from the business, handed over control to his sons and their partners and then concentrated on looking after the benevolent institutions in the locality that he had founded. George Green was as noted a philanthropist as shipbuilder and he was believed to have spent nearly £100,000 on founding a number of schools (including a secondary school), a sailors' home and a chapel (both on East India Dock Road) and a row of almshouses, opened in 1849, the year of his death. On the day of his funeral, all the shops in Poplar closed, a crowd seemingly equal to the entire population of the district lined the funeral route and ships on the river and in the India Docks flew their flags at half-mast (Survey of London 1994, p. 194; *Illustrated London News*, 3 March 1849; Finch 1996, p. 81; papers in THLH collection, ref. 902).

Blackwall was, for many years, the largest yard on the Thames, employing around 500 men at a time when the average level of yard employment was closer to 20 or 30, but a series of disputes, centred on Money Wigram's desire to build iron ships (Survey of London 1994, p. 571), culminated in the collapse of the complex partnership agreement between the Greens and the Wigrams. In 1843, a wall was 'thrown up straight across the yard', almost overnight, and the yard and business subdivided.

R. & H. Green took over the less historic, and less well-appointed, eastern part of the Blackwall yard. Its main assets were three building-slips and a dry-dock, but considerable efforts had to be devoted to the building-up of the basic facilities and of even the entrance gate. The Greens were determined to continue to build only wooden ships and they carried on making and operating Blackwall frigates and tea-clippers and some more specialised craft, including three lightships, which were quite unusual at that time.

Money Wigram & Sons accordingly took the western half of the yard, including the more historic and better-appointed parts, the main entrance and the house, and continued to build wooden ships and also a small number of iron ships including the *Royal Albert* (663 tons) in 1844, the *Mererva* the following year, and the *Ripon* (1509 tons) in 1846 and Indus (1386 g.t.) in 1847, iron paddle-steamers for P & O's eastern mail services.

Samuda (Orchard Place, Blackwall, prior to moving to Yard 4)

Jacob and Joseph Samuda (the latter b. 1813, d. 1885), the sons of a broker and East and West India merchant, went into the engineering and ironwork trade together in 1832 at Southwark, initially to make marine engines, although they then became interested in developing atmospheric railways and worked on lines from Forest Hill to Croydon and in Ireland and Paris. In 1843, despite some renown and partial success in this area, they decided to extend their activities to iron shipbuilding and they accordingly laid out a suitable yard at Orchard Place, Blackwall, in close proximity to Ditchburn and Mare.

Iron shipbuilding was, however, a highly dangerous venture and in November 1844 one of their first ships, the *Gypsy Queen*, burst a steam joint, killing Jacob, the elder brother and nine other people. Only four months later, there was further tragedy when an apparently 'strong and substantial' boiler, recently bought by Joseph Samuda for supplying steam to a factory engine, exploded. The engine house in which it stood was destroyed, there was widespread local damage to property and large parts of the boiler parts and one unfortunate workman were all hurled more than 150 yards across the river. Two other employees were killed and several were badly injured (*Illustrated London News*, 8 March 1845; *Times* 6 March 1845, p. 6). Despite these tragedies, Joseph carried on and successfully established the business at Orchard Place.

Rennie (Yard 5: Norman Road, Greenwich)

John Rennie had started up in business as an engineer in Holland Street, Blackfriars in 1791, and carried out work in connection with bridges, canals and docks. His sons, George and John, took over the business on his death in 1821, as G. & J. Rennie, casting a wide range of iron goods (including the first biscuit-making machine) in their foundry and, from 1837, they began to specialise in making locomotive engines. Their works was not ideally suited to this, however, and they then moved on to marine engineering, making the machinery for a Russian naval arsenal on the Black Sea. They also made marine and land engines for the British and several foreign navies, including those for the *Archimedes*, the first screw steamship introduced into the Russian navy.

George was also very interested in shipbuilding and started a shipyard at Norman Road, Greenwich initially as J. Rennie, after his father, and then as G. Rennie and Co. He was the first person to persuade the Admiralty to try the screw propeller, when he converted the river paddler *Mermaid* into HM screw-steamer *Dwarf* in 1842, and much of his work concerned propellers and paddle wheels (Bowen 1948, p. 616). The great majority of his Admiralty contracts were also for machinery and, although he did make ships, many of the early ones were small river passenger vessels, although in 1842 they did build a 217-ton iron paddle-yacht, the *Queen*, for Admiralty visits of inspection and 'social trips on the Thames' (Bowen 1948, p. 616).

Other firms

David Napier was one of the pioneers of iron shipbuilding on the Thames, although his actual output was modest. He decided to retire from active business life on the Clyde, where he thought the level of competition excessive and let his premises at Lancefield, on the south bank of the river to his cousin, Robert in 1835. He believed that London would provide better opportunities, for 'the building of iron steamships had only been recently commenced on the Thames [and] passenger traffic there was [capable] of great extension' (Napier 1912, p. 36) and he bought undeveloped land on the banks of the Thames at Millwall for two reasons; firstly 'for the purpose of making experiments in steamers' (Napier 1912, p. 21) and secondly to teach his sons to construct iron vessels that embodied his thinking.

He bought a large site at Millwall, adjacent to William Fairbairn's shipyard, which cost him a good deal of money. He also incurred 'much additional expense' on adapting the ground for its intended purpose and also in providing building-slips, workshops and the necessary machinery

(Napier 1912, p. 37). He also built Napier House, in which he lived, on the same site. Once the yard was established, there was a period of experimentation and it was not until 1839 that his sons, John and Francis, started business as J. & F. Napier, engineers and shipbuilders, building their first ship, the 80-ton *Eclipse*, which was capable of 16 knots and of carrying up to 500 passengers on the Blackwall–Margate route. David Napier was an innovative engineer, and the Napiers did build other notable ships such as the *Rocket* in 1841, the *Isle of Thanet* in 1842 and *Waterman 9*, but it is clear that 'Napier Yard' was never used to anything approaching its full capacity.

Fletcher Son and Fearnall was one of the oldest firms on the Thames, having been started by Mr Fletcher at the Hog Yard, Shadwell in the eighteenth century, before the firm moved to a much larger, new yard at Limehouse in 1818, which became known as Union Dock and where they built three dry docks. One had unsatisfactory foundations and they decided in 1833 to sink an old 1200-ton East India ship to form the bottom and lower sides of the dock, an arrangement that proved entirely suitable for moderate-sized boats in need of repair. They were pioneering steam shipbuilders, appointing Thomas Ditchburn as their manager from 1822–37, and obtained many orders from the East India Company, the mail packet companies and British and foreign governments but they wished to build only wooden ships and their business gradually turned to engineering and ship repair-work.

Finally, the noted engineers and marine engine makers, Miller and Barnes, who had started at Glasshouse Fields, Ratcliff in 1822 (and who later became Miller and Ravenhill), had been looking for a riverside site where it would be easier to install and remove ships engines, so in 1838 they moved to Orchard Wharf, where they almost immediately began to build iron ships, beginning with the *Victoria*, a Rhine paddle-steamer that was completed in 1839. They built a number of iron ships, particularly paddle-steamers for river use (Hicks 1928, p. 82) but also continued to manufacture marine engines.

CHAPTER THREE

Vertical integration, 1847–53

Taken as a whole, the UK shipbuilding trade expanded during the period 1847–53 to an average annual tonnage of nearly 150,000 tons, 18 per cent higher than in the previous period and was showing clear signs of increased growth towards the end of the period, in 1851–53 (see Table 2). The rise in the average annual tonnage constructed was due entirely to an increase in the average ship size to just under 200 tons, as the total number of vessels built each year fell by 15 per cent, again as compared with 1832–46.

Table 2: UK Shipbuilding statistics, 1847–53

	(1) **UK (no.)**	*(2)* **UK (000) (n.t.)**	*(3)* **UK tonnage per cent Admiralty**	*(4)* **UK tonnage per cent London Admiralty**
1847	935	147.8	1.3	1.3
1848	848	123.2	0.6	0.6
1849	737	120.7	2.2	2.2
1850	689	133.7	0.0	0.0
1851	673	150.1	0.3	0.3
1852	712	167.4	0.0	0.0
1853	798	203.2	0.0	0.0
Average p.a.	769	149.4	0.6	0.6
Ave. 1832–46	901	127.0	1.4	0.7

Notes: no. = number of vessels
n.t. = net tons
Displacement tons have been multiplied by 1.125 to convert them to net tons

Sources: Mitchell and Deane (1962, pp. 220–22); Banbury (1971); Lyon (1993); Brassey (1883); private listings kindly made available by David Lyon.

There are no satisfactory statistics for regional levels of shipbuilding during this period of time and so conclusions about the state of the trade on the London river have to be based upon indirect and less conclusive sources of information. Thames shipbuilders had a long-established reputation for high-quality work, from the days of wooden ships, and this continued through to the era of steam, iron and screw-driven ships, with the region concentrating on 'premium ships', such as clippers, steam yachts, and passenger steamers for the major passenger and mail lines such as Royal Mail, P&O and General Steam Navigation, rather than on more basic trade tonnage.

The list of P&O's ship acquisitions shows that, although the Thames had been a preferred supplier in the 1840s (building more than a third of P&O's boats and doing particularly well in 1845–46, when orders for five P&O ships were obtained), this did not continue into the immediately succeeding period, when an increasing proportion of P&O's business was going to Tod and McGregor and William Denny in Scotland. In the period 1847–52, only Money Wigram built any of the company's ships although in 1853, C. J. Mare was successful in obtaining the orders for no fewer than four P&O ships, *Rajah*, *Valetta*, *Manilla* and the *Himalaya* (Rabson and O'Donoghue 1988; Hawes 1978).

Royal Mail Steam Packet, after the Admiralty withdrew its ban on iron vessels in the mail services in 1852 (mail packet ships had an auxiliary naval role), started to change from wood to iron, although this did not benefit builders on the London river; of eleven ships built in the period 1847–53, four of the earlier wooden paddle steamers were made on the Thames (three by Pitchers and one by Greens) but the first two orders for iron-hulled ships in 1852 both went instead to Greenock (Bushell 1939, pp. 71, 257–8).

Perhaps inevitably, the Thames did much better with the locally-based GSN fleet; of 31 vessels owned by GSN in 1850, totalling nearly 10,000 registered tons, 27 were built on the Thames, many of them by C. J. Mare, although most were made of wood (Palmer 1982, pp. 4–5).

In the period 1847–53, as in 1832–46, the amount of UK private sector shipbuilding provided by Admiralty contracts was of little importance, averaging less than one per cent in volume terms (see Table 2). The London yards derived the benefits that were obtainable, however, building all the Admiralty's required tonnage, even though this amounted to a total of only five ships in seven years, divided between four yards (see Appendix 1 for the details).

The modest demands of the Admiralty on the private sector were again partly the result of the Navy's conservatism. The Admiralty had ordered three gunboats for the Niger from Laird in 1840 and six more iron-hulled ships in the mid-1840s (the largest of which was the 2920-ton *Simoom*) but they were not a success. Iron-hulled ships were now much more widely used for commercial work, but the Admiralty was unconvinced about the benefits of iron as against wood for combat ships, believing that 'cannon fire would shatter iron hulls' (Dowden 1953, p. 32), a view partly based on trials in 1840 that had shown that solid shot did more damage to (thin) iron plates, which they often rent wide open, than to wooden sides which they merely holed and which could then be plugged (Lyon 1980, p. 20).

For some time, shipbuilders in the London area had been highly innovative in the technologies of iron shipbuilding and the region had become an important centre for the new trade. In the period 1847–53 the process would be taken further by C. J. Mare in particular, who had lost Ditchburn as a partner, so that this time the pioneering innovations would come in the way that the business was structured, rather than in technical areas.

Despite their ability to innovate, shipbuilders along the Thames did face a number of long-term cost disadvantages as against other shipbuilding regions in the UK. London was a long way from deposits of iron and coal, the major raw materials relevant to iron production and, not surprisingly, the leading iron-masters were in the west Midlands, the north-east, Scotland and south Wales.[1] As early as the 1830s, the adoption of the Neilson hot blast process made it 'possible to work the enormous black-band ironstone deposits of Lanarkshire and Ayrshire' by using local coal, unconverted to coke, thus almost halving fuel costs for the Scottish iron industry. Iron industry labour costs were also lower in Scotland, helped by the influx of Irishmen and west Highlanders and, within twenty years, Scotland was to become the most important area of iron production (its share of British iron output rose from 5 per cent to 25 per cent between 1830 and 1845) and the lowest-cost producer of pig-iron in Britain (Cottrell 1980, p. 31; Checkland 1971, p. 18). Moreover, by 1851, Britain produced about one-half the world output of iron, with Scotland, south Wales and south Staffordshire responsible for about 80 per cent of this (Checkland 1971, p. 152).

It has often been alleged that shipbuilding labour was far more expensive on the London river than elsewhere in the UK, although there is evidence to suggest that, until the time of the Crimean War, the price of labour on the Thames was largely 'kept in check by contests', including a four or five month co-ordinated lockout by the London employers in 1851 which followed the foundation of the Amalgamated Society of Engineers and persuaded the employees to withdraw their increased demands (P.P. 1867–8, Vol. XXXIX, paras 16765, 16806–9). London was also not the only area where local shipbuilders were unhappy about wage levels; there were also claims that 'shipwrights wages were higher than elsewhere' on Merseyside (Neal 1993, p. 132) and it was apparent that the trade unions were strongly

1. See the map of 'Mineral Resources in Britain in 1851' in Checkland 1971, p. 151 for a clear representation of this.

organised in Sunderland and on the Tyne.[2] Moreover, in the shipbuilding and engineering industries as a whole, average earnings rose 6 per cent from 1850 to 1853 with many reports that wages on the Thames were almost stationary from 1822 to 1850 (Bowley and Wood 1906, pp. 185–9). There was also some compensation provided, consistent with a pervasive view that London shipbuilding was unusually high-quality work, by the refusal until 1853 of Lloyds to give any ship built north of Yarmouth a classification period of more than ten years, thus materially affecting the relevant insurance cost.

McClelland and Reid have suggested that shipbuilding is an inherently cyclical trade in which employers face fluctuations in output that are sufficiently severe to cause them to prefer labour-intensive modes of production, even when production techniques become more sophisticated and offer capital-intensive efficiencies. Thus, 'the commitment of resources to tools and machinery was restricted in an attempt to limit overheads and place the burden of the recurrent intense depressions squarely on the backs of the labour force' (1985, p. 157). This also meant that labour costs would continue to be a very important element of total production costs. Moreover, in the growth years of the 1840s, competition was still intensifying, with even Blackwall frigates often being supplied by firms on the Tyne rather than on the Thames (Banbury 1971, p. 181).

The main Thames yards

In the period 1832 to 1846, the London shipbuilding yards had been an important centre of the technical innovation and development that established the iron shipbuilding trade. The marine engine maker Maudslay had begun but not continued with the iron shipbuilding, Fairbairn and Napier had come to the area and set up yards in Millwall, Ditchburn and Mare had established their partnership initially at Deptford but then at the Orchard Shipyard and Wigram, Samuda and Rennie had all made modest contributions to the output of iron ships.

In the period from 1847 to 1853, C. J. Mare was to pioneer the vertically integrated, single-site approach to iron production and shipbuilding that provided the prospect of far more efficient production techniques, but Fairbairn, through business over-extension, and Napier, through under-use of his shipyard, both failed although their adjacent yards were taken over by the distinguished naval architect, John Scott Russell as a base for the construction of large ships. Money Wigram, Rennie and Samuda continued

2. The ship's carpenters in Liverpool had a strong trade union, particularly before 1835 and also carried out large amounts of repair work.

their operations, the latter moving to a larger yard and Charles Lungley, a shipbuilder, entered the trade by buying the former Deptford Green Dockyard.

During this period, shipbuilding made its contribution to the industrialisation that was changing the area east of the City of London. Poplar and Bromley were no longer rural. Numerous factories were being built along the Lea, while the 'other remaining trace of countryside between Aldgate and the Lea, the Isle of Dogs, was also urbanised about the year 1850' and transformed from a mixture of pasture and marshland to a 'place of five thousand inhabitants and the scene of some of the most important metallic and fictile and chemical manufactures indigenous to the Metropolis' (Rose 1973, p. 145). In 1851 it contained 510 houses and 58 manufactories and 2,850 people were employed there, 1,160 of whom lived locally (Cowper 1853, p. 61).

C. J. Mare (Yard 2: Orchard and Bow Creek Shipyard) – see also Appendix 3

Ditchburn and Mare had moved to the Orchard Shipyard in 1838, when their first yard had been burnt down. For a forced move, it had worked quite well. The business had overcome the inevitable early problems of getting established and in 1845 and 1846, after seven relatively sparse years, they had succeeded in greatly expanding both their commercial and Admiralty work, increasing their production (measured in tons), fivefold in a period of two years, to over 6400 tons in 1846.

Ditchburn's ability as a designer had helped the firm establish a reputation for reliability and successful innovation in their new and difficult trade. Although Ditchburn was the main influence on matters of ship design, Mare had major ambitions for expanding their business which Ditchburn could not accept, causing the break-up of the partnership in 1847 (Survey of London 1994, p. 673; TIQG Vol. 1, p. 3).[3] Ditchburn then went into business on his own but, surprisingly in view of his past achievements, he was not very successful.[4] Mare continued at the Orchard Shipyard, bringing in James Ash as naval architect.

Although the Orchard Yard had enabled the business to grow substantially,

---

3. The partnership was dissolved 30 April 1847, when Ditchburn's share of the goodwill was valued at £43,000 (*Times* 21 May 1856, p. 11).
4. He did some ship designing and building, but apparently on only a very modest scale and in 1856 he was building houses on East India Dock Road, where he had lived since 1839. Ditchburn had been an early member of the Institution of Naval Architects and was elected to its Council on 6 April 1870, but died only three days later.

it had a number of drawbacks. The yard was held on a low-cost but less assured leasehold basis, which did not provide the long-term security appropriate to a major expansion of the facilities. Only one ship had been constructed at the Yard that was in excess of 1,000 (draught) tons because the yard was cramped and did not permit the construction of the larger ships that had become increasingly feasible in the technical sense and which Mare believed would offer them the prospect of more substantial profits. Furthermore, the firm had experienced continual difficulty in 'obtaining iron material, as in those days railways were scarce and the charges high'.

By 1847, the iron shipbuilding business had undergone nearly ten years of considerable innovation in technical, industrial ways, but what Mare had in mind was both to continue this process, by seeking to build ships of up to 4000 tons, but also to bring about an equally radical change in the business form seen as appropriate to the iron shipbuilding trade. Mare's solution involved buying land on the other (Essex) side of Bow Creek, not merely to provide more space for the building of larger ships but also to enable the firm to produce its own iron and then vertically integrate its production operation. This had the additional advantage of enabling the firm to produce its own iron from a convenient, and at that time, plentiful supply: 'best London scrap-iron'.

Additional capital was put into the business, some from business associates and the remainder by Mare, from the substantial profits he had earned in the previous two years, and the planned expansion went ahead. Ditchburn was not the only person who doubted the wisdom of what was planned and 'to many it appeared a wild scheme'. At this time, large areas of Plaistow and East and West Ham consisted of little more than 'marsh land, cornfields or market gardens' (TIQG Vol. IV, p. 117) and the major part of the Essex side of Bow Creek, known locally as 'Frog Island', was a 'sedgy and apparently useless' swamp or marshland covered with water at high tide (*East End News* 24 December 1912).

Mare recovered this from the river at great expense, by piling down to the gravel, a depth of over 20 feet, and then marked out and constructed two slips, each of which could accommodate up to four small steamers. The ironworks, shipyard and machine shops were set out and equipped with the most modern machinery, steam plant was brought in for the rolling mills and steam hammers were purchased so that the business could start hammering and rolling the scrap iron into plates and bars that its shipbuilding operation would need (Crighton, p. 7; Banbury 1971, p. 195). A chain ferry was constructed, large enough to carry up to 200 men between the two parts of the yard, which were anything from 50 to 200 yards apart, depending on the state of the tide (Rose 1973, p. 145). In the iron shipbuilding industry, in which the capital requirements were normally of the order of £25,000, Mare's plans involved commitments at a completely different level; in 1856 it was stated that the Blackwall property, consisting of freehold and leasehold buildings, plant and machinery, had cost £225,000, although not all of this was spent at the outset (*Banking Almanac* 1856, p. 51). A little later, a railway line was 'stumped out and railed in across the meadows', which would, inadvertently, enclose the ironworks and shipyard entirely on its eastern and south-eastern sides but also provide a convenient form of inland transit (TIQG Vol. 1, p. 3).

In 1847, Mare built the *Prussian Eagle*, an iron paddle despatch vessel and the first iron vessel he had made for the Prussian Navy (TIQG vol. 3, p. 16), the following year the *Vladimir*, 1680 (draught) tons for the Russian Navy and in 1849 an iron screw frigate, HMS *Vulcan* for the Admiralty. The firm's expertise at building in iron extended beyond large vessels to include specialist and high-quality work; in 1848, Mare launched his first iron yacht, the 60-ton cutter *Mosquito*, in the judgement of at least one naval architect, 'the fastest and smartest craft of her class ever set afloat' (TIQG Vol. 1, p. 4) and in 1851 made the prestigious royal yacht *Faid Gihaad* for the Viceroy of Egypt, a vessel regarded at the time as one of the finest and most luxurious vessels built.

The larger ships were, however, far more attractive commercially; in 1850 alone, the firm built three cargo vessels of over 2,500 tons each for General Steam as well as two large paddle sloops for the Spanish government. In the extraordinarily successful year of 1853, nine vessels of over 2,500 (draught) tons were built. The largest of these, the iron screw-steamer *Himalaya*, was built for the P&O and, at 3,947 (draught) tons, was for many years one of the largest ships afloat. It cost the P&O about £130,000, but turned out to be rather unwieldy for commercial use and was later sold to the Admiralty for use in the Crimea and then as a troopship.[5] Between 1849 and 1853, Mare also built an entire fleet of 14 auxiliary screw passenger ships for the General Screw Steam Shipping Co. and several steamers for the P&O (Bowen 1944, p. 500).[6]

The firm's iron production capabilities also meant that they could meet orders for civil engineering work that was based on iron working techniques, such as bridge construction. Although the trade was competitive, co-operation between firms could also pay; Mare sub-contracted much of the contract to supply tubular ironwork for the building of the Britannia Tubular Bridge over the Menai Straights to two experienced frame benders, Westwood and Baillie (who had worked for Fairbairn from 1837–38), with

5. The *Himalaya* was, however, sufficiently well made that it provided the Admiralty with 41 years' service as a transport ship.
6. The General Screw Steam Shipping Company extended its original service to the Cape of Good Hope on to Mauritias, Ceylon and India and thus needed ships of at least 1,700 tons (*Illustrated London News* 12 April 1851).

Mare supplying much of the ironwork and Fairbairn building the experimental spans (Banbury 1971, p. 288). The railway boom also brought a good deal of work, Mare's firm producing a cast-iron turning bridge, the first railway bridge for the West India Docks, the iron roofs at Fenchurch Street station and at the London and Blackwall Railway's terminus on Brunswick Wharf. Mare and Co. also built the Albert Bridge, Westminster Bridge and the Saltash Bridge across the Tamar near Plymouth, although the firm lost heavily on the latter two contracts; on the Westminster contract, they agreed to supply the bridge for the 'exceedingly low figure of £4 per foot', about half the normal rate (*Daily Mail* 18 February 1898) and on the Saltash Bridge the eventual cost of construction was also well over estimate (Press cuttings and private papers, THLH ref. 902).

Appendix 2 shows that the firm's average annual shipbuilding tonnage was five times as high in 1847–53 as in 1837–46. In large part, this was due to the (inevitably) low output in the early years of the business, but the tonnage achieved was still 60 per cent above that in the peak years of the old partnership, 1845 and 1846. During Mare's first three years in business on his own, while the land on the Essex side of the river was being reclaimed and developed, average tonnage levels were down 30 per cent on 1845–46 but, from 1850, the yard moved to levels of output that had never been previously approached, averaging 13,900 tons a year, more than double the level even in the boom years of the partnership. Of this total, more than 80 per cent was from commercial contracts and the remainder from foreign navy rather than British Admiralty orders.

The business had expanded rapidly since the new facilities had been installed and, by 1853, the operation consisted of three yards, connected by ferry-boat, each yard being of some size and under divisional control. Ships built on the upper slips were launched into Bow Creek and those from the lower slips were launched straight into the Thames. The yards used technologically advanced equipment, including Naysmith steam hammers, steam-powered punching and shearing machines, a steam-engine of 60 horse-power for milling and planing operations and the largest cranes in the country, 'safe at a strain of 20 tons', although the use of 'best London scrap' meant that around the works were large heaps of old iron, included old frying-pans and horse-shoes (Hicks 1928, p. 79; *Illustrated London News* 28 October 1854, pp. 409–10).

At the end of the period, in 1853, when the *Himalaya* was launched, the firm had an unprecedented 43 vessels in hand and, although 13 were coal lighters and wooden barges, the remainder were more substantial. Never before had the firm's output been so high or its prospects so encouraging.

John Scott Russell (Yard 1: Millwall Shipyard): – see also Appendix 3

Although Fairbairn's Millwall works had been sold in 1848, a part of the works were retained temporarily to complete the contracts in hand, which included HMS *Megaera*, launched in 1849.

The new owners, the partners Albert and Richard Robinson and John Scott Russell, meanwhile built the Taman, an iron steamer for the Russian government in 1848 and the *Manchester*, launched in July 1849. The following year, Russell took over the business himself, building the schooner yacht *Titania* that same year and, in 1851, three gunboats for the Prussian Navy. This was a particularly busy year for Russell since he was also a promoter of and the 'indefatigable Secretary' to the Great Exhibition of 1851 (Cowper 1853, p. 71).

Russell was an unusually talented ship designer and architect and Brunel, who was adviser to the Australian Mail Company, recommended in 1851 that they build large ships for the England–Australia run and that two of them, the *Victoria* and *Adelaide* (1,350 [g] tons each) be designed and built by Scott Russell the following year. These were highly successful ships; the first-named won a prize of £500 offered by the Australian colonies for the fastest voyage from England and the latter was judged by inspectors to have achieved the best results 'hitherto obtained from the screw propeller' (Emmerson 1977, p. 61). This led Brunel to further advise the Australian company to contract for the construction of a 'gigantic iron ship' and, when 40,000 shares were taken up and £3 had been paid on each (the maximum payable on each share being £20), Brunel was duly given the go ahead.

Russell formed a group, consisting of himself, Robinson (one of his former partners) and Charles Geach, a friend, and they successfully tendered for the hull. No other tenders were submitted and the bid of £275,200 was to cover the finding of a place to build it, providing the 'very large and unusual plant and clenching for constructing the same', and then either buying the 'works and machinery necessary for launching the ship' or constructing a dock in which to build it and then float it out. The same group also tendered £44,500 for the paddle engines and boilers and £53,500 for the screw engines (Emmerson 1977, p. 69) and accepted that Russell would receive a large part of his payment in the form of 10,000 shares (one quarter of the total to be issued) in the Australian company and also that 'full control and supervision over every part of the work' was to reside in the engineer, Brunel.

Geach's support was critically important to Russell's overall position. He was a good friend, a very able businessman and he was also a partner in the leading ironworks firm of Beale and Co. who were to provide the iron, in turn accepting shares in the Australian company from Russell in part-payment of the sums that would be owed.

A serious fire began in Russell's yard, which was large enough to employ up to 1,500 men, in the early morning of 10 September 1853, however, and 'spread with fearful rapidity, so that in a short time, the splendid western half of the concern including the beautiful machinery, patterns, models, drawings, tools and stock' were consumed, along with the smithy, the building which contained the pattern loft and mould loft,[7] the engine and boiler shops and about a thousand tons of timber. The fire seriously damaged two iron ships of 600 tons each, that were on the slips awaiting launching (*Illustrated London News* 17 September 1853) and caused a loss of close on £60,000 (Cowper 1853, p. 70). The blaze also destroyed 'every vestige' of Napiers' workshops next door and finally closed that business (Banbury 1971, p. 248). The fire was by far the most extensive in the neighbourhood for some years and provided a major setback to Russell's ambitions, although some of the buildings on the other side of the yard survived, so that his business and the building of the 'gigantic ship' were still able to continue.

Money Wigram (Yard 3: Blackwall Yard) – see also Appendix 3

Richard Green and Money Wigram had split up over the question of whether or not to construct iron ships and accordingly subdivided their Blackwall yard in 1843. Since then, Green had built (and operated) only wooden ships but had been very successful, particularly with Blackwall frigates, tea-clippers and more specialised craft, such as lightships. The use of wood did not restrict the Greens to smaller ships and in 1851, before the Admiralty's position on iron mail ships changed, the firm built the *Amazon* for Royal Mail, the largest (2,256 gross tons and 300 feet long) and one of the finest wooden (paddle) steamers built.

Money Wigram, who worked in the western half of the Blackwall yard, was keen to build iron as well as wooden ships and, across the period 1847–53, generally built about three ships a year, the most significant being the *Indus* in 1847, a 1,386-ton iron paddle-steamer intended for P & O's eastern mail services, the *Ysabel Catolica*, a 1,567-ton iron paddle-ship made in 1851 for the Spanish Navy and the Parana, a large (2,934-ton) wooden paddle-steamer built for Royal Mail's Brazilian mail contract run shortly before the Admiralty accepted the case for iron-hulled mail ships. The yard was

7. Mould lofts were well-lit areas, perhaps half as long as the ships that were built, and given over almost entirely to a smooth floor on which were chalked lines, some straight, some curved, intersecting each other at angles of different degrees 'derived from the working drawings but enlarged to represent the exact dimensions and curvatures of the timbers required to form the vessel', which were then generally made up, out of thin pieces of American deal and were known as 'moulds' (TIQG Vol. 9, pp. 70–73).

also helped when the railway line from Blackwall to Fenchurch Street was converted from cable to steam propulsion in 1849 (Thorne 1937).

Samuda (Orchard Place, then Yard 4: Samuda's Yard)

Joseph Samuda (b. 1813, d. 1885) had successfully expanded his business, despite the premature death of his brother in an accident at work in 1844, but further misfortune struck in 1847, when a fire destroyed a large part of the firm's stores and other property. Joseph continued, however, to expand the business and increasingly concentrated on iron steamships for both the fighting and merchant navies, although the river frontage at Orchard Place of only 230 feet proved very restrictive. In December 1852, the firm moved to, and took out a lease at just over £500 a year on, some 'new and very large premises, not yet completed and intended to be used for the building of iron ships' at Cubitt Town which had an improved frontage onto the river of 370 feet (Cowper 1853, p. 73; Thomas, p. 3).

Rennie (Yard 5: Norman Road, Greenwich)

Rennie was by trade very much an engineer, but he was more than prepared to use his firm's skills to make a wide range of marine products, including iron ships. The firm developed a particular expertise in the construction of marine engines, supplying large numbers to the Admiralty and also to major commercial shipping firms such as P & O and the Compagnie Generale Transatlantique. They also supplied marine and land engines to a number of foreign navies, including those for the *Archimedes*, the first screw steamship introduced into the Russian Navy.

In 1849, Rennie obtained the contract to build and engine the iron paddle yacht *Peterhoff* for the Czar of Russia, although he eventually subcontracted construction of the hull to Charles Mare and supplied only the engines himself. The yard at Greenwich continued to produce a 'small output of widely-varying types' of mostly small ships, although in 1851 they did design and construct the 438-ton *Alexandria* (Banbury 1971, p. 237) and also produced other marine engineering products, including the machinery for a Russian naval arsenal on the Black Sea.

Other firms

Although Napier was a highly innovative engineer and had paid a good deal of money to establish and equip a shipyard in Millwall for himself and his sons, very few ships were ever built there and the business seems to have closed down by 1852. The serious fire that started up in Russell's yard in September 1853 destroyed the whole of Napier's workshops next door (although sparing the large dwelling-house) and brought about the final closure of the business (Cowper 1853, p. 70). Banbury suggests that the total output may have been worth as little as £35,000 and consisted of only six ships (1971, p. 218). A little later, the yard was let to Scott Russell, to provide additional space for the building of the *Great Eastern*.

The riverside industry in Millwall in 1853 included the rolling mill and iron works of Messrs Johnson, to which 'all kinds of old iron are sent from Her Majesty's yards, which is returned into store, in the shape of new rods and bars, ready for the forge' (Cowper 1853, p. 72).

The noted engineers and marine engine makers, Miller and Barnes, who later became Miller and Ravenhill, had moved to Orchard Wharf in 1838 and built quite a number of iron ships there, particularly paddle-steamers for river use and also the 865-ton HMS *Llewellyn* in 1847, although the building of ships seems to have 'fallen off sharply after 1847, and may have ceased altogether', with the firm instead concentrating on the manufacture of marine engines (Hicks 1928, p. 82; Survey of London 1994, p. 685).

Charles Lungley, who had previously built ships at Poplar and Rotherhithe, took over Deptford Green Dockyard in 1852, which had been used for the construction of warships since Napoleonic times, to build ships, nearly all of which were iron-hulled (apart from his sailing ships which had composite hulls). His constructions were generally of modest size, although his 'hull design and workmanship were both conspicuous and he had a number of very smart vessels to his credit', including several made for the Union Steam Collier Company (Bowen 1947, p. 510).

CHAPTER FOUR

The Crimean War and the first crisis, 1854–59

The standard explanation of the decline of shipbuilding on the Thames is based upon Pollard's (1950) article, which has been widely quoted. The leading shipping historian, Palmer, for example, in her recent analysis of shipbuilding in the south-east from 1800–1913, suggests that the 'Crimean

Table 3: UK Shipbuilding statistics, 1854–59

	(1) UK (no.)	*(2)* UK (000) (n.t.)	*(3)* UK tonnage per cent Admiralty	*(4)* UK tonnage per cent London Admiralty
1854	836	218.3	9.8	9.8
1855	1,191	354.4	8.8	7.3
1856	1,269	294.3	16.9	11.9
1857	1,283	252.3	0.7	0.7
1858	1,000	208.1	0.0	0.0
1859	939	186.0	0.0	0.0
Average p.a.	1,086	252.2	6.0	4.9
Ave. 1847–53	770	149.7	0.9	0.9
Ave. 1832–46	901	126.9	1.3	0.6

Notes: no. = number of vessels
n.t. = net tons
Displacement tons have been multiplied by 1.125 to convert them to net tons

Sources: Mitchell and Deane (1962, pp. 220–22); Banbury (1971); Lyon (1993); Brassey (1883); P.P. Navy Gunboats (1861); Preston and Major (1967); private listings kindly made available by David Lyon.

and US Civil Wars boosted business and encouraged the creation of new yards to build iron steamers' and cites Pollard as the basis for the view that 'in 1867, the London industry, reliant on marginal, speculative and foreign orders, collapsed in the wake of the Overend Gurney banking crisis and many yards closed'(Palmer 1993, p. 58). Palmer also quotes the comment made in 1867 by the leading shipbuilder, Samuda, that 'every single establishment that was in existence as an iron shipbuilding establishment on the Thames at the time I began business in 1851, with the exception of my own, had either failed or discontinued work as a shipbuilding establishment' in support of this perspective (1993, p. 59). Samuda's comment, made in evidence to a Royal Commission on Trade Unions is important but is probably rather broader than it at first appears and covers both the crisis of 1866, which was severe indeed in its effects on the London shipbuilding trade and on living conditions in the East End but also the time of the Crimean (or Russian) War, which was an important but under-recognised time of business failure in iron shipbuilding on the Thames.

The period 1854–59, taken as a whole, was a boom time for the British shipbuilding trade. The general tendency towards larger ships continued (the average tonnage per ship being 232 as against 194 net tons in 1847–53) and the number of new ships increased 40 per cent as well, resulting in an average annual tonnage of over 250,000 tons, 65 per cent above the average for 1847–53. The increase was particularly concentrated in the years 1855–57, however, and by 1859 tonnage levels were back to the levels of 1853–54 and falling.

There are no comprehensive, reliable data sources on regional shipbuilding during the period 1827–65 but it is clear that the real growth area in the UK in the 1850s was the Clyde, where iron was now cheaper than wood and where shipbuilders were developing a formidable reputation for the provision of screw-driven iron hulls powered by reliable steam engines. Between 1856 and 1860, over 75 per cent of all iron ships constructed in the UK were built on the River Clyde (Moss 1997, p. 17; see also Peebles 1990, p. 26; Slaven 1975, p. 132) and further competition for firms on the Thames had materialised in the north-west of England, following the discovery in 1850 of huge deposits of high-grade phosphorous-free iron in Furness and west Cumberland.

The ship listings of the P&O, Royal Mail and Union Steam companies suggest that the Thames continued to lose its pre-eminence during the second half of the 1850s, but still enjoyed a considerable amount of business. P&O still looked to the Thames for substantial iron steamers, colliers and liners, particularly for the Southampton–Alexandria service so that, in 1854–59, out of 19 ships they had built, seven were made in Scotland (mostly by Tod and McGregor) and six on the Thames, two by Samuda, two by C. J. Mare and the other two by Thames Ironworks (Rabson and O'Donoghue 1988; Hawes 1978). In the period 1854–59, Royal Mail Steam Packet only had four iron ships built, but two were constructed by Thames Ironworks (Bushell 1939, pp. 257–8).

The Union Steam Collier Company had been formed by Arthur Andersen in 1853 to carry coal from South Wales to Southampton, the port for P&O and RMSP; six iron-hulled ships were built, of 350 to 530 gross tons, all on the Thames, three by Samuda and three by Charles Lungley.[1] When the Crimean War started, the ships were almost immediately taken over by the government and, at the end of the conflict, were returned, but by then coal stocks were generally more plentiful and the company adopted a different trading policy, obtaining the mail contracts to Cape Colony and Natal in 1857, and also changing its name to the Union Steam Ship Company (Hawes 1990, p. 11).

During this period, the Admiralty had several important effects upon the private shipbuilding trade. Firstly, in 1852, their ban on the construction of iron vessels for the mail companies, whose ships were expected to fulfil an auxiliary naval role, was withdrawn and this stimulated iron construction in the UK generally (Bushell 1939, p. 71). In the case of Royal Mail, for example, their last wooden paddle-steamer was launched in 1854 by Pitchers of Northfleet (Bushell 1939, pp. 257–8).

The Admiralty was also beginning to change its views on the appropriate construction of naval vessels. Solid shot had generally been seen as a more effective form of attack on shipping than the firing of shells (hollow projectiles filled with gunpowder) but was often highly inaccurate and thus largely ineffective, although it could sometimes be devastating to wooden ships, as in the firings by Prussian field guns in 1849 which set fire to and destroyed several Danish warships (Lyon 1980, p. 20). Tests in the 1840s on the effects of solid shot on the 0.5 inch-thick iron plating then used in iron ship construction had shown that the plates tended to split and also that there could be a highly dangerous shrapnel-like effect on those on board.

With improvements in rifling, however, the firing of shells became more effective. They were used increasingly as a supplement to cannon balls, and their use by the Russian fleet against the Ottoman fleet at Sinope in 1853 made it clear how devastating shell fire could be against wooden walled ships, prompting an urgent rethink of design strategy amongst the world's navies. Britain, as the lead navy with the greatest investment, had most to lose from changes to the type of vessel in use but the Crimean War was highly instructive in this regard and had major impacts on naval design conventions and strategies.

---

1. The first, *Union*, had a composite hull, with iron frames and plates but wooden bulwarks (Hawes 1990, p21).

The war, the costliest in human terms of any involving the Great Powers in the century from 1815, was 'in many ways, not only the last of the old wars, but also the first of the modern ones. It was the first to use railways, iron-clad steamships, mines and the telegraph' (Kerr 1997, pp. 7, 178). The conflict made demands upon naval resources in a number of ways. Many of the larger ships owned by the major mail companies, Royal Mail, Cunard and P&O, duly fulfilled the naval auxiliary role that had been anticipated in the government's contracts for overseas mail delivery, chiefly by helping to transport the expeditionary force to Turkey and the Crimea and then back, an operation that finished in July 1856.

The Russian concentration of fortified bases, notably at Sveaborg, Kronstadt and Kinburn, presented the Allied fleets with considerable difficulty and a tactical dilemma. The French believed that armoured batteries were most appropriate to the situation and they built three floating batteries, covered with thick plates of iron, which were used in action in October 1855 (Kerr 1997, p. 146). The British fleet was initially deployed in the Black Sea, but a large fleet left Portsmouth in March 1855 for the Baltic that included large numbers of gunboats and mortar vessels, consistent with the British preference for dispersed fire-power, which they had achieved by building large numbers of small vessels on which heavy guns were mounted. These 'gunboats', which could also protect the floating batteries, were made with very shallow draughts, suitable for the local conditions, and their rapid construction became a pressing national objective. Their ready supply was hampered by the decision of the Admiralty to also construct an ocean-going steam battle-fleet in the Royal Dockyards (for a war with France that they thought would follow; Lambert 1990, p. 269) and the government therefore looked to the private sector, particularly the shipbuilders on the Thames, for meeting the immediate need for small, and somewhat basic, vessels for the Crimea.

This meant that in 1854–56 the Navy had a significant impact on the overall levels of shipbuilding in the private sector for the first time for many years. In 1854–56, nearly 12 per cent of private sector tonnage was built for the government, although the demand virtually disappeared in 1857.

Four classes of gunboats were ordered, beginning with six vessels in the Gleaner class in June 1854. The specifications were gradually improved and 20 Dapper-class boats were ordered in October 1854. In 1855, another 98 Dapper gunboats were ordered, as well as 20 Cheerful-class gunboats and then 12 Clown class in January 1856 (Osbon 1965, pp. 103–4). In 1855, eight armour-plated batteries were also ordered and built on the Thames (five made of iron and three of wood) along with a large number of iron mortar floats of about 100 tons each.

The vessels were all relatively basic and wooden-hulled, of between 210 and 235 tons burden and were designed to carry heavy guns (two 68-pound guns, or one 68 pounder and either a 32 pounder or two 24-pound brass howitzers, or variations thereon). The contractors were expected to do 'little more than get the hull afloat' as most of the coppering, rigging and armament work was attended to by the Royal Dockyards. The urgency was such that official supervision was minimal and even the use of green timber was allowed in the later stages, although many of the boats were not in fact completed in time to serve in the war (which was under armistice by February 1856 and officially ended, following the ratification of the Treaty of Paris, in April 1856). In the 1860s there were complaints that many of the gunboats were 'fit only for firewood' (Osbon 1965, p. 105) but in 1854–55 the government, while

> stipulating in formal terms for good workmanship and sound material, knew perfectly well that neither such material nor such workmanship was likely to be forthcoming ... neither in the stocks of the builders themselves nor in the market was there any adequate supply of sound seasoned wood ... The private yards were deficient in the necessary accommodation. They seldom had covered slips, so that, for the most part, the boats were built in the open air, although many of them were constructed in the winter and in very bad weather ... and the vessels were often planked and covered in while the timber was wet.

Less excusably, short bolts were sometimes used for fastenings and other bolts were left unclinched, consequent upon the work often being subcontracted to gangs of workmen, who 'undertook portions of the vessel at piecework rates' (*Times* 21 September 1860, p. 6).

The 156 gunboat contracts were shared amongst 16 private sector shipbuilders and four naval dockyards, but the distribution was highly uneven; 14 were built in the Dockyards, 101 by nine firms on the Thames (Pitcher 54, Green 14, Wigram 13, Mare 6, Fletcher 5, Young of Limehouse 4, Thompson of Rotherhithe 2, Joyce of Greenwich 2 and Westbrooks of Blackwall 1) and the other 41 in the north-east, at Birkenhead, Bristol and Cowes (see Osbon 1965, pp. 211–20).

The engine contracts were also important and were divided between the two best-known firms, Maudslay Son and Field of Lambeth and John Penn of Greenwich, and were important because the construction of over 150 sets of engines within two years represents one of the earliest examples of the application of mass production methods to marine engineering.

Unfortunately, the urgency and size of Admiralty demands provoked a sharp cost-inflation in shipbuilding (particularly in the cost of shipbuilding timber; Lambert 1987, p. 65) and meant that many firms, far from benefiting from the extra work, were ruined by it. Labour costs on the London river had barely changed since 1825 but, during the Crimean War, the usual rate for shipwrights of 6s 6d a day reached '10s, 12s and 15s a day' (Royal Commission on Trade Unions 1867–68, p. 30). The combination of fixed-price naval contracts and very rapid (and unfamiliar) cost increases (shipwrights' wages rose by 50 per cent in the period June–October 1855 alone) was particularly damaging to the shipbuilding firms and the situation became so bad that the Admiralty even offered bonuses of 30s per ton as a voluntary inducement to shipbuilders to continue to meet completion dates, and 'offset the unexpected increase in wages the shipbuilders were compelled to pay the shipwrights and other workmen', although the extra amounts were not large enough to avoid serious losses being made on the contracts (Lambert 1990 p. 310).

The severity of the problems at this time have not always been recognised, although Emmerson and Crighton did both recognise the difficulties facing firms in the shipbuilding and engineering industries on the Thames at the end of the war: the 'inflation of costs and wages brought devastating consequences when hostilities ended in March 1856. As the war was finishing, orders were suddenly cut back and decreased and the abnormally high wages paid during the war could not be maintained.' With poor prospects in view, unprofitable current contracts and reduced credit, many of the Thames shipbuilders either failed or closed down and 'great distress in the labour community ensued' (Emmerson 1977, p. 103; Crighton, p. 23).

The problems were compounded by the weather conditions of the time. In the winter of 1854–55, the Thames froze over so that 'the navigation of ships, steamers and boats was 'entirely stopped … ..and the distress among the labouring class caused by the suspension of labour was appalling', leading to bread riots in Whitechapel. The winter of 1855–56 was also one of 'excessive rain and snow' (Jones 1976, pp. 44–5, quoting from the *Reynolds News* 25 February 1855).

The main Thames yards

Iron shipbuilding had 'flourished' during the early 1850s, particularly on the Clyde but also in London. The prime area for construction, the Isle of Dogs, had been transformed. By 1854 it had become the centre of heavy industry in London and had a population of 5,000 people, with 530 houses and sixty manufactories (Survey of London 1994, p. 379) and to a reporter from the *Illustrated London News* in May 1857 the areas that were not built over, 'those marshy fields, sparsely studded with stunted limes and poplars, muddy ditches, with here and there a meditative cow cropping the coarse herbage, [were] not suggestive of the sublime or beautiful' (Rolt 1964, p. 266).

Some accounts and listings of firms on the Thames that built significant volumes of iron ships have tended greatly to exaggerate the number of firms involved and thus the nature of the declines of 1857 and 1866. The suggestion that very large numbers of firms went out of existence also tends to imply that general economic factors are likely to have been the main cause, even when the decline was very rapid, although it will be argued in this book that the production of iron shipbuilding on the river was always concentrated upon a relatively small number of firms (partly because of the nature of the technologies involved and the scale of operation which this in turn required) and that factors specific to those firms were as important to the decline of the local trade as general economic factors.

In the period 1854–59, there were seven iron shipbuilders of some importance on the Thames; Scott Russell, Mare, Money Wigram, Samuda, Rennie, Westwood Baillie and Lungley, far fewer than some listings have suggested.[2]

Scott Russell's fortunes were greatly shaped by the problems of constructing and launching the *Great Eastern*, the ship that was effectively to end his career as a shipbuilder, Mare was driven into bankruptcy by cost inflation at the time of the Crimean War despite the very high output levels

2. The most extensive listings of firms active in the iron shipbuilding trade in the mid 1850s are those of Hicks and Jordan, both compiled in the 1920s, who together identify 27 such firms as follows:

Millwall: William Fairbairn, J. Scott Russell, Edwards and Symes, D. Napier,
Blackwall: Ditchburn and Mare, Green, Money, Wigram and Sons, J. Watson, Miller and Ravenhill
Deptford: Charles Lungley
Northfleet: E. W. Morris, William Pitcher
Greenwich: W. Joyce, J. & G. Rennie, Maudslay Sons and Field
Limehouse: Fletcher Son and Fearnall
Isle of Dogs: Westwood Baillie Campbell and Co., Samuda Bros., Yarrow and Co.
Rotherhithe: Bilbie and Co.
Woolwich: F. Dadd
Bow Creek: Lewis and Stockwell
Cubitt Town: J. & W. Dudgeon, John Hepworth, James Ash
Canning Town: J. & W. Robertson
Chiswick: J. Thorneycroft (Hicks 1928, p. 80; Jordan 1925, p. 8).

The list includes, however, a) nine firms that did make iron ships, but not in the mid-1850s: Fairbairn (finished 1848), Napier (finished 1852), Green (in business but wood only until 1866), Miller and Ravenhill (finished iron ships 1847, but continued with marine engines), Maudslay (did not build iron ships between late 1830s and 1865 but continued with marine engines), Yarrow (started 1865), Dudgeon (started 1863), Ash (started 1862), Thorneycroft (started 1862) and b) eleven wooden or very small-scale iron shipbuilders: Edwards and Symes, Watson, Morris, Joyce, Fletcher Fearnall, Bilbie, Pitcher, Dadd, Lewis, Hepworth, Robertson.

he achieved (as was the leading contractor and wooden ship specialist, Pitcher of Northfleet), although Mare's father-in-law did continue the business successfully as Thames Iron Works. Samuda strengthened his reputation for technical sophistication and Lungley, Money Wigram and Rennie continued to make ships at moderate levels of output. Westwood and Baillie successfully formed their own business, after a long apprenticeship in Mare's yard.

John Scott Russell (Yard 1: Millwall Shipyard) – see also Appendix 3

The fire in the shipbuilding yard in September 1853 was a serious setback to Russell's hopes regarding the construction of the great ship (originally called the *Leviathan*, but later known as the *Great Eastern*) but in the long run the clauses in the contract which gave Brunel 'full control and supervision over every part of the work' probably proved to be more problematic.

Although Russell was an experienced naval architect and a shipbuilder of considerable competence and despite the fact that it was Russell's (not Brunel's) money that was directly at stake on operational decisions (once the contract price had been fixed), Brunel adopted his normal railway construction practice of 'close and comprehensive external control', in line with the wording of the contract. This proved to be a constant source of conflict; whereas Russell in line with normal practice in the shipbuilding trade routinely delegating a great many operational decisions to his senior employees, whom he had carefully picked, Brunel instead involved himself and intervened in almost everything that took place. On the *Great Eastern*, as each constructional problem was solved (and there were many, given the pioneering nature of the work) they were 'to be committed to paper to go forward to the Chief Engineer for approval and often elaboration'. As Brunel explained, he had 'made it a rule from the first that no part of the work should be commenced until it had been specially considered and determined upon and working drawings in full detail prepared and, after due deliberation, formally settled and signed' (Emmerson 1977, pp. 78–9, 83).

The most severe effects of Brunel's control concerned the launching arrangements. Normal practice in Russell's yard was for vessels to be launched, 'fully equipped ready for sea and with engines on board', a practice thought to be peculiar to Millwall (Cowper 1853, p. 71). Russell's preference for the *Great Eastern* was, therefore, to build a dry dock, even though this could cost as much as £20,000, but Brunel objected to this on grounds of cost.

Russell's second preference was to use a normal inclined slip-way for the launching, although this would have carried the keel so far inland during construction as to have probably been 'beyond the extent of the builders' premises', would have been more difficult for contractors (as the ship's bow would have been so high in the air) and would have required a restrained launching, as the ship was nearly as long as the river was wide at low tide (TIQG Vol. 2, p. 52).

The alternative sideways launch, which Brunel strongly favoured, meant instead building the ship parallel to the river and then launching it down an inclined slip. This solution occupied a huge amount of river frontage and more than Russell owned. The fire in 1853 had been very destructive of Russell's assets, but it had also so damaged the facilities of Napier next door as to finally drive him out of business, so that Russell was able to lease the major part of Napier's empty yard in 1854, sufficient to accommodate the major part of the *Great Eastern* and thereby release space in Russell's own yard for the construction of the enormous paddle engines, for a new, 40-foot-high engine shop and for other construction work. A railway line was then built, parallel to the river, along the entire length of the shipyard, which was then enclosed.

The *Great Eastern* was to be four times the weight of any previous boat, 692 feet long and was intended to carry 4,000 people (800 in first-class, 2,000 in second-class and 1200 in third), or 10,000 if fitted for troops only (TIQG Vol. 2, p. 52). Its hull was to be double-skinned and to be powered by both paddle-wheels and screw-propellers, requiring a good deal of pioneering work. Construction started on 1 May 1854, and it was expected that 30,000 iron plates (of 3/4 to 1 inch thickness and weighing a third of a ton each) and 3,000,000 rivets would be needed. The construction of the piles to support the ship while it was being built would itself require 1,200 tons of timber (*Illustrated London News* 4 November 1854, p. 440).

The sheer size of the ship also meant that relatively familiar components would be extraordinarily large, would involve unfamiliar physical stresses and thereby cause considerable organisational difficulties. The firm's machinery would inflict 'severe vibration' on houses in the nearby streets. Not many firms were willing to tender for the more specialised work; the crankshaft, for example, had to be contracted out to Messrs Fulton and Neilson at Lancefield Forge, Glasgow and even they had to build special furnaces. It took them three attempts to achieve the largest forgings that anyone had ever undertaken. The screw engines were cast in Birmingham and assembled into units weighing 500 tons. The 36-ton cast-iron propeller was carried on a shaft 150 feet long, weighing 60 tons. The engines for the paddle-wheels had four cylinders and each mould took 34 tons of molten iron (Dumpleton and Miller 1974, p. 99).

Although work on the *Great Eastern* was to be so innovative, Russell's quotation left no margin for unexpected eventualities or for the additional costs caused by Brunel's constant modifications and amendments. The quote had been only slightly above Brunel's tentative, original estimate and Brunel had a history of underestimating project costs. Russell's rather difficult financial position became positively threatening when Geach died in late 1854. This was a personal and business tragedy for Russell; he lost one of his closest friends, a colleague whose advice could be trusted and the means whereby the leading iron-makers, Beale and Co. would supply the necessary iron on a deferred payment basis.

Russell went to the commissioning shipping company in December 1854 to ask for a scheme of accelerated payments to himself for work done and, on New Year's Day 1855, when Martins Bank denied him any further credit, he sought Brunel's support. Unfortunately, at that time Brunel was thought to be resentful at the amount of recognition Russell was getting in the press concerning the construction of the *Great Eastern*,[3] and he also did not entirely trust Russell, so that their working relationship began to deteriorate (Emmerson 1977, p. 79; Rolt 1964, p. 251).

In 1855, with the Crimean War raising demand for shipping, Russell was also busy on a number of other ships, including the naval floating battery, Etna, although this was 'gutted by fire on the eve of its launch' at an estimated loss of £45,000, only partly covered by insurance.

For a time, the Eastern Steam Navigation Company's accelerated payments to Russell helped to maintain the speed of construction but by December 1855 there was another crisis. Brunel no longer believed that Russell was operating in the best interest of Eastern Steam, as six of Russell's ships were being built in Napier's yard in such a way as to delay the completion of the *Great Eastern*. Brunel also alleged that there were 'unexplained deficiencies' amounting to 1,200 tons of iron (Dumpleton and Miller 1974, p. 100).

On 4 February 1856, the Scott Russell Shipbuilding and Engineering Company announced that it was suspending payments and the following day, Eastern Steam took over the ship. At the end of the week, Russell's employees were discharged and his shipyard (into which the *Great Eastern* projected) was seized by the bank. It then took until May 1856, for the bank to give clearance for work to resume on the *Great Eastern*, and even then there were strict time limits attached, although Eastern Steam managed to ease the restrictions by making further payments to the bank (Rolt 1964, p. 265).[4]

---

3. It seems unlikely that this was warranted; sometime later, in April 1857, for example, Russell wrote to the *Times* in terms that effectively ensured Brunel received full recognition as the person responsible for the concept of building a steamship so large that it could carry its own coal even on long voyages and for the idea of using a cellular construction akin to that used on the Britannia bridge, and identified himself only as the person responsible for her 'merits or defects as a piece of naval architecture' (Emmerson 1977, p. 123).
4. An extension from 12 August to 10 October 1857 cost £2,500, for example.

The ship could now only be launched sideways, although this could be achieved either by means of a free or a controlled launch. Russell favoured the free launch, which was much simpler, at least £10,000 cheaper and could be justified by reference to American experience. Brunel instead insisted on a carefully-controlled broadside launch, with the ship slowly lowered to the water's edge at low tide and then floated off, which was safer but far more complex and more expensive of Russell's money (Emmerson 1977, p. 92).

In the light of the difficult situation with Martins Bank, Brunel decided to launch on 3 November 1857, even though this precluded adequate testing of the launching equipment. The occasion was poorly co-ordinated and was to be a public relations disaster; Brunel's stipulation of absolute quiet so as to aid co-ordination of the restraining winches and hydraulic rams (or perhaps merely to reduce his exposure to ridicule in the event of a mis-launching) was flouted by the Eastern Steam directors, who sold over three thousand tickets to a noisy and excited public in an attempt to recoup a little of their accumulating losses and gain some favourable publicity. Instead, the quite terrifying and highly public death of one of the winch operators caused chaos and hysteria and finally stopped a launching which had not gone at all well.

On 28 November, with no public onlookers, the ship moved, but only 14 feet and at some cost in 'broken tackle, chain cables and mooring chains'. Brunel was greatly troubled and approached an obscure, specialist firm in Birmingham for more hydraulic rams, despite the considerable cost involved (Hicks 1928, p. 86). On 10 January 1858, the great ship reached the high water mark and, on 31 January 1858, with four tugs in attendance, it finally floated.

Russell's original preference to build a dry dock costing perhaps £20,000 had been vetoed by Brunel as uneconomic, but the eventual cost of the controlled, sideways launch was nearer £120,000 (Emmerson 1977, p. 128). The whole operation was a serious 'engineering failure' and was partly caused by Brunel's 'fateful decision to attach rows of iron plates to the underside of the cradles running parallel to the axis of the ship to provide a surface on which they would slide along rows of ordinary railway lines to the water's edge' (Emmerson 1977, p. 122). With a set of iron bars on the upper surface of the ways and another set of iron plates on the lower surface of the cradle, the two metal surfaces 'rubbed off the lubricating stuff so that the rails simply bit one another as the wheels of a locomotive engine bite the rails', holding several thousands of tons on a 1 in 12 incline so firmly that it took several hydraulic rams, exerting thousands of tons of pressure, three months to move it to the water's edge.

Brunel had sought to avoid the binding of wood on wood but Russell saw Brunel's desire to use iron ways, rather than the traditional method of grease on wood as the real cause of the disaster. His view was that, 'had the surface on which she was carried been simply the ordinary plank surface, well lubricated with tallow and grease', the launching would have been like the launching of any large ship, as the area of ways covered by the two cradles was nearly 20,000 square feet (the ways were each 120 feet wide and 110 feet apart), a surface 'more than sufficient to conduct the weight smoothly and gently down into the water' (TIQG Vol. 2, p. 52). Instead it was 'the destiny of the *Great Eastern* to be the victim of experiments which had nothing to do with her original design, or her ultimate purpose' (Emmerson 1977, pp. 128–9).

In November and December of 1857, with the great ship stuck on her ways, the failed launch became 'the mock of every envious soul in London', and numerous suggestions were made to put her to good use where she stood, as she was large enough to house 'all the shows of London', casinos, concerts and more minor entertainments, that could make good use of the potential for 'communication services between the two ends by train and by electric telegraph' (Rose 1951, pp. 147–8).

Brunel found the difficulties very hard to take and the whole operation took the most severe toll on his health, accelerating his premature death. With a cost prior to fitting-out of £732,000, it also caused the failure of her owners, Eastern Steam Navigation, so that a new firm, the Great Ship Company, was formed in November 1858 with a capital of £300,000, to bring her to completion (Dumpleton and Miller 1974, pp. 102–8).

In mid-1857, Russell's creditors agreed with his leasing the unoccupied part of David Napier's yard, in order to re-establish his shipbuilding business (Emmerson 1977, p. 125) and, strangely, he received the contract for fitting-out the *Great Eastern*. She was fitted out and rigged at moorings at Deptford, leaving on 7 September 1859 on her first trip to Portland Roads.[5] Off Eastbourne, a terrific explosion occurred, caused by an absence of safety valves for the paddle-engine boiler funnels, and six stokers were killed and the saloon and several cabins wrecked. After repairs, a successful trial trip to Holyhead took place in early October 1859.

The *Great Eastern* was intended to be large enough to travel round the Cape to Australia and India with all her coal aboard, and thus to compete with P&O without the need for expensive coaling stations to be built en route, but she never made the journeys for which she was built. Instead, in June 1860 her maiden voyage was made to New York, followed by a number of repeat journeys, many attended by accident or high expense. The remainder of the shareholder's capital was soon lost and in 1864 the ship was sold to Glass Elliot and Co. on behalf of the bond-holders and laid up

5. Brunel was on board at the time and had a serious stroke, was taken off at Gravesend and died on 15 September, aged 54.

until 1866 when she was chartered by the Telegraph Construction and Maintenance Company, in order to lay a new Atlantic cable. The *Great Eastern* left the Medway on 30 June 1866 on what proved to be a highly successful venture, that led to other submarine cable work, including the laying of the Indian cable from Bombay to Aden. Later, she had a brief career moored in the river Mersey, 'transformed as a speculation by a syndicate into a floating palace, concert hall and gymnasium' (TIQG Vol. 10, p. 11) but was laid up in the late 1870s and eventually sold at an 'old iron' price of £16,500 and broken up on a beach on the Mersey in August 1888 (TIQG Vol. 2, p. 54; Jordan 1925, pp. 11–12).

C. J. Mare (Yard 2: Orchard and Bow Creek Shipyard until 1855) – see also Appendix 3

Mare's decision to expand his business in the late 1840s and to vertically integrate the iron production and ship construction activities was a great success. From 1850, once the adaptations had been completed, the shipyard achieved unprecedented levels of output, more than three-quarters of which was from commercial contracts, while the business also used its iron production facilities to meet large civil engineering orders, particularly for iron bridges and dock gates.

The onset of the Russian War provided even more demand for shipping tonnage, raising employment levels in the yard to between three and four thousand men (Rose 1973, p. 145) and the weekly wage bill to between £5,000 and £6,600 (these figures do not include employees working on bridge and other civil engineering constructions). At this time, improved medical services were also made available, although the cost was largely covered by contributions of a 1d a week paid by men earning over 30s a week (and half that for workers on lower rates of pay), and Mare founded the Poplar Hospital, after one of his workmen nearly died from the delays in reaching the nearest hospital, then in Mile-End Road.

Trading volumes were very high, which helped to spread the yard's overhead costs, but rapid and unprecedented rises in raw material and wage costs in the London area affected the firm's trading margins and, despite the most careful forms of accounting for tools, materials and various forms of hardware withdrawn from store and used on ship construction (*Illustrated London News* 28 October 1854, p. 410), the firm began to make heavy losses on their contracts.

In April 1855, the *Illustrated London News* (7 April 1855, p. 322) was congratulating the company for launching five vessels in a fortnight and making such 'rapid progress to completion' of the gun and mortar batteries, unaware of the difficult position in which the firm had been for some time past. It had become a common thing for the wages 'not to come down until seven or eight o'clock on Saturday nights' although work finished at six, and this provoked the men to 'cursing and swearing, hooting and threatening to wreck the offices' so that 'poor old Master Kennedy, the cashier, when he arrived with the money had to pass a turbulent crowd, often in fear of his life' (TIQG vol. 2, p. 3).

The last straw proved to be the construction of six wooden gunboats (*Nightingale*, *Violet*, *Bouncer*, *Hyena*, *Savage* and *Wolf*) of 250 tons each for the Crimea, each of which earned about £10,000 but were costing the firm far more; the firm's naval architect, G. C. Mackrow, later wrote that 'it was over these wooden vessels that Mr Mare came to grief', perhaps because the firm was less experienced at constructing wooden vessels (TIQG vol. 2, p. 3). Soon there were confrontations with the creditors, and the 2,000-ton *Pera*, under construction for the P&O's Southampton to Alexandria service, had to be hastily launched to avoid her seizure by creditors.

Mare was declared bankrupt in September 1855, at which date he had unsecured debts of £160,000 and total liabilities of £400,000, the assets being difficult to estimate at that point in time (*Times* 13 October 1855, p. 9). Even as late as mid-January, the 'voluminous nature of the accounts' necessitated a further adjournment and it was doubted whether it would be possible even within a further two months to complete the accounts so as to show the real position (*Times* 18 January 1856, p. 9).

The Official Assignee asked two works managers, Joseph Westwood and Robert Baillie (who were later to set up their own shipbuilding and repair business on the Isle of Dogs) to act as managers for a time, under his directions and on behalf of the creditors, while Mare, curiously, went to manage W. & H. Pitcher's business at Northfleet when it also failed in 1857.

Mare's examination in the Court of Bankruptcy eventually took place on 20 May 1856. It became clear that the delay in producing proper statements was partly because James Campbell, who was paid £1,000 a year to run the civil engineering side of the business, had failed to maintain the books, which did not help the business to monitor its performance (*Times* 21 May 1856, p. 11). Mare now had creditors of £437,472, nearly three-quarters of whom had taken out charges on a variety of assets as security.

Mare's business had made a great deal of money but, apart from the losses on government contracts, had also made heavy losses on building the Westminster and Saltash bridges. He was a 'warm supporter of horse-racing' (for a long time he ran racing-stables at Newmarket), he was also an unusually generous and 'open-handed' friend and he and his family did not live frugally: his wife moved in Court circles, he was a close friend of Disraeli and a 'familiar figure at Brighton during the season' (*Daily Mail* 18 February 1898).

His assets were extensive and widely dispersed and included the freehold of the original Blackwall yard (£28,800), of the new yard (£46,600) and of family estates at three sites in Cheshire (£49,000) and at Newmarket (£8,500) as well as various shareholdings, notably in the General Steam Shipping Company.

He had spent £27,350, £17,000 and £6,500 more respectively on the Cheshire, Newmarket and Staffordshire estates than they were now worth. He had also lost £3,300 on his stud of horses, £38,000 on his shares in General Steam and £16,000 on contesting an election in Plymouth and on running the *Plymouth Mail* newspaper (*Times* 21 May 1856, p. 11).

The business had also got into difficulties, with its liquid assets clearly insufficient to meet the claims of the creditors but the buildings, plant and machinery were thought to be worth at least £175,000, the business was entirely worthwhile and the creditors were keen to see it continue under different management (*Banking Almanac* 1856, pp. 50–52). His bankruptcy did, however, cost the firm the regular orders of the General Steam Navigation Co.; after his failure, GSN had their ships built in the north and in Scotland (Crighton, p. 8).

Thames Iron Works (Yard 2: Orchard and Bow Creek Shipyard from 1856) – see also Appendix 3

The business, including the Orchard Shipyard in Blackwall and the rolling plant on the Essex side of Bow Creek, was taken over in 1856 by Mare's father-in-law, Peter Rolt, a member of the committee of creditors for Mare's business, a director of the Commercial Dock Company, Conservative MP for Greenwich and Deputy-Lieutenant of Middlesex and someone with long family connections in shipping and shipbuilding (Hume and Moss 1979, p. 296).[6]

The first priority was the completion of the contracts that were still in progress, including those with the Admiralty for gunboats and four despatch-boats, which were well advanced but had stopped for lack of money. The Admiralty agreed to pay £9,700 of the agreed price to Rolt in advance of the contract schedule and this enabled the firm to finish building them (*Times* 17 November 1855, p. 11).

In early January 1856, the government ordered 20 iron mortar vessels of 100 tons each, to be completed by the re-formed business for £2,200 each, six in January, six in February and the rest in March. An order had also been received for an iron steamer for the South-Western Railway Company for the Southampton–Le Havre route, to be finished by April and a large ship was in hand for the delivery to Genoa. The Westminster Bridge contract was also proceeding satisfactorily, work levels in the foundry had recovered

6. Peter Rolt was also married to Mary Brocklebank, whose father had founded the General Steam Navigation Company.

since the bankruptcy, total wages were running at £3,500 a week and in some of the departments the workmen were being employed 'day and night' (*Times* 18 January 1856, p. 9).

Five vessels, including three mortar-boats, were launched on one tide in April 1856, the others being the *Genova*, 2,000 tons and the *Havre*, a 600-ton paddle-steamer built for the South-Western Railway and named by the daughter of the official assignee (*Picture Times* 21 April 1856).

Having coped so successfully with the completion of the contracts from Mare's era and with the more urgent orders received, early in 1857 Rolt put the business on a more assured long-term basis by re-forming it as the Thames Iron Works and Shipbuilding Co. Ltd, with an initial capital of £100,000 (*Times* 26 January 1857, p. 7). The capital was issued in the form of £5,000 shares, a strong signal that the company sought to channel the investments of connected associates and not to facilitate active dealing by a wider group of investors. The largest individual subscribers were Rolt, with five shares and the Maudslay family with three shares (Bowen 1945, p. 375; Survey of London 1994, p. 673).[7] The firm clearly intended to strengthen the links between shipbuilding and its related trades (six of the fourteen shareholders were London engineers) and D. F. Dykes, a founder member of the noted engine-builders, Humphreys, Tennant and Dykes Ltd, was recruited as one of the first directors.

The new company's first boats were a Dover and Calais steamer (*Prince Frederick William*) and a 700 ton cargo steamer (*Wolf*). They were able to meet the demands of the merchant shipping companies for mail packets, cargo steamers, cross-channel steamers and passenger ships, including the *Nepaul* and *Delta* launched in 1858–59 for the P&O. In October 1858, Thames Ironworks launched the UK's first floating derrick, an immense diamond-shaped craft built entirely of iron and weighing 5,000 tons, that was to be used for raising the sunken wrecks of vessels that had foundered off the British coasts. Also in 1858–59, the large paddle-ship, the *Paramatta*, was built for the Royal Mail Steam Packet, being one of the last ships to be launched from the Orchard Shipyard before it was sold off and operations concentrated on the Essex side of Bow Creek (Crighton, p. 23).

Money Wigram (Yard 3: Blackwall Yard) – see also Appendix 3

The Crimean War brought a great deal of business to the Blackwall Yard although much of it was for the construction of wooden gunboats; Wigram was an important builder of Dapper-class gunboats and mortar floats in particular but also constructed two larger ships for the Admiralty.

In the neighbouring yard, Wigram's former partner, Richard Green, who

7. PRO Kew, Annual Returns, BT31/219/686.

continued to build only wooden ships, also became an important supplier of ships for the Crimean War, building 14 Dapper class screw gunboats of just over 200 tons each and 11 other naval ships, including HMS *Glatton* (Banbury 1971, p. 182).

Samuda (Yard 4: Samuda's Yard)

During the Russian War, Samuda was mainly working on contracts for the railways, but did receive a contract from the Admiralty for the first armour-cased iron ship, the *Thunderbolt*, a 'monster floating battery' of nearly 2,000 tons intended to fire 20 guns of the 'largest calibre' at the stone fortifications in the Crimea. It was not, however, finished in time and instead became a floating landing stage at Chatham dockyard!

Samuda and Co. were technologically progressive shipbuilders, pioneering the construction of ships from steel and building one such vessel in 1856 for service on the River Kuban. In 1857, they built a ship of 450 tons wholly from steel for use on the Black Sea and followed this by building Spanish gunboats for Manilla, steamers for service on the Thames, Humber and Volga as well as smaller boats for the exploration of the River Amazon, all made largely from the new material (Editorial in *Engineering* 21 April 1893).

They also had a reputation for good-quality work on more conventional ships and continued to build for P&O (including the *Alhambra* in 1855 and the *Ceylon* in 1858, an iron screw barque of 2,400 tons which was seen as a very high quality boat and had a long and successful career; Cable 1937, p. 268), for Royal Mail Steam Packet and the Union Steam Ship Co. The *Leinster*, a packet for the Dublin–Holyhead route was able to achieve nearly 18 knots on its trials and earn her builders a good price (£80,000, or £46 per gross ton).

In Samuda's yard, the iron-work was done by boiler-makers and other 'iron-men' and the wood-work by shipwrights and joiners. Each man was rated at a fixed daily amount and, in typical London river fashion, jobs were generally allocated to gangs of men who drew their agreed daily rate against the specified total amount. On completion any remaining balance, or profit, was handed over to the men who had worked on the job concerned (Royal Commission on Trade Unions 1867–68 Minutes of Evidence, p. 11).

Rennie (Yard 5: Norman Road, Greenwich)

The yard at Greenwich continued to produced a 'small output of widely-varying types' (Banbury 1971, p. 237), particularly small river steamers and gunboats of up to 5–600 tons, beginning in 1859 with an order from the Indian government for several shallow-draught river steamers.

Other firms

Thomas Pitcher had been a leading shipbuilder in the late eighteenth century at Rotherhithe, building mainly East Indiamen and Admiralty warships but moved in 1788, away from the crowded, expensive 'Pool' of London to a large stretch of marshland (with good chalk foundations) at Northfleet, which provided the scope at relatively low cost to make larger ships. The business was highly successful until the discovery in 1813 that some of their warships had been built with 'devils' (iron fastenings with a copper head that were much weaker than the proper, all-copper versions), which immediately ruined his reputation and business. Two of his sons, William and Henry, later reopened the yard (and built the famous castellated gatehouse to the yard)[8] and gradually re-established the reputation of the yard. They built only wooden ships, were still building the last of Royal Mail's wooden paddle-steamers in 1854 (the *Tamar*) and then became by far the largest contractor for Admiralty warships, making 54 (more than half the total built on the Thames) of the 156 shallow-draught wooden screw gunboats required by the Admiralty for the Crimea, at a price of between £8,200 and £10,000 apiece. The increased level of business persuaded Pitcher to install additional plant, to cover some of the slipways and to also install gas lighting, so that 'the work could be carried on night and day' (Bowen 1943, p. 174). The contracts raised employment levels in the yard to around 2,000 men, but the unexpected and sharp cost inflation on the Thames made things very difficult. The war was followed by a slump and, with the downturn in business, Pitcher could not repay the money borrowed to expand facilities at the yard, leading to his bankruptcy' (Bowen 1943, p. 174). The receiver appointed as manager, C. J. Mare, 'whose Blackwall business had also been ruined by the gunboat contracts' and business activity at the yard ended three years later, following the construction of the Greek steam frigate *Amalia* and the death of William Pitcher. There were several attempts to sell the site as a shipyard and Elders of Glasgow were interested in establishing a new company, the Thames and Clyde Shipbuilding and Engineering Co. Ltd, at the site but the scheme eventually fell through.[9]

---

8. Much of the stone was believed to have come from the old London Bridge, then being demolished. The gateway building not only provided the entrance to the dockyard, but also contained a 'comfortable residence, a large library panelled in cedar and the administrative offices' (Bushell 1939, p. 40).
9. The yard was used for a variety of sundry purposes, including the making of bicycles, electrical gear and concrete barges during the First World War, before becoming the site for paper mills (Bowen 1943, p. 174; Bowen 1948, p. 290).

Young and Co. of Limehouse, previously Cox and Curling and then Curling and Young, who built four Cheerful-class gunboats and two larger vessels for the Crimea were also put out of business by the rise in costs, although three firms did start up in business at around this time.

The most successful were Westwood and Baillie, both of whom had been works managers for Ditchburn and Mare from about 1845 and then acted as managers of Mare's business for the Official Assignee under Mare's bankruptcy, who went into partnership in 1856, together with James Campbell at London Yard, Poplar, as shipbuilders, boiler-makers and ironworkers. Their yard had a frontage onto the river of 450 feet and by the end of 1857 it was 'considerably developed, with a smiths' shop, boiler shop, machine shop, iron store, engine and boiler-houses, furnace shed and offices'. Their first major contract was for the *Resistance* (6,300 d.t., 280 feet long, with ram bows and 4.5-inch armour plating) which they built for the Admiralty, although they also built a steam battery of 3,500 tons in 1858–59 and a steam sporting yacht for Prince Halem Pacha, intended to convey the Prince and his entourage up the 'shallow and intricate passages of the River Nile on pleasure and shooting excursions'. As well as steam-ships, they built part of the Sultan of Turkey's Istanbul Palace and some major bridges in the Cape, South America and India, including the Sukkur Bridge which, until the building of the Forth Bridge, was the largest cantilever bridge in the world; under construction in Poplar it could be seen for miles and attracted much attention (*Engineering* 7 April 1899). In 1858 they were building the Nerbudda Bridge for the Bombay, Baroda and Central India Railway Co. and their work was sufficiently advanced for the tests of one of the bridge spans to be attended by 'the consulting engineer to the Swedish government and several other scientific gentlemen who took great interest in the operation'. They were not disappointed; the tests using a weight of 'more than 2 tons per foot run, did not produce a deflection of five eighths of an inch, a result unprecedented in the construction of iron bridges' and the secretary of the railway company, Colonel Kennedy, 'highly complimented the firm and observed that he had never seen anything approaching their accuracy of workmanship' (*Illustrated News of the World* 18 September 1858).

Blackwall Iron Works was established in 1854 by John Stewart near Folly Wall, with a 500-foot frontage onto the river, making some ships but really specialising in marine engines, mainly for tugboats. The Victoria Foundry Company was formed in 1857 with an initial subscribed capital of £14,500 to build iron steamboats and other engines and boilers at Greenwich but the business was not a success.[10]

---

10. PRO Kew, Annual Returns, BT31/279/950

CHAPTER FIVE

Trade boom and the effects of 'shady finance', 1860–67

After the Crimean War, shipbuilding volumes in the private sector fell back, although remaining at higher levels than before the war. From 1859 onwards, however, trade began to build up again and, from 1863 to 1866, the shipbuilding trade experienced probably the most feverish boom in its history (see Checkland 1971, p. 146), as part of a surge in the economy as a whole largely due to the changes in company formation procedures in 1862, making limited liability far more readily available to investors. In 1866, the trade reached what Slaven has seen as a point of capacity saturation, from which output was bound to contract, even without the crisis in credit provision that followed the failure of Overend Gurney (1980, p. 116).

The different parts of the trade were, of course, influenced by a variety of factors. The scale economies of iron technologies, investments and facilities, for example, operated at far higher levels than those for wooden construction and tended to concentrate production in particular areas and yards, a process that proceeded more rapidly on the Thames than on the River Clyde. London-based trade sources spoke of an 'astonishing increase in shipbuilding' and of an 'expansion of the trade beyond precedent' that encouraged many builders to make 'extensive additions to their yards for the immediate laying down of keels' (*Economist* 11 March 1865, p. 20).

Prior to the slump, in 1864, the main iron shipbuilding areas in the UK were the Clyde (where 33 yards produced 170 ships with a total tonnage of 121,000 tons), the Thames (notably the Millwall and Thames Ironworks, jointly producing the major part of the 117,000 tons of iron vessels built locally), the Mersey (80,000 tons), the Tyne (51,000 tons), the Wear (25,000 tons) and the Tees (15,000 tons). These centres provided 409,000 tons out of a total of nearly 500,000 tons, with the remaining production taking place at Bristol, Belfast and elsewhere (King 1864, p. 27).

In 1866, however, UK shipbuilding output slumped dramatically, as part of the sudden downturn in the British economy prompted by a crisis in general credit provision that followed the collapse of the Overend Gurney bank. The effects were widely felt. On the Clyde, output fell by 25 per cent and there were major labour disputes, involving a sustained lock-out that led to a 'reduction of from 2s to 6s a week in the wages of all classes employed in shipbuilding' (*Economist* 9 March 1867 supplement, p. 21). On the Tyne, 1866 was also a year of 'unparalleled depression in the shipbuilding trade'; stagnation and strikes accompanied a cut in tonnage produced of a third, while Sunderland experienced similar difficulties.

It has been strongly argued in the literature, however, that the collapse of the London trade was far more pronounced than in other important shipbuilding areas; Pollard, for example, has suggested that the proportion of UK mercantile iron-ship tonnage built on the Thames declined from 28.7 per cent in 1865 to 4.7 per cent in 1866. The problem was also no temporary aberration; in September 1867, for example, there was an 'absolute dearth of work in the shipbuilding yards on the banks of the Thames' with no more than four vessels on the 'numberless slips between the steamboat pier at Millwall and the Victoria Docks, [the] ground tenanted only by poles and scaffolds', although Thames Ironworks did have a large ironclad in the course of construction for the Prussian government (*Times* 4 September 1867, p. 5) and Samuda and several other builders on the river were thought to still be 'well supplied with work' (*Times* 6 September 1867, p. 8). There was also some evidence that local orders were being lost; 21 out of 148 of the vessels built at Sunderland in 1867, for example, were for London buyers, although most of the ships built on the Wear at that time were wooden, rather than iron (*Economist* 9 March 1867 supplement, pp. 21–2).

Broad economic factors were clearly weakening the relative position of the Thames region as a major iron or steel shipbuilder but the sudden collapse of the London river trade have been attributed instead by several writers largely to business problems caused by 'shady finance'.[1] Pollard was highly critical of the activities of company promoters in the London area, following the introduction of limited liability, that encouraged firms with no secure basis of technical knowledge to spring up 'fully grown and equipped, competing for orders and for skilled men in the bubble period before the panic' and concluded that 'shady finance' had a particular and marked effect upon the prospects for serious shipbuilding in the Thames region, hastening the effects of cost differentials and other longer-term economic factors on the regional location of this important industry (Pollard 1950, p. 81).

Similarly, Palmer has suggested that, for London firms, the ease of raising capital on the local financial markets 'may have been detrimental, inducing firms to invest in modern technology and burdening them with debts not justified by market prospects' (1993, p. 60), although this is of course inherently difficult to test.

Checkland and Banbury, on the other hand, have been more concerned with the particular effects of the Overend Gurney crash in 1866. Checkland saw this as the blow from which Thames-side shipbuilding 'never recovered' (1971, p. 45) and Banbury believed this to have 'drag[ged] the Millwall Ironworks and Shipbuilding Co. and some of the greatest firms in the country down with it' (see also Palmer 1993, p. 58).

It will be argued in this book that the standard explanations of the decline in

1. See, for example, Checkland (1971, pp. 42–5), Pollard (1950, p. 79) and Palmer (1993, p. 58).

shipbuilding on the Thames from 1866 are often sound enough but that they are also misleading in three respects. Firstly, some business failures on the river took place well before 1866, following the rapid cost inflations of the Crimean War period. Secondly, some accounts have exaggerated the number of shipbuilding firms on the Thames incorporated in the bubble period of the 1860s, building iron ships and then disappearing; the number of important iron shipbuilders on the Thames was never all that large. Finally, it will be suggested that the collapse of Overend Gurney was as much the result of its active but misconceived commercial relationships with a small number of (failing) firms in the London iron shipbuilding trade as the cause of further business failures in that trade, although the crisis in credit provision did of course depress the general level of trade activity for some time to come.

The UK shipbuilding industry

The average number and tonnage of ships built in the private sector in the period 1860–67 (for mercantile and naval customers both in the UK and abroad) were the highest since 1832. Although volumes fell 8 per cent in 1866 and a further 22 per cent in 1867, as shown in Table 4, the level of production in 1867 was still 40 per cent above that of 1860. Ships also continued to grow in size.

Moreover, the Admiralty was now changing its views on iron warships. In tests, the thin iron hulls used on five frigates built in the 1840s had shown poor resistance to shot (Brownlee 1985, p. 6) but it was the successful deployment of batteries, heavily-armoured with 4-inch thick plates, against Russian forts that changed naval perceptions. The French started building the frigate, *La Gloire*, the first seagoing[2] iron-clad warship and announced a construction programme for another 16 similar vessels.

The British Admiralty had been reluctant to innovate, as a general policy, as it had the greatest accumulated investments in ships made with existing technologies, but the French programme effectively forced Britain into building iron ships. The French policy also seemed strategically rather foolish, as their own iron industry had very limited capacity, at that time being 'unable to provide enough iron for more than one iron-hulled ship per year' whereas Britain was the world's leading industrial power with a massive iron-producing capability (Gardiner 1992, p. 53).The Admiralty therefore decided to change their position on iron ships and to compete with the French technologically, confident that the technical capability and capacity of their own iron industry and shipbuilders would prove decisive.

The *La Gloire* was iron-clad and iron-decked, but it was also wooden-hulled, which had limited the design advances that could be achieved and the Admiralty called on the leading shipbuilding firms (and ostensibly the

2. As distinct from the armoured floating batteries used by France and England during the Crimean War.

Royal Dockyards as well) for designs for a new class of iron-clad ship (Brassey 1883 Vol. 1, p. 58).

The Admiralty's design specification, heavily influenced by the Surveyor, Admiral Sir Baldwin Walker, was for a 'frigate of 36 guns cased with wrought iron plates', 4.5 inches thick, from the upper deck to 5 feet below the load water-line. It was issued on 27 January 1859 and sent to the seven Royal yards, although they built primarily in wood, and to the eight leading iron shipbuilders in the private sector (Thames Ironworks, Mare, Scott-Russell, Samuda and Westwood and Baillie of London, Laird of Birkenhead, Palmer of Jarrow and Napier from Glasgow). The accompanying letter stated that as

> iron appears to be the most suitable material for a ship of this kind both as regards strength and durability, the design should be for an iron ship, but if it is considered by any of the parties called on that a more satisfactory arrangement could be made with wood than iron, a plan and the particulars of a wooden ship may be forwarded for consideration (Lambert 1987, p. 18)

a form of wording designed to propitiate the dockyards without disguising the government's intention to actually look to the private yards for the important design initiatives.

The first of the ships built under this programme, HMS *Warrior*, has been described as the 'greatest single development in the history of warship design'. A highly advanced ship, *Warrior* was 'powered by steam, built with the scientific precision of iron, armed with rifled breech-loading guns, protected by solid wrought iron plate 4.5 inch thick and powered by the largest set of marine engines yet built, with sail reduced to an auxiliary role' (Gardiner 1992, p. 58), its specifications well suited to the British economy's strengths. She was effectively a fast armoured frigate and could achieve a speed of 13.5 knots. The ship, when constructed, was highly successful and prompted additional orders from the Admiralty for large and small ships alike and also provoked an investigation in 1861–65 of the Special Committee on Iron (Fairbairn was one of its six members), into the 'application of iron to defensive purposes in warfare' (Pole 1970, p. 345). The battle of Hampton Roads in the American Civil War in 1862 also 'dramatically demonstrated the superiority of the iron-clad for war [so that] the end of wooden walls was in sight' (Checkland 1971, p. 143).

Although the ship was highly successful and an enormous advance on what had gone before, there were still some residual problems. The marine fouling of iron-hulled ships had not been solved, so that the *Warrior* had to be docked about every ten months, in order to avoid her top speed being greatly reduced. Not only did this take the ship out of commission at regular intervals, but the absence of docks of sufficient size outside the British Isles also seriously limited its strategic deployment. The Admiralty therefore continued to order the construction of wooden ships, to be clad with iron, at least until 1866, although wood was not as plentiful as it had been (Jordan 1925, p. 6; Marder 1964, p. 5).

It soon became clear that soft and tough, rather than hard and brittle, iron plates were the most effective. Iron plates could be either hammered or rolled; when plates were hammered, as in the case of HMS Warrior, heated iron from either scrap or puddled bars were shaped by being placed under heavy steam hammers. In the case of rolled plates,[3] the process used for ordinary boiler plates was utilised,

Table 4. UK Shipbuilding statistics, 1860–67

	(1) UK (no.)	(2) London (per cent)	(3) UK (000) (n.t.)	(4) London (per cent)	(5) UK tonnage per cent Admiralty	(6) UK tonnage per cent London Admiralty
1860	1,018		222.4		4.7	4.6
1861	978		225.1		10.7	3.0
1862	1,062		257.4		6.2	2.5
1863	1,165		389.9		7.4	5.8
1864	1,251		439.4		1.7	0.9
1865	1,312		434.8		4.5	1.8
1866	1,407	9.5	400.1	12.4	5.1	5.1
1867	1,221	6.6	310.7	7.2	1.5	1.5
Average p.a.	1,177		335.0		5.2	3.2
Ave. 1854–59	1,086		252.2		6.0	4.9
Ave. 1847–53	769		149.4		0.6	0.6
Ave. 1832–46	901		126.9		1.4	0.7

Notes: no. = number of vessels
n.t. = net tons
Displacement tons have been multiplied by 1.125 to convert them to net tons

Sources: Mitchell and Deane (1962, pp. 220–2); Banbury (1971); Conways (1979); Brassey (1883); Palmer (1993); Board of Trade Annual Statements of Navigation and Shipping, 1867–68.

3. In France, armour plates were made in 1855 for three floating batteries used in the Crimea and rolled armour plates for warships were first produced in Britain later that same year by the Parkgate Steel and Iron Co., when they made 3-inch plates for HMS *Terror* (TIQG Vol. 1, p. 52).

but on a much larger scale. Iron sheets were heated, placed on one another and then passed between rollers which used immense power to roll them into one solid plate of the intended size. The Navy tested the two approaches and found that the more uniform and gradual application of force used in the rolling process produced plates that were softer and more uniform, although the degree of welding between the various layers was not always satisfactory. The best shape was the simplest, a single plate of uniform thickness with a plain surface, while the use of wood as a backing material deadened the shot vibration, reduced the fracturing of bolts and rivets, spread the blow more widely and also enabled broken pieces of armour-plate to become embedded in the hull rather than lost.

The cost of iron-hulled or sheathed ships inevitably prompted a cautious approach on the part of the Admiralty; 'where steam had cost its tens of thousands, iron cost its hundreds of thousands'. The cost of a 36-gun frigate, prior to the use of steam, was about £40,000, the cost of 36-gun steam frigate was about £80,000, but the cost of a 36-gun iron-cased frigate was of the order of £200,000 to £250,000 (TIQG Vol. 2, p. 43); thus the cost of HMS *Warrior* was 'nearly six times the price of its eighteenth-century counterpart, the first-rate wooden sailing ship-of-the-line'. This was of course a process that would continue; improvements in ordnance, armour and steam engineering over the next quarter-century would result in very substantial cost increases (Sumida 1989, p. 8).

Moreover, given the location of the new technologies, an increase in the Navy's demand for iron ships was bound to change the relative importance of the Royal Dockyards and of the major shipbuilders in the private sector. The Royal Dockyards lost work and the yards at Deptford and Woolwich (which never built any iron ships) closed in 1869, although new capacity (for increasingly large ships) was created at Portsmouth, Chatham and Sheerness.[4] The major builders in the private sector gained work; if the state's overall level of demand, 4.7 per cent of total private sector shipbuilding tonnage, was still modest it was now on a far more stable basis and no longer effectively confined to war-time crises. London continued to fulfil the major part of the Admiralty's orders, although to a lesser extent than previously.

Attempts to analyse the regional effects are handicapped by the lack of detailed statistics on shipbuilding, based upon Board of Trade Annual Statements of the Navigation and Shipping of the UK, until 1866. It is

4. The dockyards were converted into, respectively, a metropolitan cattle market and a military store (Jordan 1925, p. 9). The closure at Woolwich caused particular distress in its locality.

therefore, impossible, to calculate the fall in London shipbuilding tonnage from 1865 to 1866, although the 57 per cent decline from 49,515 tons in 1866 to 21,268 tons in 1867 was very severe and two-and-a-half times the rate of decline in the UK trade as a whole. As shown in Table 5, the proportion of UK tonnage built on the Thames, thus fell from 12.4 per cent in 1866 to 7.2 per cent in 1867, a very pronounced decline but less precipitous than has sometimes been suggested in the literature.

Table 5. Ships built on the Thames, 1866–67

	1866		**1867**	
	no.	**net tons**	**no.**	**net tons**
Domestic wooden sailing ships	69	3,902	34	1,376
wooden steam ships	3	104		
iron sailing ships	6	4,286	2	336
iron steam ships	31	9,360	27	3,851
	106	17,548	66	5,667
Foreign merchant ships	20	3,932	12	9,510
	126	21,480	78	15,177
Foreign war ships	5	7,477	2	2,396
Admiralty ships	3	20,558	1	4,695
Totals	134	49,515	81	22,268

In 1866 and 1867, London's shipbuilding was as shown in Table 5, which suggests that the largest decline was in naval shipbuilding, although commercial (domestic and overseas) orders still fell by 29 per cent.

If less direct sources are used, such as the fleet lists of the major overseas mail companies that were inclined to deal with builders on the Thames, they tend to confirm Banbury's view that there was a rather sudden shift in the demand of major commercial customers away from the Thames and that it took place at about this time (Banbury 1971, pp. 64–68). Although Scotland had emerged as the most important area for large-scale UK commercial tonnage in the 1850s, between 1860 and 1865, eleven of the thirteen ships bought by P&O direct from shipbuilders were from firms on the Thames and none were from Scotland (ten of the eleven ships were substantial iron passenger steamers and liners of over 2,000 tons) but, after that, the Thames never built another ship for P&O[5] and Glasgow came to dominate the trade, with the remaining orders going mainly to Southampton.

P&O's trade with firms on the Thames in 1860–65 was mainly with Thames Ironworks, who built six ships (including the last two, the *Nyanza* in 1864 and the *Tanjore* in 1865) and Samuda, who built three. Samuda' shipyard did suffer one accident, on launching the *Rangoon*, caused by the failure of the drag chains and this meant the ship spending a day stranded on the East Greenwich bank of the river in 1863, but this could hardly have cast serious doubts on the facilities on the Thames in general.

Moreover, out of four ships built for the Panama, Australia and New Zealand Royal Mail Co. in 1865 and 1866, three were built on the Thames, one by Dudgeons, one by Millwall Ironworks and the other, the 1,560-ton *Kaikoura* by Charles Lungley. In 1864–65, the first of RMSP's large iron screw ships came into use, the *Douro* (2,824 g.t.) launched at Greenock in 1864 and the *Rhone* (2,738 g.t.) at Millwall Ironworks in February 1865 (Bushell 1939, p. 102) but these, and the 2,000-ton iron paddle-steamer *Danube*, were the last RMSP ships to be built on the Thames; thereafter nearly all the company's ships were built in Scotland or in yards in the north-east of England.

The Union Steam Ship Company, awarded mail contracts to Cape Colony and Natal in 1857, ordered ten ships between 1860 and 1866, eight of which were built by Charles Lungley, but again these were the last to be built for the company on the Thames; thereafter this company's ships were also made in Scotland or the north-east (Hawes 1990, pp. 21–31).

The promotion of joint-stock companies

Traditionally, in the shipbuilding industry, firms had been organised as family businesses or as partnerships, with little outside capital or outside influence being either sought or needed, but the development of iron shipbuilding techniques brought a substantially increased demand for capital and thereby encouraged incorporation, particularly when the owner's liability could be limited (Slaven 1980, pp. 122–3). This applied across the UK shipbuilding industry, although the formation of new companies was thought to have been more common in the older river locations, particularly the Thames and Mersey.

After the passing of the 1856 Companies Act, new companies were being

5. Except for two very small and rather specialised boats, a 55-ton iron tug built by J. & G. Rennie in 1874, to be shipped out and reconstructed in Bombay, and a 10-ton steamer launch built in 1881.

formed at a rate of about 375 a year, but the greater availability of limited liability under the Companies Act 1862 encouraged the number of company formations to 748 in 1863, 970 in 1864 and 1,002 in 1865 although, after the crisis of 1866, they fell back towards the levels of the earlier period.[6] The number seeking funds from the public fell sharply from an average of 277 in 1863–65 to only 44 in 1866 and 27 in 1867 and total, newly authorised capital rose from £17.8m in 1860 to £235.8m in 1864 and £203.7m in 1865, before falling back to only £28.5m in 1867.[7] Many companies failed after a short existence and Pollard and Robertson found shipbuilding to have been the least stable industry for newly formed companies, after banking and finance (1979, pp. 72–5, 266).

Checkland wrote of an 'astonishing increase [in shipbuilding] in 1863 and 1864', when many new yards were constructed and a 'frightening number of new companies, under limited liability' were called into being (1971, pp. 42–3). The names of the new joint-stock companies brought before the public, during the boom years 1863–67, were listed in the *Economist*'s annual 'Commercial History and Review',[8] which shows one company in 1863, seven in 1864 and three in 1865 as being UK shipbuilding businesses. Between them, they sought total amounts of capital of £100,000 (out of £78.1m that year), £4,450,000 (£235.8m) and £1,000,000 (£203.7m) respectively, amounts that do not seem disproportionate to the general importance and size of the shipbuilding industry. Of the eleven public companies identified above, three were located on the London river: Millwall Ironworks, Thames Ironworks and the London Engineering and Iron Ship Building, each formed in 1864.

The picture this provides is consistent with the two standard analyses of company structures during this period. Using a slightly broader definition of 'companies',[9] Hunt identified (1936, p. 149) 17 out of 1,334 companies formed in 1863–65 as being in the shipbuilding industry and Shannon, from an analysis of 'effective' company formations, found that four new shipbuilding companies were formed in 1863, seven in 1864, six in 1865 (and one in 1866), out of annual totals of 360, 500, 474 and 364 respectively (1933, p. 312).

The London shipbuilding trade part of Kelly's Post Office directories,

---

6. The total number of companies *registered* in any given period is not very meaningful, as it includes large numbers of companies that were merely 'abortive or ephemeral' and never became active.
7. Levi (1870, p. 14), also Todd (1932, pp. 56–7) and Hunt (1936, pp. 144–6).
8. *Economist* 20 February 1864, pp. 36–9; 11 March 1865, pp. 36–9; 10 March 1866, pp. 35–9; 9 March 1867, p. 35; 14 March 1868, p. 39.
9. As 'those registered, excluding abortive and small companies'.

Board of Trade lists of registered companies and the individual company files held at the Public Records Office, Kew were also checked, but no other incorporated shipbuilding firms were found in the London area in the period to 1866.[10] Finally, the list of major shipbuilding firms in the area was confirmed indirectly by two witnesses to the Royal Commission on the Trade Unions: Wigram who identified two limited liability companies, Thames and Millwall Ironworks (Royal Commission on Trade Unions 1867–68, paras 16693–5) and Samuda who identified Millwall Iron and James Ash's businesses as those 'started on a large scale who had not grown to that scale by experience' and yet were supported by 'Overend Gurney and all these financial companies' (Royal Commission on Trade Unions 1867–68, paras 16817–21).

Overend Gurney

The collapse in limited liability registrations in 1866 was largely due to the failure of the great banking house of Overend Gurney, 'the greatest instrument of credit in the kingdom' (Sheppard 1971, p. 65), precipitating the panic of 'Black Friday'; no single bankruptcy had ever caused 'so great a shock to credit' and there ensued the 'greatest agitation ever known in the City'. Several banks failed within days, the Bank Act of 1844 was suspended and the minimum discount rate was raised to the crisis level of 10 per cent for more than three months.

The failure prompted two different types of reappraisal: an immediate reaction against some of the general features of the time that were thought to have contributed to the problem, and a slower and more detailed investigation into the internal management practices and arrangements at Overend Gurney that had made the collapse possible.

Overend Gurney were seen to have been 'infected by the madness of the time' and to have departed from normal banking ventures into risky ventures connected with the remarkable spread of limited liability company promotions (*Bankers Magazine* March 1867, pp. 222–3); over two hundred company promotions were abandoned as 'a universal outcry against all joint-stock companies broke forth' (Hunt 1936, p. 154). There was widespread criticism of the factor which was most thought to have increased speculative

10. Other firms trading on the river at that time did subsequently incorporate, including Thorneycrofts, Yarrow and Forrestt. One other company was formed during the period in question, Victoria Foundry Co. Ltd in July 1857, before the 'bubble' period, and with a very modest issued capital of only £14,500. The company had an address in Greenwich but did not appear to have been active on any real scale (PRO Kew, BT 31/279/950).

pressures, that is, the ability of equity holders to realise the whole of the gain on a share for which they might have subscribed only a modest proportion by way of a 'first call' and also a reaction against the 'unsound and extravagant financing operations of railway companies and contractors', that led to a major curtailment of 'excessive' railway promotion. Any recognition that the banking firm had very substantial investments in the local shipbuilding industry was delayed until the liquidation proceedings of the bank were well advanced.

Overend Gurney and Co. Ltd was registered as a business in July 1865 with an authorised capital of £5,000,000, to take over the previous, unincorporated business that had traded under virtually the same name. There was some continuity of management, the managing directors, for example, Henry Gurney and Robert Birkbeck, having been prominent in the old business (*Economist* 29 September 1866, p. 1136). The new business provided considerable incentives for financial success: the two managing directors had contracts that offered them each £2,500 pa and 10 per cent of the surplus profits beyond a defined level.[11]

For half a century, until the late 1850s, all had gone smoothly; the bank generated business transactions of £70,000,000 a year, that yielded substantial profits, of the order of £190,000 a year. The principal managers of the old establishment had been Samuel Gurney and David Barclay Chapman but the former had died in 1856 and the latter retired in 1857, after which time changes in the senior personnel and in the direction of the firm took place (*Economist* 16 June 1866, pp. 697–8). By 1859, Overend Gurney, while continuing the 'legitimate and regular business of the firm' in money dealing and bill discounting, also began to commit themselves to 'various transactions by way of investment, loan or discount, which were entirely extraneous to the legitimate concern of the business, connected with various advances made to companies and firms engaged in the shipping, shipbuilding and timber trades and comprising also loans made to railway contractors'(*Times* 2 February 1869, p. 7). These transactions, many of which were poorly judged, transformed the firm's business 'beyond recognition', so that they became in part 'grain traders and speculators, iron-masters, shipbuilders, ship-owners, large-scale railway financiers and partners in almost every kind of speculative and lock-up business, much of which had only the flimsiest prospect of even ultimate success' (King 1936, p. 247).

D. W. Chapman had been particularly negligent and irresponsible and was thought to have had quite unsuitable cronies in an underworld of sham paper finance. He was excluded from the business in 1865 (Sheppard 1971,

11. After payment of a dividend of 7 per cent and a transfer to reserved funds of 20 per cent of the profits; Articles of Association, Overend Gurney and Co. Ltd, PRO Kew, BT 31/1128/2280c.

p. 79) but by then the firm was already insolvent, probably by some £4m (*Economist* 16 June 1866, pp. 697–8); for several years past Overend, while maintaining its reputation, had been in reality 'a finance shop of the worst possible character' which was not spending the public's money on the discounting of ordinary trade bills, but was instead 'squander[ing it] in advances upon wretched steam navigation companies, preposterous manufacturing companies, advances to American railways and the support of a race of reckless contractors and schemers, utterly unfit to be treated with' (*Economist* 9 March 1867, supplement, p. 4).

The management at Overend Gurney was also sufficiently crass as to antagonise the Bank of England in a highly public dispute in April 1860 and thus reduce the likelihood of institutional support when a crisis eventually came about (Kynaston 1995, pp. 235–40, 436).

The extent and nature of Overend's departure from normal banking ventures into risky ventures connected with the sudden rise in limited liability company promotions (*Bankers Magazine* March 1867, pp. 222–3) was shown all too clearly by the lists of bad debts and losses that were published when they went into liquidation and the *Times* concluded that 'a taste for shipping and railways had been its ruin' and that its mismanagement had been 'so gross as to be almost incredible' (*Times* 28 November 1866, p. 6). In one case, they lent £144,000 to the Greek and Oriental Steam Company, which had 'no assets, no security, no information, not even any person or persons accountable' so that Gurney's liquidator was unable to trace the office of that company or even any shareholders (*Times* 30 January 1869, p. 9).

Although Overend's failure ruined the great railway contractors, Peto and Betts (Sheppard 1971, pp. 79, 138, 148), the largest amounts (in excess of £500,000) owing to the business all related to shipbuilding and shipping were; Millwall Iron Works (which was in liquidation) £566,000; the Atlantic Mail Steam Packet Co. (in liquidation) £848,000 and the East India and London Shipping Co. (in liquidation) £578,000 (*Bankers Magazine* January 1869, pp. 121–30).

The Atlantic and East India shipping companies had become in effect Overend Gurney's subsidiary companies; Atlantic had only paid a little over £10,000 by January 1869, at which time nothing further could be anticipated, while the debts of the East India and London Shipping Company produced no more than £100,000. Of the amounts owed by Millwall Ironworks, only £7 10s had been received by January 1869, although the banking company did hold the 'equity of redemption of the works, plant and machinery' (*Economist* 23 January 1869, pp. 85–6); *Bankers Magazine* January 1869, p. 134).

The directors were found to have not acted fraudulently over the reforming of the banking business as a limited liability company and calls were duly made for the unpaid balance on the shares (generally £35 on each £50 share) with the liquidation process finally coming to an end in 1893.

The crisis of 1866

We're all froze out,
we've got no work,
we've got no work to do.

There was a very severe depression in the trades that operated in the East End of London in 1866 and the resulting unemployment turned the East End of London into a byword for poverty (Pollard 1950, p. 83). The numbers on Poor Law relief rose from 107,864 to 147,756 between Lady Day 1866 and 1867, and the numbers for Poplar in particular rose 76 per cent (Jones 1976, p. 46).

There were several causes. The harvest had been bad, the winter was severe, a number of trades were in a state of cyclical depression and, most important of all, the London shipbuilding industry had collapsed into a depressed state that was 'one of the most painful and severe of the century'. Engels wrote of the 'removal of the iron shipbuilding trade from the Thames to the Clyde' as being sufficient in itself to 'reduce the whole East End of London to chronic pauperism' (cited in McGrath 1983, p. 11) and Jones of the collapse of the Thames shipbuilding industry in 1867 'firmly establish[ing] in the public mind the image of the East End as a nursery of destitute poverty and thriftless, demoralised pauperism' (Jones 1976, p. 15).

On the other hand, Pollard's claim that '27,000 shipbuilding workers on the Thames' were unemployed at the end of November 1866 (1950, pp. 82, 88), which has been quite widely quoted[12] is surely a considerable exaggeration of the real position. The local shipbuilder, Samuda, in his evidence to the Royal Commission on Trade Unions, estimated the labour lost by the failed firms in the iron shipbuilding trade across the entire period 1851–67 (in which every iron shipbuilding establishment on the Thames except his own had 'either failed or discontinued') at about '4000 heads of families' (who might have been supporting up to 20,000 people; Royal Commission on Trade Unions 1867–68, para. 16749), although the contrast between the boom conditions of 1865 and 1867 was very sharp indeed.

There were other causes of the severe social distress. The level of business, particularly in the shipbuilding and building trades, was always liable to be affected by the state of the weather and Jones has argued that 'some of the worst periods of distress in Victorian London were the result, not so much of cyclical trade depression, as exceptionally hard winters' (Jones 1976, p.

12. See, for example, Jones (1976, pp. 24, 102, 105)

44). In 1866–67, the weather was most unhelpful;

> the outstandingly cold and wretched summer of 1866 had been followed by a hard winter, and in the East End the distress, always great towards Christmas and the New Year was abnormally severe. Work on the river came to a standstill through frost and the shipyard workers and dockers paraded through the streets, jangling tins for coppers and singing their dirge of 'we're all froze out, we've got no work, we've got no work to do.' (Rose 1973, p. 148).

The combination of a financial crisis and an exceptionally hard winter also ended the boom in building, particularly since by 1868, there were 800 empty houses on the Isle of Dogs, close on half the total stock (Survey of London 1994, p. 4).

The nearby Millwall and Surrey docks were also affected by particular seasonal influences that caused employment levels to fluctuate quite considerably; the arrival of grain and timber, particularly from the Baltic, peaked in the autumn through until Christmas and the three months after Christmas were normally 'almost completely slack'. In January 1867, again partly because of the harsh weather, '20,000 dockers were unemployed, together with lighter-men, coal-whippers and all other workers who depended on riverside employment (Jones 1976, pp. 36, 103).

The silk-weaving industry had been one of the largest in London, employing 50,000 people in 1824, but the industry declined severely in the 1830s and the 1860s represented its 'final agony'; in twenty years from 1860, employment in the trade fell from 9,500 to only 3,300 (Jones 1976, p. 101).

As if to add insult to injury, there was a very severe outbreak of cholera in the East End in August 1866 (having already been experienced in Bristol, Liverpool and Southampton) that 'carried off nearly 12,000 souls' (TIQG Vol. 3, p. 15). Not surprisingly, Jones saw the 1860s as a 'watershed in the social history of London' (1976, p. 15) and from this time the incidence of cholera and of the general death rate were both to decline continuously.

The supply and price of labour

The supply and price of labour in the London shipbuilding industry at this time became a highly politicised issue, partly because the Royal Commission, set up in 1867 to enquire into and report on the organisation and rules of trade unions, paid considerable attention to arrangements in the shipbuilding trade on the Thames.

It was a particular view of employers generally at the time that shipbuilding was expanding on the Clyde at the expense of the Thames and that this shift was largely due to the effect of the local unions on the supply and cost of labour, even though there were many other factors that affected the demand for ship construction in the various parts of the country.

It was, in any case, difficult to disentangle business trends from more random variations, particularly in a trade, like shipbuilding, that was undergoing rapid technological changes, that was inherently cyclical and was actually composed of several sub-trades, each with its own characteristics and market potentials. Individual businesses often operated in several trades at once (thus 'iron shipbuilding' firms often built wooden ships as well as other iron products, such as bridges) and their success or failure as organisations were also as vulnerable to individual entrepreneurial judgements as to matters of more general economic significance.

Higher wage levels were, however, widely seen as contributing to the decline of shipbuilding on the Thames, even if the evidence was complex; the certainties of some contemporary commentators accordingly appear to have been largely partisan.

Glover (1869, pp. 290–91), for example, stated that the cost of labour was 22.7 per cent higher on the Thames than on the Clyde, that establishment charges were probably twice as high and concluded that high (nominal) wages had destroyed the trade, providing a clear exemplar of what happened 'when the men become masters'. Glover's precision was the more surprising because the customs of the London trade were unusual and based upon a combination of daily wage and 'job work' payments, rather than on simple wage rates, making regional cost comparisons much more difficult (Royal Commission on Trade Unions 1867–68, para. 16691).[13] The daily wage rates on the Thames were based on a scale devised in 1825, that had risen temporarily during the Crimean War before returning to previous levels (Editorial in *Engineering* 21 April 1893). This apart, the standard wage rate on the Thames had remained at 6s to 6s 6d a day from 1824 until February 1866, at which time the unions sought to raise the rate to 7s. This was agreed to by the employers but it was very short-lived; by 1867, the unions on the Thames were accepting reductions of about of 10 per cent (Royal Commission on Trade Unions 1867–68, p. 23).

Slaven's view was that, after 1850, wage 'differentials narrowed but remained significant in traditional grades of work', with shipwrights earning 24–26s on the Clyde, 30s on the Mersey and north-east coasts and 42s on the Thames, but 'in the new grades of work, near-uniformity was evident' (1980, p. 120; see also Campbell 1980, p. 190). Between 1850 and 1860, wage rates increased about 12 per cent in the Clyde, Tyne, Wear and Belfast areas but were largely static on the Mersey and Thames.

Although wage rates have been seen as important, labour malleability

13. The shipbuilder, Clifford Wigram, believed that the union system had a beneficial effect upon the quality of the work done but also operated to prevent him from contracting with shipwrights who could employ and supervise cheaper artisans.

was probably more important. Although wage rates had advanced on the northern rivers, narrowing differentials across the UK, the major changes came during the slump. Wage reductions, of the order of 10 to 20 per cent, were achieved in the iron and iron shipbuilding trades in the Midlands and North, but only after protracted strikes which, on the Tyne, Wear and Tees lasted from July to November (*Economist* supplement 9 March 1867, p. 2). In Scotland, however, and particularly in Govan, near Glasgow, there was less resistance. In Govan, the only major employer prior to the arrival of the new shipbuilding firms – Dixon's, an iron and coal firm – had since the 1830s banned its employees from being trade union members and the new shipbuilding firms adopted similar policies, enforced with lock-outs in 1867 (Campbell 1986, p. 2). Here and elsewhere in Scotland, during the slump, the masters drove the men's wages down to 4s 6d in many cases whereas, in London, major wage reductions were resisted (Royal Commission on Trade Unions 1867–68 Minutes of Evidence, p. 12 and para. 16739).

Class-based anxieties were rarely all that remote from the debate; the potential for disorder amongst the inhabitants of the East End, once described by Matthew Arnold as 'those vast, miserable, unmanageable masses of sunken people', clearly caused considerable concern amongst the well-to-do, particularly since the localised system of poor relief represented a poor solution to geographically concentrated, persistent unemployment, at least until the arrangements made by the Metropolitan Poor Act of 1867 eased intra-parish inequities (Jones 1976, pp. 241–2, 249–50, 253).

To some extent, labour supply issues on the Thames became a struggle that was as much symbolic as it was substantive. The *Economist* (9 March 1867 supplement, p. 2) thought it 'probable that 1866 will be hereafter referred to as a turning point in the relations of Capital and Labour in this country, and as marking at least a pause, if not a reaction, in the advancing tide which for a long period has promoted the rise of wages' and, a year later believed that the 'slack trade of the last two years has brought to a stern test the pretensions of the Trades Unions in this country' (14 March 1868, supplement, p. 3).

On the other hand, the unions on the Thames were far more resistant to accepting a reduction in the official daily rates than in the real value of particular jobs, where market resistance was more quietly accepted. The long-established shipbuilder, Clifford Wigram, argued that, since local wages had not risen in any general sense since 1825 (except during the Crimean War),[14] the costs of similar ships built on the Thames, Clyde, Mersey and at Jarrow were 'remarkably close' and within 3 per cent of one another (Royal Commission on the Trade Unions 1867–68, para. 6669) but that the 'general

14. See also Dudgeon's evidence regarding the 25 years to 1868 (Royal Commission on Trade Unions 1867–68, para. 16947).

impression that unionism does drive work from the Thames has acted prejudicially, and people have gone elsewhere from that impression', an effect he attributed to 'the people who talked about the union and not by the union themselves' (Royal Commission on the Trade Unions 1867–68, paras 16662–3).

Others also argued that wage levels were more important in the political than in the commercial arena. Even Samuda, who clearly resented his inability to determine wage rates, due to the power of trade union involvement, did not estimate wage levels on the Thames at more than 15 per cent above those elsewhere or the wage component of total costs as beyond 30 per cent, resulting in a final cost differential of no more than 5 per cent (Royal Commission on the Trade Unions 1867–68, para. 16788). These judgements were reinforced more recently by Pollard and Robertson who thought London's distance from the main sources of raw materials was far more important (1979, pp. 52–3, 65).

Moreover, as Palmer has pointed out, the cost of labour and the pricing of contracts had almost always been higher in the Thames area and had not previously prevented the local shipbuilders from attracting sufficient work,[15] although labour and other cost disadvantages were coming to matter more in the later parts of the nineteenth century, in an era of national rather than local competition in which London was less able to rely upon local demand for tonnage (1993, pp. 57–9).

Others believed that it was the lack of demand rather than high wages that had caused the slump in work levels on the Thames, while Dudgeon, a noted London shipbuilder, instead attributed the major part of the decline in trade to the unsound state of the financial world and to the 'unsound operations which induced us all to overwork ourselves in 1865' and to take contracts they could not perform (Royal Commission on the Trade Unions 1867–68, pp. 24–6).

The main Thames yards

The period 1860–67 brought growth, feverish boom and finally desolate slump conditions to the areas that were most dependent upon shipbuilding work. The main centre, the Isle of Dogs, had been industrialising rapidly, with much of the impetus provided by shipbuilding both directly, due to its own output, and because of the stimulus it provided to its ancillary trades; in the new industrial town of Millwall, for example, heavy cable for the new ships was

15. In 1740, for example, Thames contractors were paid 10–15 per cent more per ton than contractors in Liverpool and Hull (Banbury 1971, p. 42); see also Slaven 1980, p. 120 and Pollard 1950, pp. 72–6.

manufactured by steam, using Riga hemp and iron, in place of the old hand-twisted ropes.

The development of new sources of power also meant the disappearance of the windmills along the river bank, that had given Millwall its name (Rose 1973, p. 147). By 1860 the periphery and some of the inland areas of the Isle of Dogs were almost continuously taken up by manufactories, although some areas of the adjacent hinterland still remained as pasture, primarily because its low-lying marshy character made it unpopular as a site for businesses or for housing. When John Scott Russell was in business in his shipyard, he was well aware of the 'beautiful cattle feeding on long, fine grass, almost surrounded by manufactories on all sides (Guillery 1990, p. 3), but by 1868 only 26 acres of the Isle of Dogs were still used as either permanent meadows or were under crop (Survey of London 1994, p. 379).

The low-lying nature of the surrounding areas could also be problematic in other ways; in October 1864, a powder barge exploded off Plumstead Marshes, 'which blew the river wall away for some hundreds of yards but happily it was at low water, otherwise the whole of the marshes would have been flooded. With great presence of mind the Sappers and Miners turned out from Woolwich' and managed to fill the breach before the tide rose sufficiently to constitute a problem (TIQG Vol. 2, p. 117).

Further development of the area took place when the Royal Assent for the building of Millwall Docks was obtained in July 1864, effectively extending the water frontage for 'manufacturing, especially shipbuilding and ship-repair' (Guillery 1990, p. 5). Early in 1865, '2,000 men and boys and 300 horses, aided by every feasible mechanical appliance, steam engines, cranes, lifts, wagons and tramways' were on site (Guillery 1990, p. 16) and extensive but informal markets began to develop just outside the gates. There was something of a lull in late 1865, however, when interest rates rose from 3 per cent to 7 per cent and many of the shareholders were unable to pay the second call, while the failure of Overend Gurney in 1866 made this the most difficult of times to be 'seeking the money that the Millwall Company so desperately needed' (Guillery 1990, p. 11). Work resumed in 1867, however, and the docks opened for business in March 1868.

The activities of the iron shipbuilders in particular were very different from what had gone before and the essential brutality of the technologies involved provided much fascination to contemporary observers who commented on the

> myriads of carpenters, sawyers, caulkers and various other artisans which the building of a wooden vessel seldom failed to call into existence have disappeared, to be replaced by miniature armies of swart-featured, brawny-armed mechanics, furnace-men, blacksmiths, hammerers, riveters, roller-men and other trades which form the rank and file of our great iron industry (*Working Man* 10 February 1866, pp. 81–2).

At least until the slump, the slips leading to the river were busy with vessels in different stages of progress, and each slip was surrounded by an intricate maze of scaffolding, which ceaselessly vibrates with the shock of the workman's ponderous hammers, as stroke upon stroke rings upon the massive bolt-heads with which are riveted together the enormous plates used in forming the sides of the vessels. Look around where he will, all is bustle and activity ... with forges hissing and roaring away ... the rolling mills where the stubbornness of the metal is overcome and made to glide forth in sheets of the desired thickness ... while in the workshops the iron is being cut, bent, twisted, hammered, filed and polished into almost every conceivable form and size.' (*Working Man* 10 February 1866, p. 82).

The 1860s were a time of considerable change in the iron shipbuilding trade. The severe downturn in trade in 1866 was not, however, as ruinous as it might have been to business survival on the river. The major losses were the closures of the major producer, Millwall Ironworks, which was owned by Overend Gurney from 1862 and of James Ash's business, also financed by Overend Gurney, while London Engineering and Iron Ship Building, formed in 1864 to take over Westwood, Baillie and Campbell's business, found the slump very difficult. Most other businesses were able, however, to stay in business; Rennie was succeeded by his two sons and Dudgeon, Wigram, Samuda and Thames Ironworks all continued, albeit at lower levels of output. Moreover, two new shipbuilding businesses, Thorneycroft and Yarrow, started up in this period in a trade that was to bring them much renown in future years.

John Scott Russell (Yard 1: part of Millwall Shipyard until 1861)

In mid-1857, Russell had leased the unoccupied part of David Napier's yard in an attempt to re-establish his shipbuilding business. He had obtained the contract for fitting-out the *Great Eastern* and in 1860–61 completed two small Admiralty ships and two commercial vessels, the Merial and the *Anette* (a 600-ton auxiliary Chinese clipper) but he was unable to attract sufficient further business. He was an extremely able designer and naval architect, helping the Admiralty to develop the concepts used in the revolutionary armoured iron warships, HMS *Warrior* and HMS *Black Prince* and he therefore decided to leave the commercial side of shipbuilding and became a consulting engineer at Westminster, where he was able to make a considerable contribution to the development of his profession.[16]

---

16. Previously, he had formulated the 'wave-line' form of construction, based on experiments concerning the resistance of floating bodies under propulsion. In early 1860, he convened the meeting that led to the establishment of the Institute of Naval Architects and in 1865 he had published an enormous three-volume set on the theoretical aspects of ship design (Russell 1865).

Messrs C. J. Mare and Co. (Yard 1: Millwall Shipyard until December 1862)

Mare's shipbuilding business at the Orchard and Bow Creek Shipyard had got into difficulties over government contracts at the time of the Crimean War and he was bankrupt by September 1855. He spent some time managing W. & H. Pitcher's business at Northfleet when it also failed in 1857 but, by 1859, Mare had attracted sufficient backing to try to revive his business fortunes. In 1859, he took over the site formerly occupied by Scott Russell before he went bankrupt and initially operated the business under the name Messrs C. J. Mare and Co. Millwall.[17]

The yards that Mare took over were very substantial, covering 22 acres and having a frontage of 1,500 feet, nearly opposite the Deptford dockyard and Humphrey's, where engines and boilers were often fitted (Hume and Moss 1979, p. 24; Banbury 1971, pp. 268–9) and providing plenty of scope for Mare's belief in manufacturing iron and rolling ship-plates and armour on site (unlike Thames Ironworks who produced hammered armour). Rolling required only three heatings and relied upon the gradual application of pressure, producing softer and less brittle iron than hammering, where the heating was often repeated and the hammering constant. John Hughes followed Mare from Bow Creek to become the resident iron-master (although he was later to leave to set up new ironworks in Moscow and Kiev), in charge of the building of substantial rolling mills that would have an annual capability of 20,000 tons and provide the armour plate and bars for ship, boiler or bridge construction (Hicks 1928, p. 80).

In 1861, Mare also took over the part of Napier's yard that Scott Russell had used in an (unsuccessful) attempt to re-establish his shipbuilding business. The business was carried on in Mare's name until the end of 1862 (see letter from Mare in the *Times* 30 January 1869, p. 9) but, when the creation of limited liability companies became easier, Overend Gurney bought out Mare's interest in the business.[18]

---

17. A newspaper report of the time records a fatal accident in late July 1860 'in the shipbuilding yard of Messrs Mare and Co. Millwall, when a large iron tug-boat, being built for work in the Red Sea, was being prepared for its run off the stocks but slipped prematurely', killing or seriously injuring five of the men underneath (*Times* 30 July 1860, p. 7). A metal plaque can also still be seen on the walls of one of the buildings in the area which refers to 'CJM and Co., 1860'.
18. Mare was bankrupted for the second time on 21 December 1867 (*Bankers Magazine* January 1969, p. 131) and, after this, he had a 'haphazard career' and 'simply disappeared and none of his relatives or friends could find any trace of him'. He is known to have worked from 1880–83 as a marine boat-building inspector on the river and was still a subject of great interest to

Millwall Ironworks and Shipbuilding Co. (Yard 1: Millwall Shipyard from December 1862 until 1866) – see also Appendix 3

The business was reformed in December 1862 as an incorporated business, Millwall Ironworks and Shipbuilding Co. Ltd, with an authorised capital of £300,000, consisting of 300 shares of £1,000 each, a denomination clearly not intended for active share dealings by the investing public (Crighton, p. 26; Emmerson 1977, p. 125). The first call was £500 and, apart from one share taken up by the manager and one by the auditor, all the capital was provided by eight shareholders: Robert Birkbeck, managing director of Overend Gurney and three others from the same address, David and Arthur Chapman and Charles Pelly (an associate director of Overend Gurney), and the noted railway contractors, Peto and Betts and Thomas Brassey and his son.[19] The firm appointed experienced and able people to the senior management positions and was soon a very substantial employer, with 4–5,000 men on the payroll, and also a relatively progressive one that provided half-holidays from one o'clock each Saturday (Banbury 1971, p. 211) and made available a range of facilities including a rowing club, cricket club and band, a dining and reading room and library and, for workmen who did not live nearby, a 'spacious dining-hall with a large stove' (Barry 1863, p. 223).

The company also took over land to the south of Russell's main yard (that had originally been leased by Fairbairn) and laid it out again for shipbuilding. By 1864 the works had grown by 'many alterations and additions', both permanent and make-shift and covered 27 acres of works and shipyards, with a river frontage of 1,900 feet and were also accessible by means of the river steamers of the Waterman Company or by railway from the West India Dock station to Fenchurch Street. The works consisted of machinery and erecting shops, foundry and copper shops, wood-work shops and an armour-plate bending and preparing shop. Across the street, but connected by a tram-road and several teams of horses, were two rolling mills (one for angle and bar iron and one for plates and heavy bars and costing around £100,000), both driven by powerful horizontal engines, a forge (which contained six of the largest steam-hammers available, costing about £6,000 each, and which could produce individual wrought-iron forgings weighing 60 tons), armour-plate mills, a boiler shop, an armour-plate planing shop and a circular saw

---

shipworkers when he visited their yards. He died in poverty in 1898, although a marble memorial was later provided by subscription, with the support of the West Ham Borough Council and of Thames Ironworks (*Daily Mail* 18 February 1898; TIQG Vol. IV, p. 118).

19. Millwall Ironworks and Shipbuilding Co. Ltd, Annual Return, PRO Kew, BT 31/725/151c.

area for cutting hot bars. The engine shed had a capability of producing engines with an aggregate of 3,000 hp a year. The vessels were built in the open air and the foundry was 'old-fashioned' but the installation of a new one was being contemplated (King 1864, p. 28).

In March 1864, a call of £500 on each share was made and paid but on 5 May 1864, the shareholders agreed to dissolve the company and immediately form a new company, the Millwall Iron Works, Shipbuilding and Graving Docks Co. Ltd,[20] in order to take over the assets of both the old business and those of a nearby dry-dock. The assets of the old business were taken over at a substantially increased price of £575,000 and the company issued 40,000 £50 shares (£5 called) to the public, with David Chapman of Overend Gurney initially being the largest shareholder. In the first year, the company had about 950 shareholders, but holdings began to concentrate, particularly after widespread sales of small holdings in late June and early July 1864. The following year, the number of shareholders fell to about 280 and Robert Birkbeck, managing director of the bankers, Overend Gurney, emerged as by far the biggest shareholder with 18,950 shares.[21] The chairman and his deputy were J. Lubbock and D. Chapman, bankers, of 15 Lombard Street, close to Overend's head office and, if they and their fellow directors had been successful, they would have been handsomely rewarded for their efforts; a total of £6,000 per annum, together with 20 per cent of the surplus profits after a 7 per cent dividend had been paid, was set aside as their annual remuneration.[22]

In November 1864, Charles Lungley, an experienced shipbuilder who is thought to have been the person who first persuaded the Admiralty that it was sensible to use screw steamers for mail ships, was appointed as managing director of Millwall Ironworks, as part of an arrangement linking the Ironworks with his own shipbuilding and engineering works at Deptford, giving Millwall additional capacity and 'control of the most extensive dry dock in the Thames' (*Times* 1 December 1864, p. 5; Banbury 1962, p. 207; Bowen 1947, p. 512; Smith March 1924). In 1865, Millwall Ironworks appointed John Napier who, since building iron ships in the area in 1839, had been working in Australia and then managing a shipyard in Govan, to manage part of their operation, effectively the works on his former yard (which was still known at that time as Millwall's 'Scotch yard').[23]

In 1864, Millwall Ironworks was described as the largest iron shipbuilding

---

20. 'Graving' docks are those where the water is removed, after a vessel has been floated into the dock.
21. There were five other holdings of over 1,000 shares, the largest of which was 3,350 shares.
22. Articles of Association, PRO Kew, BT 31/946/1252c, para. 66.
23. John Napier later managed the extensive Canada Works in Birkenhead, before

works in England (with Thames Ironworks the second largest) in a report drawn up by the US House of Representatives, which noted that both firms were unusual in that their operation integrated ironworking and shipbuilding. Both firms were of course equally distant from major iron deposits, although this disadvantage was reduced by their practice of reconstituting the iron from old scrap metal (for which London was the 'great mart') rather than by smelting iron ore:[24] the construction of steamships from the 'pig metal, scrap and bar iron entering the gates ... was ... a combination peculiar to these great yards and not to be found elsewhere either in Great Britain, on the continent or in the United States'.

Banbury suggests that Millwall Ironworks built only 17 ships in the period 1862–66, most of them of some importance although this is almost certainly a very conservative estimate. Barry states that 13 were under construction or just completed at one particular point in time in 1863 (1863, p. 226) and the company's prospectus claimed to have contracts with the British Government, the Ottoman Government, Royal Mail Steam Packet, the Intercolonial Royal Mail Steam Packet and to be building twelve screw steam ships for private merchants (Prospectus, Millwall Iron Works, Ship Building and Graving Docks Co. Ltd, 1864, p. 2, Guildhall MS 19096).

The output included the 3,000-ton Italian naval corvette *Affondatore*, the *Centaur*, in 1864 the largest merchant-sailing ship built on the Thames, two ships for P&O (*Golconda* and *Baroda*) and two for Royal Mail Steam Packet (the *Rhone* and the *Danube*). The first iron ships for the Russian government were also built at Millwall Ironworks, in 1862–64. Mare's rolling mill at Millwall was smaller than its equivalent at Thames Ironworks, so that some of the iron-wrought plates for the ships had to be bought-in, from Gadsby's Ironworks, Aberdare. In 1864, the company also finished a 'monster iron shield' for the Russian government as an enhancement of the Cronstadt fort defences. The shield was to be fixed in position on the parapet of one of the outer forts, was 43 feet long, 10 feet high and built of bars of wrought iron, 12 inches by 12 but was only 15 inches thick, much thinner than a masonry shield of similar capability, which enabled the defensive guns to be fired at a more satisfactorily raked angle (*Illustrated Times* 5 November 1864).

---

moving back to Glasgow again in 1867 to establish (with his brother Robert) the firm of Napier Brothers, where he remained until his death in 1880.

24. The prospectus of a company formed in 1854, the Millwall Iron Company, claimed that Millwall was the cheapest locality in London for the manufacture of iron and that the cost disadvantage of distance from coal deposits was 'more than counterbalanced' by the fact that scrap iron required only half the coal for its conversion and that its quality once produced was greatly superior (Millwall Iron Company Prospectus, Guildhall MS 19096).

The company was particularly keen to attract Admiralty orders in order to make proper use of their considerable capacity (Checkland 1971, p. 143) and are thought to have sponsored a book by Barry in 1863 which tried to 'boost' private sector firms at the expense of the Royal Dockyards.[25]

One of the company's naval contracts was, however, to have seriously negative consequences for the business. A slip on the land to the south of the main yard was used to construct HMS *Northumberland* (the yard becoming known as Northumberland Yard in the process) but the launching scheduled for 17 March 1866 failed in front of a 'brilliant and numerous assembly' including the Prince of Wales. The ways were built over a dam built across the lower end of the ship to keep out the tide and the piles of the dam were driven more closely and firmly than the other piles and stood firm under the weight of the ship when it began to travel down the ways. Those either side did not, however, and instead 'yielded and so caused a depression on each side of the dam, that effectively stopped the way of the vessel'. The grease had also apparently been forced out so that the bare wood surfaces cohered and the ship stuck fast, despite the efforts of four tugs. At the luncheon immediately afterwards, held in one of the buildings in the yard, the Chairman, Sir John Hay explained that this was the heaviest boat (7,000 tons with nearly all her armour plating fitted) to have ever been launched in this way, from an excavated slip, but it provided only the smallest of consolations to those concerned.[26] Four immense wooden camels or tanks were made at Woolwich Dockyard to lift part of the hull as the tide rose and 'after four weeks work, night and day' the ship was successfully launched on 17 April 1866.

Millwall Ironworks had been doing well enough to have paid an interim dividend of 8 per cent per annum for the half-year to 30 June 1865 (*Times* 15 September 1865, p. 5) but the initial launching failure of the *Northumberland* was very expensive, costing over £12,000 (TIQG Vol. 2, p. 50) and helped to close the business and bring about the failure of bankers Overend Gurney (Crighton, pp. 26–8) in May 1866.

The Ironworks made substantial calls on their shares which led, predictably, to the default of many of the major shareholders (including Robert Birkbeck of Overend Gurney) and to the forfeiture of their shares

25. The book does not appear to have been part of a wider conspiracy; Thames Ironworks for example, thought the 'style of the whole is so scurrilous that they [the board] decline to have anything to do with it' (Banbury 1971, p. 269).
26. The *Great Eastern* was heavier but was launched sideways on. The sister ships HMS *Agincourt* and *Minotaur* were floated from dock and launched without iron plates, respectively (Crighton, p. 27).

but very little new money was forthcoming.[27] The company was formally wound up in January 1872.

Thames Iron Works (Yard 2: Orchard and Bow Creek Shipyard) – see also Appendix 3

Thames Ironworks obtained the order for the first all-iron ship, HMS *Warrior* in 1859, partly because they were known to make 'hammered armour of proven quality' (Hume and Moss 1979, p. 23)[28] and began building it on 25 May 1859, the same day that John Penn and Sons of Greenwich were awarded the contract for the *Warrior*'s twin-cylinder horizontal single expansion trunk engines.

The *Warrior* was the largest warship in the world (at 9,210 displacement tons, 380 feet long and with 1,250-horse power engines) and had the largest iron hull to have been constructed apart from the *Great Eastern*. More importantly, it was the 'biggest advance on previous warship designs made in the history of naval warfare ... her iron construction enabled her to be so big that she could carry the heavier guns and the proof armour and be subdivided into water-tight compartments below, a thing not possible in a wooden ship'.[29]

The *Warrior* was originally scheduled to be launched eleven months after construction started and then completed for sea in another three, i.e. by July 1860, but it soon became clear to all concerned that these dates were far too optimistic, particularly given the design changes which the Admiralty made while the work was in progress. Nonetheless, the *Warrior* was completed with less delay than the *Black Prince*, which was being built on the Clyde and its construction, using the longitudinal system, was a 'great novelty to all ship constructors' (Bowen 1945, p. 375).

Its plates were to be 4.5 inches thick (plates less than 4 inches thick were

---

27. The early calls of £7 10s 0d per share raised £205,850 and the later calls for a further £10 per share raised less than £20,000; PRO Kew, Annual Returns, BT 31/946/1252c.
28. Also known as 'best London scrap iron'. HMS *Warrior* was clad with armour plates, 'forged under a steam hammer on the premises and not rolled' as then became the practice (Jordan 1925, p. 15).
29. Archibald 1971, p. 8; see also Gardiner 1992, pp. 54–7. HMS *Warrior* was quite a gamble for the Admiralty and for Thames Ironworks alike; on her launching, the First Lord of the Admiralty, Sir John Pakington, later Lord Hampden, voiced his wonder that he ever 'mustered sufficient courage to order the construction of such a novel vessel' and Mr Rolt that he often wondered how he mustered sufficient courage to 'undertake the construction of such a novel vessel' (TIQG Vol. 1, p. 4). The *Achilles*, the first iron vessel ever built by the Admiralty was later to be constructed at Chatham Dockyard.

known to provide ineffective protection) and were to be 'bolted to the 5/8 inch skin of the iron hull through 18in of teak, composed of two 9in baulks laid crossways, the whole to be recessed into the side of the ship, leaving the external surface of the armour flush with the hull plating of the areas that were not protected. Each plate was 3ft wide and 12ft long, (Lambert 1987, p. 67) and, during construction, the Admiralty decided that the horizontal joint faces of the plates should be made to interlock, in 'tongued and grooved' style, to provide more strength, a modification which was very difficult to implement and caused much of the overall delay period.

In September 1860, a serious fire broke out which destroyed a good deal of property in the Middlesex yard and seriously set back that yard's shipbuilding programme. Virtually all the sawing, moulding and planing mills and related machinery (driven by a steam-engine of some 60 hp) was destroyed, along with £10–15,000 worth of recently delivered teak, mahogany and oak in a huge bonfire at the dead of night, which was visible for eight to ten miles around. The fire was thought to have started in the engine-house and, despite its early discovery by the night watchman, it spread rapidly. Despite the help given by the working population from the adjacent Trinity-wharf, the dockyard of Mr Green and the efforts of the fire-crews, the fire burnt until 5am. The tangible losses were covered by insurance, but these were 'as nothing compared with the costs of the inevitable delays to the progress of a war steamer of prodigious dimensions and strength, called the *Warrior*', which was well advanced. The dislocations did not only affect the owners: until shipbuilding could continue, about 500 of the 2–3,000 men working in the yard were immediately thrown out of work (*Times* 3 September 1860, p. 10).[30]

The ship's launching on 29 December 1860 'marked the beginnings of the modern British screw fleet' (Graham 1958, p. 48) and the launching arrangements made were very different from those devised by Brunel for the *Great Eastern*, representing a minor triumph of the modest but highly apposite traditions of the trade. When the launching was to take place, it was very cold and the grease froze on the ways, despite the bogie fires that burned night and day along the side of the way and the ship stuck fast on the launching ways. The naval architect, G. C. Mackrow, wrote later of how

> in those days they were a bit fond of a little powder, minus the shot ... and we prepared a small gun (as used for starting yacht races from Blackwall) as it was thought that a few blank charges fired in the cold frosty air would set up a considerable vibration and tend to release the vessel ... after a couple of rounds she began to move slowly and eventually took her plunge into her cold bath very grandly'.[31]

30. Fires were quite common in the industry; another one in December 1861, destroyed Thames Ironworks comparatively new mould loft, although it was soon rebuilt.

Their main concern had been over the width of the stream and the risk of the ship striking the far bank, to check which they had floated 30–40 pine logs as a movable buffer. This was just as well, as the vessel struck the logs 'on which scores of curious folk had ranged themselves and the logs were set rolling over each other up the bank, causing the greatest consternation to all, but happily with no hurt other than a ducking which, considering the weather was not over-enjoyable'. Sir (later Lord) William Armstrong was an interested spectator of the proceedings (TIQG vol. 2, p. 50). The ship's measured mile performance of 14.3 knots 'set a record for fighting ships which was not exceeded for some years' (Emmerson 1977, p. 164) and the advanced nature of her design clearly impressed many people; the following year, among the stubby wooden hulls of the Channel Squadron, she seemed 'like a black snake among rabbits' (Emmerson 1977, p. 164).

The original contract sum for the hull of the *Warrior* from Thames Ironworks was £190,225 but this did not cover the major changes required by the Admiralty during its building. On 16 March 1861, six months before the *Warrior* left the Thames, the firm sent the Admiralty a bill for extras for £40,808. When all was finished, further additional costs had been incurred and the firm suggested that they be paid cost plus 12.5 per cent, subject to a full investigation of the books by the Admiralty's accountants, as the company's resources had been at the disposal of the government for more than two years, but the Controller of the Navy instead paid an additional £12,000 on the basis of cost plus 5 per cent (*Times* 13 March 1863, p. 12).

The eventual total cost of the ship to the Admiralty was £357,291 (Lambert 1987, p. 30) and Thames lost £61,400 on their part of the contract (TIQG vol. 2, p. 45) although the company's success in building such a ship established its reputation and 'brought more persons of note to the works than had, perhaps, ever visited a private dockyard before', including Grand Duke Constantine, Prince Frederic Wilheim (father of the subsequent emperor of Germany), the Duke of Cambridge, Lords of the Admiralty and a host of Ambassadors and Naval Attaches from foreign courts. This in turn led to orders for the first armour-clads ever possessed by the Governments of Russia, Turkey, Germany, Spain, Portugal, Greece and Denmark (TIQG Vol. 1, pp. 3–4; *Engineering* vol. 80, 13 December 1894, p. 567).

In October 1861, they also received orders for two Danish gunboats and launched a paddle vessel for the Paraguyan Government Transport Service. In 1863, they had in hand the armour-clad *Pervenetz* (3,300 d.t.), the first

---

31. This account, which appears to be reliable, is slightly different to Emmerson's, which says it took six tugs an hour to pull her into the water (Emmerson 1977, p. 164).

armoured warship built for the Russian government, the *Vittoria* (7,000 d.t.), for many years the flag ship of the Spanish Navy, a Turkish frigate (6,400 d.t.), a very fast cruiser yacht for the Sultan of Turkey (*Izzeddin*) that could achieve 16.5 knots, and the first of what was to be a line of steamers for the Egyptian government (*Charkieh*). They also built HMS *Minotaur* (10,690 displacement tons) which, at 400 feet, was longer than HMS *Warrior*, had ram bows and armour plating that was 5.5 inches thick and used 1,800 tons of armour plate, as against 900 tons for the *Warrior* (Barry 1863, p. 217).[32]

Thames Ironworks had invested considerably in improved facilities and the works 'doubled in area and resource' in the three years to 1863 (Barry 1863, p. 219). The yard was large, although inconveniently divided into two sections by Bow Creek; the Middlesex side consisted of five acres of offices, plumbers' shops and timber yards and material had to be taken across to the 20-acre Essex section, which was well laid-out but 'far more compact than the Royal Dockyards', with five building slips, the largest capable of taking a ship of up to 12,000 tons, interspersed with workshops. The coal that was needed was brought to railway sidings or by colliers that were unloaded at the pier and then distributed round the yard on internal railway lines (Barry 1863, p. 219).

The processes in use at the works were very interesting to contemporary eyes. An account in a journal of the period suggests that 'if a battle were raging, the scene could hardly be one of more strife and noise; heavy blows resound on every side' and there were real risks of injury from 'stalwart hammerers fighting with all their might against obstinate bolts. Hoarse and angry shouts from the men are answered by shrill cries from the boys who, armed with long pincers, rush madly past you with red-hot bolts and take flying leaps over dark bottomless-looking abysses, like so many young imps.' The ship appeared to be 'on fire in fifty places, and this gave the whole scene a strange character of wild and imposing fierceness and power' (*Temple Bar* vol. 1 March 1861, pp. 235–6). Similarly, when John Penn and Co. were making their larger marine engines, they frequently cast cylinders weighing 20–30 tons, work which involved machinery of the 'most ponderous character' to hold the molten iron and the manipulation of the huge masses 'with the delicacy required in winding up a watch'. The pyrotechnics involved also had their own charm, at least to the onlooker:

> the hitherto dark foundry being suddenly lit up with the glare of the rivers of liquid iron running over the lips of the cauldrons, the most beautiful coruscations of fire fly about in all directions; the air is positively full of coloured sparks;

---

32. The *Minotaur*, most unusually, had five masts. The problem of how each should be named was a 'great puzzle' to the local naval officers (TIQG Vol. 2, p. 50).

while the bright glow of the molten iron, almost white in its intense heat, lights up the features and forms of the workmen and numerous visitors in a wondrous manner.' (*Illustrated London News* 7 October 1865)

The shaping of the metal was carried out with the help of three rolling mills and forging by means of seven large steam-hammers. The steam-hammers at the Thames Ironworks plant were based upon Nasmyth's design of 1840, whereby a hammer-head weighing several tons is drawn up by means of a piston-rod and then allowed to fall by its own weight, descending with a 'rapidity and power that literally shakes the earthen floor'. The largest hammers delivered blows with a force of 90 tons onto metal which had just been swung across from the furnace by means of a powerful crane. The hydraulic plant for curving the metal plates could also exert enormous pressure and the forges could produce the heaviest of keels, stems, stern-posts and machinery for the ships under construction (*Working Man* 17 February 1866, p. 98). The rolling operation used white-hot metal drawn from the furnace and subjected the roller-men and furnace-men to intensities of heat and light that were recognised at the time to 'operate prejudicially' to the men's health and which profoundly discouraged the consumption of alcohol by those involved. The rolling process was 'as dangerous as it is grand' and involved several repetitions (involving the manipulation of the sheets with giant pincers) to convert the lumpen mass of iron into metal sheets or angle-irons of the required thickness, ready for shearing (trimming) and cutting (*Temple Bar* Vol. 1 March 1861, p. 238).

In 1863, despite having such impressive iron-working facilities and being one of the leading shipbuilding firms in England, they were actually 'in an exceedingly critical position', with liabilities of £178,904, greater than their share capital of £150,000. They decided to reform the business and at the beginning of 1864, a formation of a new company, Thames Iron Works, Shipbuilding, Engineering and Dry Dock Co. Ltd was announced.[33]

The capital of the new firm was in a far more easily transferable denomination of £100 per share and by 1866 there were about 190 shareholders, who had contributed almost £400,000. Twelve of the shareholders held over 100 shares apiece, including Peter Rolt who had 237. The directors were Rolt (Chairman), Captain John Ford (Managing Director), Lord Alan Spencer Churchill, Frank Clarke Hills, William Jackson and John Margetson. The assets of the old business had been taken over at a valuation of £275,000 (purchased for £150,000 in shares and the remainder in debentures) and the additional funds raised by the new company enabled them to construct two dry-docks, 'at a cost of over a quarter of a million

33. PRO Kew, 31/913/1080c. The company taken over was Thames Graving Dock Co. Ltd, PRO Kew, BT 31/255/843.

pounds, the bigger one capable of taking any ship then afloat' (Bowen 1945, p. 375) and provide the facilities that were lacking in the Thames and had caused ships to be sent from the river to Southampton and even to Liverpool for repair work (Prospectus, Millwall Freehold Land and Docks Co., 1865, p. 2). Eight acres of land immediately adjoining the works were also purchased to increase the frontage onto Bow Creek and the Thames (Prospectus, Thames Iron Works, Ship Building, Engineering and Dry Dock Co. Ltd).

At full capacity, the company employed 5–6,000 men and business was at a good level for four or five years until 1866. Thames Ironworks (whose company motto was 'no work no pay') was not using the 'gang-contract system' that had been common practice in the London area and thus did not pay over any contract profits to the shipwrights (Pollard 1950, p. 86). On the other hand, they did pay a slightly higher official wage than elsewhere, supplemented by piece-work, and the efficient layout of the yard meant that the men could earn 'remarkably good money', which enabled the company to 'skim the cream of London shipyard labour' (Bowen 1945, p. 375).

The company continued to use engines supplied by the noted Thames firms of John Penn and Maudslay, Son and Field and in February 1865, they launched the *Napoleon III*, one of the largest (4,000 tons) and most powerful paddle-steamers afloat which they had built for the Compagnie Generale Transatlantique (*Times* 13 February 1865, p. 12). They retained the custom of P&O and Royal Mail until 1865, but then P&O's business disappeared almost overnight, after the construction of the Tanjore. G. C. Mackrow, the firm's naval architect, attributed the sudden loss of P&O's business to two things: acrimony over the intended succession of Captain Ford (whose health at the time had seemed to be in decline) as Assistant Managing Director by the P&O's Captain Engledue, an outcome that was blocked even after he had bought a large number of Thames Ironworks shares and secondly, the reinforcement of the P&O board at that time by 'gentlemen from beyond the Tweed', who encouraged the company to place more of their orders with Scottish shipyards (TIQG Vol. 2, p. 118).

In 1866, however, general commercial trade virtually disappeared, employment at the firm had to be cut from 6,000 to 2,000 and the company was able to keep going only because of its British and foreign naval work (*Times* 18 January 1867, p. 10) and because their civil engineering division had secured a major contract to construct the arched bridge at Blackfriars.

In 1867 they were building the 9,600-ton armour-clad *Fatikh* (whose armour was 8.5 inches thick) for the Turkish government, but they could not pay for it and arrangements were made for Prussia to take her over as the *Konig Wilhelm* (TIQG Vol. 2, p. 119). While the vessel was being built, it was inspected by Emperor Frederick III, Crown Prince of Prussia although at this time it was the only vessel on the slips, which were looking 'woefully bare' (TIQG Vol. 3, p. 58). Despite the dismal prospects, the company was able to pay a dividend of 2.5 per cent, at a cost of £15,000, in March 1867.

By now the original Orchard Shipyard had become too small for the ships that were now in demand and, when the lease expired in 1867, Thames decided to further concentrate their business on the larger slip-ways on the Essex side of Bow Creek and take out an annual lease on only part of the yards on the Middlesex side, the remainder being taken over for a while by the shipbuilder, Henry Green (Crighton, p. 23).

Money Wigram (Yard 3: Blackwall Yard) – see also Appendix 3

Money Wigram did use the traditional Thames system of contracting with shipwrights for the building of ships at an agreed job-rate and also offered iron shipbuilding work to the shipwrights at the same price they would have got it done by boiler-makers and iron shipbuilders. Not surprisingly, the yard had a history of being able to avoid strike action and any labour problems tended to be far more between the shipwrights and other workers than between the shipbuilders and shipwrights (Royal Commission on Trade Unions 1867–68 Minutes of Evidence, pp. 8–9).

In the 1860s, Wigram built four ships for the London, Chatham and Dover Railway, several other commercial vessels and five ships for the Admiralty, including the biggest they were to build, the troop-ship HMS *Crocodile*, that was well over 4,000 tons.

At times, Wigram's yard had employed up to 1,200 people but they suffered a marked decline in trade in the winter of 1866–67, when their wage bill fell from about £800 a week to £200 (Royal Commission on Trade Unions 1867–68 Minutes of Evidence, p. 10).

Samuda (Yard 4: Samuda's Yard)

Samuda was well-known for building fast steam packets, particularly for the Holyhead to Ireland run, and iron-clads for foreign navies, including the Russian, German, Japanese and Brazilian, but they also built more specialised craft and became pioneers in the use of steel in shipbuilding.

In the early part of the 1860s, Samuda often had as much as 16,000 tons of shipping in hand and built the Admiralty's iron-clad cupola ship *Prince Albert* and the transport *Tamar*, two vessels for the P&O, two for the Viceroy of Egypt and four for foreign governments and steam navigation companies (Barry 1863, p. 298). Their commercial customers also included Royal Mail, General Steam, the Folkstone and Boulogne Services and the Messageries Imperiales of France.

As a result, Samuda invested in increased capability by taking over more land between their main yard at Cubitt Town and Stewart's engine-works, which extended their frontage onto the river to more than 500 feet.

In 1865 the firm built a 400-foot yacht of high quality, the *Mahroussa*, for the Viceroy of Egypt, which was for many years the largest steam yacht afloat. In that same year, Samuda became an MP.[34] In 1867, they built a frigate for the Prussian Navy, the *Kronprinz*, partly of steel and weighing 3,400 tons and the following year, an innovative 'floating fire-engine' that was to be stationed at Southwark Bridge, but employment levels fell below 200, as against a normal level of 1,200 and occasional peaks of 2,000; only their ability to attract work from foreign navies enabled them to survive the 1866 crash (Royal Commission on Trade Unions 1867–68 Minutes of Evidence, p. 13).

Rennie (Yard 5: Norman Road, Greenwich)

In 1862, Sir John Rennie retired from active business and all the marine and mechanical engineering facilities were moved to Greenwich, with only civil engineering remaining at Blackfriars. The Greenwich yard was capable of excellent work and during the 1860s, at the time of a famine in India, built and engined a dozen twin-screw supply vessels for the Indian government in about the same number of weeks (Bowen 1948, p. 617). John Rennie died in 1866 and was succeeded by his two sons, who were interested in warship design and construction and built the floating batteries *Cabral* and *Colombo* in 1866 for the Brazilian government, who were then at war with Paraguay.

Dudgeon (Yard 6: Dudgeon Wharf, Cubitt Town)

John and William Dudgeon, who were thought to have once been blacksmiths, left the north of England and moved to the Sun Iron Works, Millwall in 1855 to make engines, boilers and marine machinery. In 1860 they obtaining a 40-year lease at £300 a year and also leased a site on the river in 1863, close to the pier at Cubitt Town, with a frontage of 350 feet and a depth of nearer 600 feet, which was properly laid out as a shipyard. (Survey of London 1994, p. 429).

The firm then helped to pioneer developments in twin-screw propulsion

---

34. At first he represented Tavistock, then Tower Hamlets until 1880. He also served as Lieutenant-Colonel of the 1st Tower Hamlets Rifle Volunteers, helped to establish the Institution of Naval Architects and became a member of the Institute of Civil Engineers (*East London Observer* 24 September 1910).

with the construction of *Flora*, a 400-ton blockade runner built for the Confederates in America, the first vessel fitted with two screws and engines working independently, an arrangement which provided excellent manoeuvring capability. The twin-screw system was 'a big selling point on long-distance services where there was a great fear of broken shafts'. Dudgeon also developed a reputation for being able to turn out ships with very light hulls and machinery that could travel at high speed, but without any sacrifice of strength or reliability (Bowen 1950, p. 54). From March 1862 to 1865, they built 20 twin-screw vessels of an average size of 500 tons, twelve of which were blockade runners (Pollard 1950, p. 78) and in 1865 they made the armoured gunboat, *Viper*, one of the first twin-screw ships in the Navy. They also built the first packets for the Great Eastern Railway, when it obtained Parliamentary powers to run its own steamers between Harwich and Rotterdam.

The best year was probably 1865, when 850 men were employed in the shipbuilding yard and 650 in the engine works. They survived the crash of 1866 with some difficulty and continued to make ships and engines, including those for the armoured gunboat *Waterwitch* launched by Thames Ironworks in 1867, but levels of employment fell drastically to 175 in the shipyard and only 25 in the engine works.

Thorneycroft (Yard 7: Chiswick)

John Thorneycroft had shown an unusual aptitude for shipbuilding when he was still very young: at 19, he finished building a steam launch, the *Nautilus*, that was the only steam launch capable at that time of keeping up with the 'eights' in the University Boat Race. His father bought him a piece of ground at Chiswick, known as Corney's Reach and he made several launches there including two, the *Ariel* and the *Slaney*, which were very fast. He then left and started work as a draughtsman in Palmers Shipyard, Jarrow, studied engineering at Glasgow University and then worked in the drawing office of a shipyard at Govan. In 1864, he returned to Chiswick and built several ambitious, fast steam launches, including the 50 foot *Miranda*, which achieved the 'then incredible speed of over 18 knots' and later would build a steam launch for Baroness Rothschild which achieved nearly 24 mph. His first iron launch was the *Water Lily*, launched in 1866.

Yarrow (Yard 8: Folly Shipyard, Poplar)

Alfred Fernandez Yarrow (1842–1932) was apprenticed at 15 for five years to Ravenhill and Salkeld of Glasshouse Fields, Ratcliffe, London (formerly Barnes and Miller and then Miller and Ravenhill), who built marine engines and river steamers. He was an unusually able and enthusiastic apprentice, helping to form a society (the Civil and Mechanical Engineers Society) for the 'reading and discussion of papers on engineering and kindred subjects' (*Engineer* 29 January 1932, p. 133), developing with a friend called Hilditch a link between their houses by 'electric telegraph on the over-house wire system, this being the first telegraph of the kind in London', and also designing and patenting a steam plough with obvious commercial prospects.

At the end of his apprenticeship, he was then employed by Messrs Coleman, agricultural engineers, to look after their newly opened London office. His employers also agreed to take on the manufacture and sale of the steam plough. In 1865, Yarrow built an experimental steam launch, *Isis*, with Hilditch, largely for their own interest (*Engineer* 29 January 1932, p. 133; Banbury 1971, p. 296) and, later that year, went into partnership with Robert Hedley, an engineering foreman, who had no capital but did have contacts in the trade that could be expected to generate ship-repairing work. Yarrow put up the capital of about £1000, from his royalties on the steam plough, from his own savings and from two unexpected bequests.

They rented an area of about half an acre at Folly Wall on the eastern side of the Isle of Dogs that consisted of a small barge-builder's yard (known as Hope Yard), work-shed and tools as well as a recreational space used for quoits and as a tea garden. The combined site had a river frontage of 3–400 feet and was about 350 feet deep but the usefulness of the area was limited by the Folly public house,[35] which stood in the middle and was served by two rights of way. The boundaries of the area could not, however, be readily extended because they were determined by the world's largest gasometer (owned by the South Metropolitan Gas Company), by Samuda Street, Folly Wall and a draw-dock (Banfield 1897, p. 470; Barnes 1924, p. 43).

The partners built a small machine shop and were able to employ twelve men in their first year. They started by constructing pumping machinery for the docks at Rio de Janeiro and their sales for the year totalled £2,800 but their costs were £2,900 (including labour £800 and materials £1,500), resulting in a small loss (*Kentish Mercury* 12 January 1900). Their work was very diverse; as well as repairing ships, they also built a 'thief-proof door for a safe in a jeweller's shop in Brighton, apparatus for roasting coffee and repaired the boiler in a jam factory (*Engineer* 29 January 1932, p. 133). In the following year, they tried to both concentrate on ships and to expand the scale of their operations but they 'lost on almost every contract', the total amounting to £2,000 over the year as a whole and the firm's prospects began to look rather bleak (Barnes 1924, p. 48).

---

35. Nell Gwynne had lived in the pub during Charles II's time, which was much used by smugglers; if caught they were liable to be hanged at Blackwall Point, opposite and in full view of the pub (*Listener* 15 January 1930, p. 98).

Other firms

Richard Green had always been committed to the construction of wooden ships, many of which were of some size. The business deteriorated during the 1860s, even before the general slump and, some time after Richard Green's death in 1863, the firm began to build iron ships as well as wooden. Their first iron ship was the 365-ton *Superb*, launched in 1866 and after that the yard was properly 'adapted to produce a variety of iron ships' (Survey of London 1994, p. 572) although most of their vessels were still made from wood. In 1867 they launched one of the largest ships ever built at Blackwall, the 4,175-ton HMS *Crocodile*, an Indian troop-ship.

Maudslays, the well-known engine makers were now facing much stiffer competition for engines than hitherto and, in 1865, they started to also make ships at East Greenwich, a practice that lasted until 1872.

London Engineering and Iron Ship Building Co. Ltd was formed in July 1864, at Millwall with a nominal capital in £50 shares of £500,000. Their paid-up capital was far more modest, however (£24,000) until they took over 'the shipbuilding ironworks and engineering business of a respectable house, Westwood, Baillie and Campbell of London-yard, Millwall' towards the end of 1865, at which point, £65,000 was subscribed and 4,000 other shares issued, fully paid, to Westwood and Baillie (Campbell had left the business, after a domestic quarrel with Westwood) as payment for the assets they had transferred to the company. Westwood, Baillie and Campbell had got into financial difficulties in 1862, when they were building the *Valiant*, sister ship to the *Resistance*, and they asked to be relieved of the contract, which was taken on by Thames Ironworks (TIQG Vol. 2, p. 94). At first, the company attracted quite a lot of business, making iron lock gates, railway swing bridges and iron footbridges for the nearby India Docks (and making a £5,000 profit in the six months to April 1865: *Times* 23 May 1865, p. 12), but they only survived the 1866 crash with some difficulty.

James Ash and Co. was not an incorporated business, yet had one of the 'most extensive and impressive office and works of any of the private Thames shipyards' (Banbury 1971, p. 159; Barry 1863, p. 299). The yard, north of Pier Street in Cubitt Town, had a considerable river frontage and a depth of 650 feet and was set up in 1862 by Ash, with financial support from Overend Gurney. Ash had been naval architect to C. J. Mare for eleven years and a ship designer at Thames Ironworks for six and, in his first year, several ships were launched, including two for the P&O, a steamer for the South Western Railway Company for the Channel Islands trade (the *Normandy*, launched June 1863), two paddle-wheel steamers of 770 tons and a yacht for Arthur Anderson, chairman of P&O. (Barry 1863, p. 300; *Times* 18 June 1863, p. 8). In September 1863, the firm launched a 'splendid iron screw steam-vessel, the *Nutfield* ... in the presence of a large number of spectators'; the 1,770-ton ship was to be used for river passenger traffic in Australia (*Illustrated London News* 12 September 1863). The business lasted only four years, however, when Ash was forced to close by the failure of his main financial backer, although he had never been far from collapsing; his bankruptcy investigators 'found that his costs exceeded his income by the whole amount of wages paid out' (Pollard 1950, p. 82).

In 1863, Nathan Thompson established the National Company for Boatbuilding by Machinery Ltd, in a newly-equipped yard on the marshes at East Greenwich. The aim, to secure a quarter of the national boatbuilding market, proved totally unrealistic and the business failed in 1865. Maudslay, the engine-maker, took over the premises and started shipbuilding on his own account, although he made only a small number of ships, mostly iron sailing clippers.

The Blackwall Ironworks on the Isle of Dogs added a large new foundry to their facilities in 1863, on ground adjoining the main factory. The business was now more focused on engine and boiler manufacture, providing the engines for Arthur Anderson's (the chairman of P&O) 340-ton yacht and several other ships built by Thames Ironworks and Charles Lungley, but the owner, John Stewart, got into financial difficulty and was made bankrupt on 18 May 1865.

Charles Lungley had excellent dry-dock facilities and considerable experience as a shipbuilder and repairer at his yard at Deptford Green. He began to make his own marine engines when his previous supplier, Dudgeon, began to make ships, but his particular interest was in building 'unsinkable' ships, where the lower part was divided into a number of water-tight compartments divided horizontally and accessible only from the upper decks. In 1864, he began to build and engine cross-channel packets of 4–700 tons for a number of companies and he also built eight iron ships for the Union Steam Ship Company, over the period from 1860 (the 1,055-gross ton *Cambrian*, Union's first mail ship) to 1866 (the 1,439-ton *Celt*) and some ships for the Admiralty, including HMS *Vixen*. Lungley joined Millwall Ironworks in November 1864, as managing director but resumed work in his own yard when the Ironworks failed in April 1866.

CHAPTER SIX

The long slump, 1868–88

In 1866, the shipbuilding trade reached its point of capacity saturation, from which output was then to contract. The 57 per cent decline in London shipbuilding tonnage, from 49,515 tons in 1866 to 21,268 tons in 1867, was more than twice as severe as the rate of decline in the UK trade as a whole. As a result, the proportion of UK tonnage built on the Thames also fell from 12.4 per cent in 1866 to 7.2 per cent in 1867.

During the next 20 years, UK annual shipbuilding volumes were to advance by 50 per cent as compared with 1860–67 (see Table 5) although there were very considerable cyclical variations around the generally rising trend.[1] By 1869, world trade, particularly in grain, was expanding again and Britain was able to gain an increasing share of the growing world market (Checkland 1971, p. 47), aided by improvements in steam technology, in the availability of the more economical compound engines and the opening of the Suez Canal. The UK shipbuilding trade peaked in 1874 at an output of 620,700 tons (40 per cent above the previous boom of 1864–65) but collapsed quickly to only 413,400 tons in 1876 (a third lower), when the major shipbuilding areas were in the grip of trade recession. By 1882 there were clear signs of a revival (*Times* 26 December 1882, p. 9), the following year conditions were 'buoyant' in the trade and an unprecedented output of nearly 900,000 tons was achieved in the UK but three years later, output had fallen by 56 per cent and there were 'desperate conditions on the Wear and Tyne; for the nation as a whole, 20 per cent of shipyard workers were idle' (Checkland 1971, pp. 56, 66).

The leading firms in the industry had typically been formed in the 1840s and 1850s and 'all had adopted an organisational structure based on functionally specialised departments … relying increasingly on specialised departmental management' (Slaven 1980, pp. 123–4). Most remained as family firms, with only 17 out of the 90 iron shipyards being run by public companies. The main iron shipbuilding yards in Britain in 1871 employed, on average, 575 workers (Pollard and Robertson 1979, p. 81) and, according to Slaven, aimed at a profit norm of about 10 per cent on cost, although

1. The historical trend of increasing vessel size continued; although tonnage volumes were 50 per cent up on 1860–67, 10 per cent fewer ships were built.

actual out-turns varied considerably around this figure (Slaven 1980, p. 121).[2]

By 1870, iron ships constituted some five-sixths of the total UK fleet (Checkland 1971, p. 146) but the increasing use of steel in shipbuilding (recognised as a suitable material by Lloyds in 1877), particularly as the quality of the material improved and its price fell, brought about a major shift from iron to steel as the main construction material for ship's hulls.

In 1870, the six or eight largest firms had each invested about £250,000 in their business facilities (six times as much as the smallest firms), although the growing importance of steel raised the 'price of keeping up with the competition', requiring further investment to re-equip the yards concerned and introduce new 'bending rolls and cranes capable of handling the larger plates and sections' (Moss 1997, p. 21; Peebles 1990, p. 33).

The availability of the new, more sophisticated material also brought about major changes in naval strategy, with consequent effects upon the relationship between the shipbuilding industry and the Admiralty. Capital ships were still important and their requirements for armour plating brought benefits to the heavy end of the steel industry, particularly in Sheffield (Checkland 1971, pp. 47–8), but the strategic and cost benefits of dispersed firepower and of speed at sea meant a much increased demand for vessels that could be built by smaller, more specialised firms (*Times* 30 May 1877, p. 3). British naval demand does not appear, from Table 6, to have been particularly important to shipbuilding firms until 1885, representing under 3 per cent of total demand, although in some years (for example, 1869–70 and 1876) and to some firms the work could be far more important. Admiralty orders did, however, have a value beyond purely volume terms, as they acted as a signal of quality and reliability that helped the firms concerned to tap potentially lucrative foreign markets. Moreover, in the years 1885–88, there was a marked increase in naval demand, which took nearly 9 per cent of shipbuilding capacity, suggesting that the British government was heading for a much closer working relationship with technically advanced firms in the shipbuilding and steel-producing trades.

The complex pattern of cyclical variations around a generally rising output trend was also subject to considerable regional variation. The leading areas were clearly Scotland and the north-east; in 1871, some 24,000 men were employed in shipbuilding on the Clyde and 13,000 in the Northeast, as against 8,800 on the Thames (Slaven 1980, p. 107; see also Palmer 1993, p. 59 and Pollard 1950, p. 88) and both areas increased their market share during the

---

2. An Inspector of Factories report identified 48 shipbuilding works in England and Wales in 1871, employing 20,467 people. By county, the major centres were: Durham 15 (employing 9,564), Chester 7 (3,417), Northumberland 7 (3,746), Middlesex 6 (1,441), Essex 3 (893) and Kent 3 (479) (Inspector of Factories 1871, p. 22).

period under examination. On the Clyde, the larger screw steamships were being made more cheaply, helping to raise the average size of ships launched and they also advanced their share in the more specialised markets for smaller boats; the fleet records of one of the largest river steamer operators on the Thames, the Woolwich Steam Packet Company for example, show that whereas the first 26 steamers (over the period 1834 to 1861) were all built in the London area, Scotland was able to attract the orders for half the ships built from 1862 to 1875 (Burtt 1949, pp. 40–41).

Even the more successful areas suffered during trade slumps, however and on the Clyde, output fell to only 63,000 tons in 1867, rose to a new peak of 262,000 tons in 1874 but by 1875 'the whole of the Clyde shipbuilding industry was in the grip of another trade recession' and output fell back to 169,000 tons (Peebles 1990, p. 31).

Table 6: UK Shipbuilding statistics, 1868–88

	(1) UK (no.)	(2) London (per cent)	(3) (000) (n.t.)	(4) UK London (per cent)	(5) UK tonnage per cent Admiralty	(6) UK tonnage percent London Admiralty
1868	1,130	4.8	371.5	4.5	2.5	0.4
1869	1,075	5.4	417.3	3.4	7.0	1.7
1870	1,082	6.2	428.3	5.2	7.9	1.6
1871	1,026	3.3	406.6	4.0	3.9	1.9
1872	1,076	4.5	478.7	2.1	0.8	0.1
1873	932	3.1	454.6	1.6	0.2	0.2
1874	1,082	5.1	620.7	8.0	2.7	2.5
1875	1,007	3.8	490.5	7.2	3.8	2.8
1876	1,065	3.8	413.4	2.5	8.6	1.3
1877	1,162	6.4	457.4	1.2	1.4	0.0
1878	1,207	8.5	488.1	0.7	3.6	0.0
1879	938	10.7	412.8	2.9	1.5	1.5
1880	1,000	10.2	478.1	1.2	1.0	0.4
1881	1,099	11.7	615.2	1.6	1.0	0.4
1882	1,154	13.4	786.3	1.5	0.4	0.2
1883	1,415	10.5	898.7	0.9	0.7	0.2
1884	1,199	10.3	589.7	1.0	0.4	0.1
1885	988	8.0	471.4	4.9	6.5	3.8
1886	756	8.5	394.8	1.7	16.0	0.7
1887	742	5.5	424.0	5.1	11.1	4.6
1888	887	7.2	578.1	0.8	1.8	0.1

Average p.a.	1,049	7.2	508.4	3.0	3.9	1.2
Ave. 1866–67	1,314	8.1	355.4	9.8	3.3	3.3
Ave. 1860–67	1,177		335.0		5.2	3.2
Ave. 1854–59	1,086		252.2		6.0	4.9
Ave. 1847–53	769		149.4		0.6	0.6
Ave. 1832–46	901		127.0		1.4	0.7

Notes: no. = number of vessels
n.t. = net tons

Sources: Mitchell and Deane (1962, pp. 220–22); Banbury (1971); Conways (1979); Brassey (1883); Palmer (1993); Board of Trade Annual Statements of Navigation and Shipping, 1868–88.

Cost factors tended to work in favour of the two leading areas. By the mid-1870s, the Cleveland area was producing one-third of UK iron output, closely followed by Scotland, making one of the basic materials cheaper to local shipbuilders. Until 1871, profits had been low in the coal industry but thereafter prices and profits picked up, to the relative detriment of the Thames region; 'the price of coal in London reached an extraordinary level, costing over fifty shillings per ton for the first time since the coming of the railways' (Checkland 1971, p. 47).

The evidence on comparative wage levels is less conclusive. Shipmasters on the Clyde appeared to have a greater ability to enforce wage cuts on their workers during trade slumps and to hire and fire many of their workers at very short notice (in each case because of the size of Glasgow's pool of unemployed workers) and were thought to have been able to pay wages 10 per cent lower than those on the Tyne and Mersey (Campbell 1986, p. 3). It has often been suggested that shipbuilding on the Thames was discouraged by its wage levels but the differentials involved can be exaggerated; between 1860 and 1874, wage rates on the Clyde rose 31 per cent, in the north-east and Belfast 25 per cent, on the Mersey 16 per cent and on the Thames only 7 per cent, by which time Slaven thought that labour-rate differentials in the dominant iron sector were 'small and certainly less than 10 per cent between districts' (Slaven 1980, p. 120). Labour relations in the industry could be very corrosive, however; worker's demands in 1877 for a 10 per cent increase were broken with lock-outs in a dispute which lasted over thirty weeks. Six months later, the employers instead sought a 7.5 per cent cut in wages and an extension of the working week from 50 to 54 hours, which they achieved after a twenty-week dispute.

The main Thames yards

During this period, cost factors tended to work against the Thames region: iron was becoming cheaper in Scotland and the north-east, prices in the coal industry were rising generally and were reaching extraordinary levels as delivered into the London area. Wage levels were higher and, perhaps more importantly, were widely believed to be considerably above rates in the other major shipbuilding centres, due partly to the inflation of the official figures on wage rates on the Thames (because of an increased proportion of repair work on ships using the London docks, which was always less predictable and thus more expensive work) and partly to politically based hostilities and anxieties.

The London shipwrights were well organised and highly resistant to wage reduction measures, even during trade slumps, and they were a persistent target for those who feared the rise of trade union power (and working-class intransigence more generally), a theme of considerable political importance in the early part of the period under examination. Moreover, in the latter part of the period, the greater volumes of traffic in the London docks, and the difficulties of selling new shipping tonnage, meant that shipbuilding increasingly gave way to repair work on the Thames and that the employment of all types of ship-workers became more and more casualised. Seasonal influences on employment were to some extent offset by the fact that accidents to ships requiring repair were more common in the winter, but this also increased the vulnerability of work levels to adverse weather conditions. In 1885–86, for example, the winter was very severe; the February temperatures were the lowest for thirty years and those working for building, dock and shipbuilding firms in the area suffered 'intense distress', leading to the famous riot of 8 February 1886 in which property in Pall Mall was extensively attacked (arousing fears of a 'rising of the casual poor' in London) culminating in the battles in Trafalgar Square on 'bloody Sunday', 13 November 1887 (Jones 1976, pp. 291–6).

Factors affecting shipbuilding volumes were, however, at least as important as relative cost levels. Table 6 shows the overall levels of tonnage constructed each year in the UK and in the London area in the period 1868–88 and can be read in conjunction with Table 7, which shows the main categories of ships built on the Thames during this period (together with comparative figures for 1866 and 1867), based primarily upon data contained in the Board of Trade Annual Statements of Navigation and Shipping and in Admiralty contracts. The data in these two tables fully supports the arguments of Pollard and Palmer and evidences the very severe collapse in shipbuilding in the region after 1866. They also make apparent the extent to which the initial decline in 1867 became permanent, because of the failure of the region to recover during the subsequent trade booms. As a result, whereas Thames shipbuilders produced 9.8 per cent of UK tonnage in 1866–67, this fell to an average of only 3 per cent in the following twenty years.

Pollard was particularly concerned at the London shipbuilder's loss of normal mercantile orders. Commercial work was not, of course, necessarily more profitable on a contract-by-contract basis, as it tended to provide lower, if less risky, returns than Admiralty contracts,[3] but it was less variable in its incidence than naval orders (which were vulnerable to changing political and strategic considerations). Above all, it provided throughput volume in an acutely cyclical trade, that helped to keep facilities and employees in use and absorb the overhead charges consequent upon earlier investments in operating facilities. This perspective is again supported by the evidence set out in Tables 6 and 7: in only four years between 1872 and 1888 did London's share of annual output rise above 3 per cent (1874, 1875, 1885 and 1887) and in each of those years the improvement was due to the completion of either foreign or Admiralty warship contracts.

Across the period 1868–88, orders for iron vessels for the British commercial market provided 31 per cent of London's shipping tonnage, but the proportion was falling from 35 per cent in the first of those decades to 24 per cent in the second. Indeed, in some years, such as 1877–78, 1880–81, 1884 and 1887–88, in which less than 2,000 tons were produced, the Thames was losing its position as an important producer of mercantile iron or steel shipping.

The London shipbuilder, Samuda, argued as early as 1867 that wages were almost bound to be higher in London, because of higher local costs, notably for housing, and that shipbuilding on the Thames would therefore really only pay for high-quality or speciality work (Royal Commission on Trade Unions 1867–68 Minutes of Evidence, p. 13). The most specialised work was probably that carried out for the Admiralty and in the twenty years to 1888, this provided 38 per cent of London's shipping tonnage. The reliance on Admiralty orders for the limited tonnage that could be obtained was also increasing, from 33 per cent in 1868–78 to 51 per cent in the following decade although, more ominously, in the twenty years to 1888, competition was increasing such that the London area attracted a much smaller proportion of Admiralty tonnage (30 per cent: see Table 6) than in earlier periods. Moreover, the growth in Admiralty work did not prevent a decline by a third in the total tonnage built on the river from 1868–78 to 1879–88.

In the twenty years after the collapse of 1866, the local trade, particularly in commercial tonnage, was generally very depressed. Thames Ironworks struggled to exist on very small volumes of output and was 'in constant

---

3. See Peebles (1987, pp. 38–40, 57–9, 79–81), Campbell (1980, pp. 66–9) and More (1982, pp. 176, 181).

fear of grounding' for much of the period, Wigram stopped building ships and sold his yard in 1877, Joseph Samuda's death in 1885 threatened the continuation of the business, Rennies stayed in business making small boats while J. & W. Dudgeon failed in 1879, following the serious illness of one of the partners and the death of the other. The more specialised shipbuilders, Thorneycroft and Yarrow, however, both greatly expanded their business, most of which was with the Admiralty and a number of foreign navies.

Millwall Ironworks and Shipbuilding Co. (Yard 1: Millwall Shipyard)

The largest yard to have failed, Millwall Shipyard (owned in turn by Fairbairn, Scott Russell and then Millwall Ironworks until 1866), did not reopen for shipbuilding on any significant scale. For several years, alternative buyers for the site were sought but without success and, in May 1872, the stores, materials and tools were sold off. The 'grand old armour rolling mill, that rolled the armour for HMS *Northumberland*', was also disposed of, at scrap metal values, to be reinstalled in the Thames Ironworks yard (TIQG Vol. 3, p. 14).

The former Napier yard was leased to a number of local barge and shipbuilders, iron-workers and scrap-metal firms, generally on a short-term basis, on into the 1880s and the former Northumberland Yard, used for the construction of the ship of that name, was taken over by a group of London and Tyneside shipbuilders and converted into graving docks. That venture did not last very long, however, and Dudgeon and Co. took over the same yard in 1878, but they too went out of business in November 1879.

Finally, some of the former Millwall Ironworks buildings were taken over in the 1880s by a firm of engineers, Joseph Westwood and Co. and the remainder became part of Burrell's Wharf in 1888.

Thames Ironworks (Yard 2: Bow Creek Shipyard) – see also Appendix 3

After the 1866 crash, the amount of business coming to shipbuilders on the Thames declined sharply and Thames Ironworks, in particular, experienced great difficulties. In the 1850s they had been producing in excess of 8,000 tons a year of commercial tonnage (see Appendix 2) and were able to look to occasional orders from the Admiralty as welcome additional business. During the period 1860–67, however, volumes fell just over 40 per cent and the company looked to orders from overseas governments as necessary compensation for a sharp decline in mercantile business, which represented about a third of total output. In the following twenty years, commercial tonnage went into free-fall, and construction levels (at 756 tons a year) were less than a tenth of their volume in the 1850s and represented only a little more than 15 per cent of output.

In the whole of the 1870s, the commercial trade amounted to only 4,540 tons, almost half of which consisted of three cargo boats built in 1871 for the Russian Steam Navigation Company. Indeed, after the launching of a passenger vessel of just over 1,000 tons in 1873, the remaining orders were merely for tugs and small paddle-steamers, only one of which exceeded 150 tons. An informed and expert view was that of their naval architect, who submitted countless, unsuccessful bids and concluded that it was their price that 'always led to our being ruled out, as the North Country and the Clyde were making rapid strides, putting down new machinery and doing their utmost to economise labour' (G. C. Mackrow, TIQG Vol. 4, p. 56).

The works was accordingly in a generally depressed state. In 1871, the employment level fell to 1,100 although, in 1873 with HMS *Rover*, the *Mesoudiye* and the *Castalia* in progress, the works looked 'pretty busy again', Canning Town (which was very dependent upon employment at the Thames Ironworks shipyard) had 'brightened up again' and the Victoria Dock Road, 'always an index of the prosperity or otherwise of the Thames Iron Works, seemed to be endowed with fresh life on Saturday nights' (TIQG Vol. 6, p. 5). In August of that year, the rolling mill taken over from Mare broke down, however, with 'evident signs of foul play, as several of the teeth of the large cog-wheel were broken off', stopping the mill for five months (TIQG Vol. 6, p. 5).

They even tendered for the construction of cattle boats and in June 1877, had five small boats in hand (including three Customs vessels for the Portuguese government) which 'made a pretty sight, but the slips were woefully bare' (TIQG Vol. 7, p. 63). Some orders were better than none, although 'little profit [was] made out of such work at [our] establishment', as it had the facilities (and overhead charges) more appropriate to vessels of 10,000 tons (TIQG Vol. 7, p. 6).

To get business, boats often had to be designed to suit highly specific circumstances; in 1877 a small twin-screw cargo boat was made for trading in ivory and other goods on the east coast of Africa, which had to come in on the surf towards shore stern first, so as to be able to steam out head first against the surf. The two shafts and propellers also had to be designed so as to keep the same speed, as the boat's owner, Mr Price, 'feared a kaffir native would not be equal to handling two separate pairs of engines, that is one pair to each shaft' (TIQG Vol. 7, p. 4).

Such specialist work did not, however, provide very substantial volumes and the company became almost totally dependent upon its naval work, which amounted to over 54,000 tons in the ten years from 1868, 60 per cent of which was for the British government. During this time, they built five ships of about 3,500 tons each, mostly iron screw corvettes. HMS *Cyclops* was completed in November 1871, a month under contract time, which earned the company a premium of £4,200, although overtime working cost them twice as much. They also built for overseas governments, including three armour-clads in 1876, ordered initially by the Turkish government, one of which was sold to the UK government at the time of the Russian war scare for £453,000, becoming HMS *Superb*.

In 1878–79, the company built the first torpedo gunboat in the world, the *Zieten*, for the German Navy and also tried making a torpedo boat hull from 'Parson's metal', a manganese bronze which had the strength of mild steel without its corrosive qualities, but the vessel never achieved its required speed and was taken over by the Admiralty for experimental purposes (TIQG Vol. 7, p. 61).

At the start of 1879, business at the works was 'about as low as could well be' and the only orders were for a couple of barges for Aden and a small tug for service in South Africa. Later in the year, the firm also built the *Middlesex*, a Great Eastern Railway ferry for service between north and south Woolwich, a caisson for Rio de Janeiro, HMS *Swift* and *Linnet*, two composite gunboats, but plans to build a double-turret warship for the Peruvian government were abandoned when that government ceased to be at war with Chile (TIQG Vol. 7, p. 114).

The 1880s started with the company 'still among the shallows and in constant fear of grounding' (G. C. Mackrow, TIQG Vol. 8, p. 4), although their naval work was more diverse than hitherto, consisting of a large number of small gunboats (two of which, for the Royal Hellenic Government, had complete hulls of iron, sheathed with wood and then covered in zinc; TIQG Vol. 8, p. 6), mine layers, torpedo boats, cruisers and customs vessels. In one case, the company only obtained the contracts despite their higher prices, by agreeing to time penalties of £100 a day if they went beyond a four-month construction time: on signing the contract in October 1880, the company's naval architect 'went to bed but not to sleep, the heavy penalties bec[oming] a nightmare, as the vessels were not large and the profit but small and a few days default would swallow up all the profits. Still we wanted work badly as the forge and rolling mills were all but idle and our workmen were in great need.' The Christmas break was cut to three days and they had to launch another boat that was in the way, in a 'fearful snowstorm', but the contract was duly completed in time (TIQG Vol. 8, pp. 6–10).

Two Spanish cruisers, launched in August 1881, were to be built complete with searchlights, which were at the time a 'great novelty to us as just coming into vogue' and their testing caused members of the company to spend 'several late nights in the Victoria Docks after dark' (TIQG Vol. 8, p. 57).

The firm also built the British battleships HMS *Benbow* and *Sans Pareil*, both over 10,000 tons. The order for HMS *Benbow*, the most powerful vessel of its day, was received in September 1882 and this 'was a great cheer for us, as we seemed to have entered upon a new era for the Works' (G. C. Mackrow, TIQG Vol. 8, p. 152). The ship's design was highly controversial, as it required no armoured protection at either end but did specify a belt of compound armour 18 inches thick and 150 feet in length, covering the side of the vessel from 2.5 feet above to 5 feet below the low water line. Similarly, in April 1885, when the order for the *Sans Pareil* was obtained, the Company ran up the flag on the flag-staff to announce the fact as this was 'always an occasion of general rejoicing in the neighbourhood and no wonder, when we remember that some £3–5,000 are paid in wages by the Company weekly, most of which, if not indeed all, is spent in the district' (TIQG Vol. 9, p. 57). The state of the company's order-book could also affect some people in the locality for much of their working lives; in 1888, for example, George Johnson retired as master shipwright, having been born and bred in the 1830s at Orchard House and having joined Mare and Ditchburn 'as a lad', first as gate-boy and then as apprentice shipwright (TIQG Vol. 10, p. 112).

Shipbuilding was not an easy trade but it did have its pleasing rituals and occasions: on the launching of the Portuguese corvette *Affonso de Albuquerque* in July 1884, for example, the visitors were 'more than the Board Room could well seat, so lunch was served in a marquee, the weather being very fine' (TIQG Vol. 9, p. 54). It also brought a surprising amount of contact with European royalty. In February 1885, Prince George of Wales, who was studying at the Royal College, Greenwich, was keen to inspect HMS *Benbow* and, with the help of Messrs Humphreys, who supplied a steam yacht, this was duly accomplished; 'the sight of the vessel as we steamed into the mouth of Bow Creek was very imposing, as the full depth of the vessel was towering above the blocks' (TIQG Vol. 9, p. 56). It is also clear that a degree of co-operation applied between shipbuilders who were competitive in seeking contracts but, once these had been awarded, often provided helpful advice to one another, as indicated by the visit of G. C. Mackrow, the firm's naval architect, to Armstrongs when the latter were building the *Victoria*, sister ship to the *Sans Pareil*, and his comment that 'there were many points we had to discuss' (TIQG Vol. 10, p. 14).

The trade could also involve unexpected complications; in early 1885, Thames Ironworks were repairing and modernising two Peruvian cruisers, *Socrates* and *Diogenes* (each of 1,765 d.t.) which had been built in Germany at the time of the Peruvian–Chilean War, ostensibly as passenger steamers for a private company. The Chilean government became aware of the real position, however, and the ships were embargoed and not allowed to leave Germany until the war was over. In 1885 it was, and the ships were being brought up to date, but no one in government had thought to remove an earlier British embargo requested by the Chilean government. As a result, Thames Ironworks had to request Admiralty permission to take the ships to the mouth of the Thames for trials on the Maplin Sands. The Admiralty duly assented, but required the ships to have 30 'blue-jackets' on board and to be accompanied by a British gunboat, in order to ensure that the vessels could not 'steal away from the British Isles, as did the *Alabama* in the days of the American War of 1864'. When the work was completed, the *Diogenes* was renamed the *Lima* but Thames took the sister ship *Socrates* in part payment for their work and eventually sold it on to the American government, who renamed it the *Topeka* (TIQG Vol. 9, p. 56).

The difficulty of obtaining orders for mercantile vessels of reasonable size, taken in conjunction with the receipt of occasional naval orders, meant that Thames Ironworks was often dealing with a highly divergent set of vessels; in 1888, for example, the yard contained HM battleship *Sans Pareil*, a Portuguese transport ship, three Romanian Customs boats for service on the Danube and a water boat for the Indian government (TIQG Vol. 10, p. 112). The company's civil engineering work also extended from suspension bridges (including the Hammersmith) to caissons and dock entrance gates (including those for the Kidderpore Docks).

The difficult trading position of the company during this period also had its effect upon the constitution and ownership of the business. In 1871, the 'Thames Iron Works, Shipbuilding, Engineering and Dry Dock Co. Ltd' was re-formed and became the 'Thames Shipbuilding Graving Docks and Ironworks Co. Ltd' , valued at £250,000. Shortly afterwards, in May 1872, the business was re-formed again, under the name, 'Thames Ironworks and Shipbuilding Co. Ltd'.[4]

By now, although Rolt and Lord Churchill were still on the board of directors, their share-holding had fallen considerably and influence over the company's policies was shifting to F. C. Hills, a successful manufacturing chemist from Deptford, who had been a large stakeholder for ten years and now had £100,000 invested in the company's £50 shares and £97,000 in their debentures. A year later, in March 1873, the change in control was much clearer as there were now only eight shareholders: Lord Churchill, John Bulmer and six members of the Hills family. Arnold Hills, one of Frank Hill's three sons, was then at Harrow; after reading Classical Moderations and Modern History at University College, Oxford (and also showing outstanding athletic prowess, winning the English mile and representing his University at football) he joined the board in 1880 at the age of 23 at the beginning of what was to prove one of the most eventful careers in the local shipbuilding industry.

4. PRO Kew, BT31/1597/5338; BT31/1722/6293.

Wigram and Son (Yard 3: Blackwall Yard) – see also Appendix 3

The Wigrams were ship-owners as well as builders, but they found the latter trade very difficult after the slump of 1866. During the first half of the 1870s, business revived a little and they built five or six fairly substantial ships, including HMS *Sappho* and HMS *Daring* for the Admiralty, two composite screw sloops of around 1,000 tons each. The largest and the last of these ships to be built was the *Kent*, 2,484 gross tons, launched in 1876.

They then decided to concentrate on ship-owning, have their steamships built in the north of England and give up shipbuilding (Banbury 1971, p. 290) and in 1877 they duly sold their yard to the Midland Railway Company for £80,000. The new owners filled in the old slips and dry-dock in order to build railway yards and warehousing and then built a new Poplar Dock particularly suited to use by colliers (Elmers and Werner 1989, p. 18).

Samuda (Yard 4: Samuda's Yard)

Samuda Bros. were well-known for the construction of high-quality iron ships, ranging from yachts to warships. The yard was well-appointed and contained the most sophisticated equipment, including machinery for bending armour plates with a pressing power equal to 4,000 tons, but the shipwrights in particular were opposed to the equipment because they thought that it reduced the level of employment (Crory 1876, p. 12).

The yard had a good reputation with overseas navies. In 1872, they built the Austrian imperial yacht *Miramar*, in 1874 the *Fu-soo*, the first Japanese armour-clad and in 1875 the *Kaiser* and *Deutschland* for the Emperor of Germany. The last-named had a total displacement tonnage of over 7,500 tons and were the last warships built in Britain for the German Navy. Samuda's also fulfilled orders for two small corvette iron-clads from the Turkish government although, in 1877, the Admiralty instead decided to buy them for £240,000 each, renaming them HMS *Orion* and *Belleisle*.

Samuda had previously been an MP for Tavistock and he represented Tower Hamlets as a Liberal from 1868–1880 but eventually lost his seat, apparently to the combined opposition of a combination of interests; Jews who objected to his 'secession from the faith of his fathers', Liberals who found his support for a 'Disraelian foreign policy' incompatible with their beliefs and shipworkers who disliked his use of modern machinery (papers in THLH, ref 902).

The firm also continued to attract orders for commercial tonnage and in 1880 built 'about the fastest thing afloat', the *Albert Victor*, for the South-Eastern Railway's service from Folkestone to Boulogne, chartering a special train to take the guests to Gravesend for the trip to Folkestone (*Times Weekly*

Edition 9 July 1880; *Times* 14 March 1882, p. 11). The yard at Poplar was often quite busy and in 1882, for example, they had in hand a steel turret vessel for the Brazilian government, three screw and one paddle vessel for the Admiralty and two paddle-wheel ships.

Joseph Samuda died in 1885, however and, once existing contracts had been completed, including those for the construction of small steamers for the South Eastern Railway Company, the yard closed. A limited company (Samuda Brothers Limited) was then formed in August 1885 and £60,000 subscribed in share capital to take over the assets and sell the business as a going concern, but without success. That same year, in September a fire of 'alarming character' broke out in the early morning and destroyed a large, two-floored building used for storing masts and rigging, spread with great rapidity and was not subdued until the late morning (*Times* 8 September 1885, p. 4).

In late 1887, at the third annual general meeting, shareholders heard how the business continued to be affected by the depressed state of the shipbuilding trade in the country; in their first year, receipts had been only £12,000 and in their second year, orders amounted to only £32,000 although they were hopeful of large orders in the near future for the construction of iron-clads and dredgers.

Rennie (Yard 5: Norman Road, Greenwich)

From 1868 until 1887, the Rennies concentrated increasingly on general and marine engineering work and built only a small number of ships, including six steamers for India and a number of gunboats for the British, Argentinian and Mexican governments. In 1887, however, they decided that their engineering facilities were becoming out of date and they decided to abandon engineering work and concentrate instead on shipbuilding (Bowen 1948, p. 618). Their output was almost entirely small vessels, ranging from lighters to high-speed river boats, although they also built sailing vessels and barges. The firm's reputation was enhanced by the steel lighters they made for Wm. Cory's coal business, which were generally regarded as the best on the river (Bowen 1948, p. 618).

Dudgeon (Yard 6: Dudgeon Wharf, Cubitt Town)

In 1869, despite the general deterioration in trade, J. & W. Dudgeon bought a disused yard to the south of their own, thereby increasing their river frontage to 500 feet. Unusually, the firm was prepared to accept orders for unorthodox boats, but it also built a number of screw and paddle tugs as well as, in 1870, the monitor HM *Abyssinia* for the defence of Bombay.

Dudgeons built three ships of about 1,600 tons apiece and a fourth, rather larger ship, for an Italian firm, the Compania de Navigacion a Vapor Italo Platense, each to run between Genoa, other Italian ports in the Mediterranean and the River Plate, their owners having obtained a contract from the Italian government for carrying the mails (*Times* 2 February 1870, p. 7). The first two ships, the *Italo Platense* and *La Pampa* were to 'inaugurate the emigrant traffic between Italy and the River Plate' and the ships were named 'in a very graceful manner by Madame de Murietta' and blessed according to Italian custom by the Bishop of Troy, before being launched from the slipway (Bowen 1950, p. 54).

Dudgeons were also successful in attracting orders for cross-Channel packets, notably from the London, Chatham and Dover, and London and South-Western companies. The yard was almost entirely given over to iron shipbuilding and built only one wooden-hulled ship, the schooner *Richmond* for the Board of Trade in 1868.

In 1874, the firm took on by far their largest ship to date, the 9,310-ton *Independencia* for the Brazilian Navy. John Dudgeon was very anxious about its weight and provided three launching ways on each side, to be thinly coated with grease at the time of the launch (Bowen 1950, p. 54). The launching took place on 16 July 1874, before a large company of onlookers but, halfway down the slip, 'she brought up and defied all the tugs that came to her rescue. The launching way had necessarily been carried over the foreshore wharf on piles, the intention being to withdraw the piles after the launching'. As a result, the temporary piles may not have been driven so firmly as the permanent ones but, whatever the cause, 'as the tide receded, she was supported for a while by the piles, but eventually she settled down on them and they crushed completely through the bottom in the engine and boiler-rooms'. A more distressing sight was never seen, 'each tide leaving its deposit of mud inside and she looked a complete wreck. After some months work, however, they managed to dam round the injured part and float her off, when she was taken into Woolwich Dry Dock and repaired by another shipbuilder, Samuda' (TIQG Vol. 6, p. 6). Before completion, she was instead bought for £600,000 and renamed HMS *Neptune* by the Admiralty.

Her builders had insured against launching problems but the misfortune was still costly and distressing and the following year one of the partners, William, died and John fell ill, his reason affected by the unfortunate events of the previous year, thereby closing the business and its two yards.

A company (Dudgeon and Co. Ltd) was formed in January 1878 to restart the business and take over the nearby premises of the Northumberland Graving Docks and Engineering Co. Ltd, that had gone into liquidation in April 1876, but the venture was not successful and the company went into voluntary liquidation in November 1879.[5] The engine and boiler works at Millwall were taken over by another firm, J. & A. Blyth, who retained the old name of the Sun Engine Works but the machinery from the yard at Cubitt Town was sold off piecemeal and the riverside yard auctioned in 1880 and then used for oil storage.

Thorneycroft (Yard 7: Chiswick)

At first, Thorneycroft built only a small number of ships but they did develop an early reputation for speed, their launch *Sir Arthur Cotton*, reaching a speed of over 21 knots in 1873. In that same year, Thorneycroft's brother-in-law, John Donaldson became a partner in the business in an arrangement which brought together Thorneycroft's innovation and flair for design with Donaldson's organisational ability (Jeremy 1986, p. 514).

At first, they specialised in the construction of steam launches but, at about this time, torpedoes were coming of age as naval weapons and Thorneycroft, with their experience of making fast launches, were well placed to take advantage of the situation. Torpedoes, mounted on small, fast vessels, offered considerable benefits to lesser naval powers who could not compete on large ship provision and Thorneycroft produced the first launch 'designed specifically to act as a high-speed torpedo boat' for the Norwegian government in 1873–74 and then for the Admiralty in 1876 (Yarrow 1897, p. 293). The Admiralty boat was 86 feet long and reached 18 knots and Thorneycroft went on to build 77 similar (or slightly longer) boats in the next five years, many of which were for foreign buyers. The firm was also very highly rated by the British government, and they received the contract for exactly half the 54 torpedo boats ordered by the Admiralty in 1885, raising employment at their six acre yard at Chiswick to nearly 1,700 men.

Yarrow (Yard 8: Folly Shipyard, Poplar) – see also Appendix 3

Yarrow and Hedley had tried in 1867 to concentrate their business on shipbuilding, rather than on general engineering work, but they lost money on nearly every contract. In the spring of 1868, they decided to try making small steam launches, similar to the *Isis* that Yarrow had once made. They received their first order very soon after placing an initial advert and, although they lost about £50 on a contract price of £145, they more than made this up on subsequent buying and reselling of the same boat. They carried on building the launches with scarcely a pause, making about 350 between 1868 and

5. PRO Kew, BT31/1905/7734 and BT31/2400/11995.

1875. Their prices varied from £140 to £2,000, which provided them with a reasonable return, and their launches were unusually well made and luxurious enough to appeal to customers like the Sultan of Turkey.

The firm developed two other specialisms in this period, torpedo boats and stern-wheelers. Primitive 'spar' torpedos, 40-foot poles mounted on launches about 30 feet long, and carrying a container like an oil drum, packed with 80 pounds of gun-cotton, had first been used during the American Civil War. The carrying launch could run up at night close to a ship (with the crew's faces carefully blacked to reduce the risk of being seen), the pole lowered and the charge ignited by electricity, a procedure which could blow a hole 12 feet in diameter through a 1-inch plate (Banfield 1897, p. 471).

In 1871, Yarrow began to take a renewed interest in the construction of fast boats that might be used to carry spar torpedoes and the firm built their first torpedo boat in 1873–74. The 'torpedo' now consisted of a spar 25 feet long, run out over the bows with a copper cylinder at the end of it, containing about 60 lbs of explosive charge, which could be lowered under the water. On contacting the ship's side, the short-circuit caused an explosion, far enough below the surface of the water as to cause 'little danger to the launch itself, if well built and properly handled' (*Illustrated London News* 6 February 1875). The device was tested to the firm's satisfaction by blowing up a barge on the upper Thames (Yarrow 1897, pp. 293–4).

The Argentine government was particularly interested in the use of torpedoes and in obtaining fast, manoeuvrable craft to which spar torpedoes could be fitted. Yarrow duly obtained the Argentinian order in 1875, supplying 55 foot boats suitable for the purpose, although they were in fact 'neither larger nor faster (12.5 knots) than some pleasure boats already built by the firm' (Borthwick 1965, p. 21).

Yarrow then started to put more thought into the design of really fast naval ships, an area of activity that would earn the yard a 'world-wide reputation and set them on a course they were to follow for close on ninety years' (Borthwick 1965, p. 20). Yarrow believed in careful research as the means of acquiring the ability to build fast ships, and the tests he carried out overturned the conventional wisdom that larger propellers reduced slip and increased speed, leading to a decision to make rather smaller propellers than previously was thought to be sensible (Borthwick 1965, p. 22).

Torpedo technology was now advancing rapidly. Whitehead had sold the rights to his propelled torpedoes in 1871 (for £15,000) and, by 1877, the possibilities provided by their use from fast ships rendered spar torpedoes obsolete and changed naval strategy overnight:[6] 'Within months, the fleets

6. Whitehead's locomotive torpedo was later to be seen as 'unquestionably the most far-reaching' of the important naval developments of the 1870s in its later influence on history and naval architecture' (Ballard 1952, p. 30).

of the world were frantically interested in torpedo boats. Small navies as well as big were determined to own the fastest torpedo-carrying craft which could be devised' (Borthwick 1965, p. 22).

Yarrow and Co. now built enormous numbers of mobile torpedo boats. Russia ordered designs that would enable them to build 110 boats at their Baltic works in St. Petersburg, along with as many sets of engines and boilers as Yarrows could build at Poplar before the onset of winter (Borthwick 1965, p. 22). The 75-foot boats were duly supplied, after Admiralty approval had been obtained, although two 100-foot boats under construction for the Russian government were taken over by the Admiralty when the Turkish–Russian war began. The Russians used the Whitehead torpedoes in the conflict, although with 'very feeble results' and one of the torpedoes missed its target and ended up on the shore and thus delivered the secret designs to the Turkish government, without the need for payment (TIQG Vol. 7, p. 10).

The torpedo boats also 'figured conspicuously' in the Naval Review in the Solent in 1878, taking the Prince of Wales for his first high-speed trip afloat and providing Yarrow with favourable publicity that did much to secure the long-term future of the company (Barnes 1924, p. 92). The boats were now in demand world-wide and, in 1877–79, the firm was able to sell an enormous number of boats to the French, Italian, Austrian, Spanish, Japanese and other navies, at quite lucrative prices.

The speed of the boats was dependent upon both their weight and on the use of forced draughts and the boats had to be constructed with great care. The hulls were only 1/16 to 3/16 of an inch thick and, in order to achieve uniform stiffness and keep the weight down, the firm always hammered their steel plates into shape cold, since the bending of plates by rolling or heating tended to increase the weight of the boat (Yarrow 1897, p. 301). The use of forced draughts was also crucial to the speeds achieved but could make the boats very dangerous to the engineers and stokers who sailed in them; the latter in particular worked in very confined spaces and faced almost certain death by burning or scalding, if the tubes gave out (TIQG Vol. 7, p. 62).

In 1880, Yarrow developed the first properly sea-going torpedo boat, the 100-foot *Batoom* and began a new era. The new ship was far more robust than previous torpedo boats, which were light craft built for speed and unsuitable for the open sea for any period of time, but was still capable of 22 knots.[7] The Greek government ordered six in 1881 with heavy penalties for late delivery. Yarrow, characteristically, would accept the contract only if it included matching premiums for early delivery, which the firm achieved,

7. The *Batoom* was sufficiently seaworthy that it was able to steam unaccompanied from London to the Black Sea.

earning an additional profit of £12,500 (Barnes 1924, p. 98).

In the latter half of the 1880s, Yarrows continued to supply torpedo boats to foreign governments, and in 1885 made one of the largest such boats of all time for the Japanese government, the 166-foot-long *Kotaka*, which was partially protected by armour. Also in 1885, Yarrows were awarded the contract for 22 of the 54 torpedo boats ordered by the Admiralty and were now describing themselves only as 'Torpedo Boat Builders' although, in fact, they continued to make other boats, particularly stern-wheelers.

Yarrow has been seen as the 'father of stern-wheelers' (Banfield 1897, p. 471) and the firm began to develop a good reputation for making them and other types of river steamers soon after the partnership between Yarrow and Hedley was dissolved in 1875. Hedley started up another business nearby, which did not succeed, and Yarrow, now trading as Yarrow and Co., began to specialise in the construction of 'steam and side or stern wheeled steamers', particularly river steamers (as well as in the making of torpedo boats). Stern-wheelers are typically light ships, with a very shallow draught, and Yarrow built them from 50 to 180 feet long (and from 8 to 36 feet wide). They sold particularly well with South American governments, who found them useful in developing trade along their rivers and, in 1883, they built the stern-wheeled *Le Congo* for the King of the Belgians, in which Stanley went up the Congo.

Yarrow also built a range of special craft, including other types of shallow-draught boats suitable for use in rivers marked by shoals and rapids. Some of them, including the *Itala* (built for the anti-slavery work of the Nyassa Mission and believed to be the first steamer launched on an African lake) were built in sections and could be converted into small wagons, transported by road and then reconstructed on site. Others were made in sections that would float, so that reconstruction could take place more quickly in water.

In 1874, Gordon ordered, through the Governor of the Equatorial Provinces, four stern-wheeled boats from Yarrow that would cope with the floating vegetation on the Nile, and these were eventually used in the defence of Khartoum and sent down the Nile to meet Lord Wolseley's relief force. Yarrow and Co. also built a very luxurious stern-wheeler for the King of Burma in 1876, and three 100-foot stern-wheel steamers for the carriage of mails on the river Magdalena in the South American state of Colombia (one in 1877 and two in 1879) with a draught of only 12 inches to suit even the shallow parts of the river (*Times* 3 November 1879, p. 10). They also made (in conjunction with Messrs Siemens) an experimental battery-operated electric launch.

The firm achieved very good results despite being based on a small and difficult site. Space became very tight when employment levels reached 1,200 and the Folly public-house in the middle of the plot of land presented additional problems as the shipyard workers were 'constantly found within its doors' (Barnes 1924, pp. 56–7). It was very much in Yarrow's own interest to close the pub and free up some additional space but the demand from his own workers helped the pub's trade and the owners were well aware of the position and would not sell, except at a prohibitive price. The ground-landlord, who owned the reversionary interest in the freehold that was due to fall in ten years later, died in 1875, but there was little commercial benefit in buying up the interest, given the dilapidated state of the public-house and Yarrow was accordingly able to arrange for a friend to purchase it at modest cost. His friend duly served notice on the landlord to meet the existing conditions of the lease and, in particular, to make good the accumulated deterioration of the property. The tenant-publican was highly discomfited at these demands and opened negotiations with Yarrow to sell the building, at a far more reasonable price than hitherto!

The purchase of the pub, and the conversion of its front room to a drawing office (Barnes 1924, p. 56–8), also provided the impetus for the firm to buy up the freeholds on some adjacent land and the yard was then redeveloped, with new workshops being built and open sheds provided over the boat-slips. The enlarged site was known thereafter as the 'Folly Shipyard' although in 1881 the former public-house was demolished, thus opening up more space. Finally, in 1885, after the death of Joseph Samuda, Yarrow and Co. were able to lease part of Samuda's yard, and thereby increase their river frontage by about 150 feet.

Other firms

Many of the smaller firms on the river experienced difficulty after the slump of 1866. The London Engineering and Iron Ship Building Co. had, by 1870, raised £135,000 of paid-up share capital, but trading opportunities were very limited and they went into voluntary liquidation in February 1871.

Maudslay and Co. operated the east Greenwich yard of the National Company for Boatbuilding by Machinery (Limited) as a shipyard until 1872, but it was then turned into a boiler works.

Westwood and Baillie resumed control of their 'London Yard' in 1872, but concentrated on the construction of prefabricated iron and steel bridges rather than on shipbuilding. In 1883, after Westwood died, Robert Baillie carried on the business in his own name, but still continued to make bridges (including the Sukkur Bridge for the Indian government) rather than ships.[8]

8. In 1891, Robert Baillie sold his business to a limited company and retired from business and two years later the yard (which was near to Samuda's old yard) and its extensive holdings of equipment, boilers, winches, cranes and plate-bending presses were sold off (*Westminster Budget* 20 October 1893).

Greens, who had once shared the old Blackwall Yard with Wigram, had virtually lost interest in government contracts and it was not until 1875 that they built their first Admiralty ship, HMS *Assistance*, since the Crimean War. The firm had always concentrated on the construction of wooden ships and it was not until 1875 that they built their third iron ship, the *Melbourne*, of 1,975 gross tons, apparently from surplus iron plates from the recently completed HMS *Assistance* (Banbury 1971, p. 183).

In February 1876, the firm embarked upon the construction of a major new graving dock but Henry Green died later that year and his son Henry and cousin Joseph decided to make mainly dredgers, hopper barges, launches, schooners and tugs. In 1877, they formed, with Anderson, Anderson and Co., the Orient line of steamers, an independent service to Australia, which soon became the Orient Steam Navigation Co. Ltd, although some shipbuilding and repair work continued at the yard. In the 1880s, they continued to build small-tonnage vessels, including coastal paddle-steamers, ferry steamers and lightships (Banbury 1971, p. 183) and to expand their very profitable repair work (Bowen 1932, p. 4), although in 1882 they did built HMS *Sphinx*, a composite paddle gunboat used to suppress 'slaving and gun-running in the Persian Gulf' and a large (2,900-ton) merchant marine ship, the *Suffolk* (*Times* 26 December 1882, p. 9). In 1885, they built a series of 20 troop lighters for the British government and in 1888 launched a steel paddle-steamer for Messrs Cousens of Weymouth and two new powerful Woolwich ferry steamers for the Metropolitan Board of Works (*Times* 10 May 1888, p. 3).

Table 7. Ships built on the Thames, 1868–88

	Total		Wood		Iron or Steel		Foreign Merchant		Foreign War		Admiralty	
	(no.)	(n.t.)	(no.)	(n.t.)	(no.)	(n.t.)	(no.)	(n.t.)	(no.)	(n.t.)	(no.)	(n.t.)
1868	54	16,685	31	2921	12	4,647	7	1,300	2	6460	2	1,357
1869	58	14,298	20	752	19	3,823	12	439	5	2354	2	6,930
1870	67	22,246	2	2983	31	8,006	12	3,424	1	807	2	7,026
1871	34	16,335	4	281	15	6,411	13	1,813	0	0	2	7,830
1872	48	10,240	9	627	16	3,384	21	5,657	0	0	2	572
1873	29	7,362	9	447	15	4,832	4	1,025	0	0	1	1,058
1874	55	49.826	6	1,275	29	19,655	7	2,031	12	11,644	1	15,221
1875	38	35,124	8	713	20	9,617	2	900	6	10,141	2	13,753
1876	40	10,133	16	751	23	3,903	0	0	0	0	1	5,479
1877	74	5,282	27	1,251	19	676	21	437	6	2,882	1	36
1878	102	3,426	38	1,469	19	1,192	29	399	14	260	2	106
1879	100	12,163	38	1,594	18	3,423	28	971	12	164	4	6,011
1880	102	5,888	31	884	24	1,857	39	1,193	5	149	3	1,805
1881	129	9,758	33	1,400	28	1,256	25	1,310	39	3,276	4	2,516
1882	155	11,534	34	1,346	65	7,540	32	537	22	411	2	1,700
1883	148	7,879	31	1,144	39	2,832	48	1,510	26	218	4	2,175
1884	124	6,092	36	1,021	32	1,547	39	1,714	16	968	1	842
1885	79	23,033	13	425	29	2,135	27	975	7	1665	3	17,833
1886	64	6,798	5	138	39	3,235	4	82	11	484	5	2,859
1887	41	21,573	10	471	13	554	5	345	10	576	3	19,627
1888	64	4,571	21	1,379	27	1,877	3	167	11	623	2	525
Av.1868–88	76	14,297	21	1,108	25	4,400	18	1,249	10	2,052	2	5,488
Av. 1868–88	50	15,843	14	959	19	5,591	11	1,466	4	2,553	1	5,274
Av.1879–88	101	10,929	25	980	31	2,626	25	880	16	853	3	5,589
1866	134	49,515	69	3,902	37	13,646	20	3,932	5	7,477	3	20,558
1867	81	22,268	37	1,480	29	4,291	12	9,510	2	2,396	1	4,695

Notes: no. = number of vessels
n.t. = net tons

Sources: Board of Trade Annual Statements of Navigation and Shipping, 1868–88; Conways (1979); Brassey (1883, 1909).

CHAPTER SEVEN

An excessive dependence on the state, 1889–1915

In the 25 years before the First World War, the British shipbuilding industry achieved unprecedented levels of tonnage (see Table 8); the annual average for the entire period, of 966,300 tons, was 90 per cent higher than the average for the 20-year period that had followed the crisis of 1866.

For the first time, following the passing of the 1889 Naval Defence Act, Admiralty orders constituted a substantial (10.3 per cent) and regular component of the output of the private sector shipbuilding industry and were to have an increasing influence upon the way that the industry was structured, encouraging the leading firms to integrate their steel production, ship construction and armament provision.

Output in the industry was, as ever, cyclical with particular downturns from 1893–97 and 1908–10, although the overall trend was clearly upwards, leading to three years in 1911–13 in which production exceeded all previous levels.

The influence of Admiralty orders on private sector shipbuilding

Admiralty orders were important in volume terms (see Table 8) and also provided an important source of high-value work, but also raised two interrelated issues of considerable political importance: the regional allocation of contracts and the provisions made for 'fair wages'.

Warship construction had always been an expensive business and advances in technology tended to increase this rather than to provide cost savings; in 1894, for example, the 'average cost of the materials worked into the hulls of first-class battleships completed at the Royal Dockyards was £27 per ton', four times the average price of products in the iron and steel industry generally (Marder 1964, p. 25).

There is a good deal of evidence that Admiralty contracts provided higher profits, perhaps twice as high (as a proportion of contract price) as commercial work, although equally naval work was usually more innovative and could go badly wrong.[1]

1. See Peebles (1987, pp. 38–40, 57–9, 79–81); Campbell (1980, pp. 66–9) and More (1982, pp. 176–81).

The passing of the 1889 Naval Defence Act signalled the arrival of a new era of more substantial and predictable government contracting and provided for the construction of 70 vessels, 8 first-class battleships and 2 second-class, 9 first-class cruisers and 33 second-class, and 18 gunboats. The construction of these boats was to be shared between the Royal Dockyards, who were to build 38, and the private yards who were to build the other 32 (including 4 of the first-class battleships). There were further expenditure commitments during the build-up to the First World War and, during the period 1889–1914, £134.6m was spent on the construction of Royal Navy ships by firms in the private sector (Pollard and Robertson, 1979 pp. 213–15).

Inevitably, the regional allocation of major government contracts was a political issue, although the Admiralty naturally claimed to be even-handed in all their decisions. In its investigations in 1885, however, the Ravensworth Committee had identified four transactions where the lowest tenders (of those made by experienced shipbuilders) had not been accepted, so the area remained controversial.[2]

The Admiralty of course looked primarily to established suppliers who were both technologically advanced and reliable as far as delivery was concerned, requirements which meant a concentration of demand on a limited number of suppliers. Pollard and Robertson, for example, identified ten important builders of the larger iron-clad ships: Laird Bros. of Birkenhead, Vickers of Barrow, Thames Ironworks, Earles of Hull, Napiers, Fairfield, Clydebank and Scotts on the Clyde and Armstrong-Mitchell and Palmers in the north-east (1979, p. 84).

The higher levels of government contracting also encouraged significant changes in the organisational structure of the industry. The major steel producers began to buy up companies that would provide an integration of armour plate and armament production with shipbuilding and engine-making activities, enabling an individual contractor to build and arm an entire ship without having to factor in major components. Vickers, who had made all-steel armour plate since 1889, pioneered the new form of vertical integration in 1897 when they bought the Naval Construction and Armaments Company of Barrow, but this was soon followed by Whitworth's merger with Armstrong Mitchell, by John Brown's acquisition of the Clydebank yard, making the latter 'essentially the shipbuilding division of a vertically-integrated coal, metal engineering and armaments combine' and by Beardmore's takeover of Napiers in 1900 (Slaven 1993, p. 176).

2. Ravensworth Committee (1885 Cmd 4498), cited in Pool (1968, pp. 223–4).

The 'fair wages' issue

The allocation of naval contracts was made more controversial because of its linkages with issues concerning the payment of 'fair wages'. On 13 February 1891, the House of Commons had passed a resolution that:

> in the opinion of this House, it is the duty of the Government in all Government contracts to make provision against the evils recently disclosed before the Sweating Committee, to insert such conditions as may prevent the abuse arising from sub-letting, and to make every effort to secure the payment of such wages as are generally accepted as current in each trade for competent workmen.

Table 8: UK shipbuilding statistics, 1889–1915

	(1) UK (no.)	(2) London (per cent)	(3) UK (000) (n.t.)	(4) London (per cent)	(5) UK tonnage (per cent) Admiralty	(6) UK tonnage (per cent) Admiralty
1889	1,095	4.7	877.5	0.4	2.6	0.0
1890	1,098	8.3	882.3	2.5	7.9	1.7
1891	1,173	6.7	872.1	1.8	7.2	1.3
1892	987	5.0	951.3	2.7	15.7	2.5
1893	914	11.2	587.9	1.4	0.5	0.5
1894	1,076	11.0	677.9	1.3	1.2	0.6
1895	1,134	10.5	761.1	1.1	14.9	0.1
1896	1,285	13.0	817.4	2.1	9.9	0.3
1897	1,308	16.5	699.2	2.5	7.8	0.3
1898	1,588	18.3	988.4	4.0	11.9	2.5
1899	1,503	14.1	1,042.1	1.8	8.9	0.1
1900	1,447	19.5	995.0	1.8	5.1	0.0
1901	1,417	18.3	1,223.1	5.3	19.6	3.9
1902	1,438	19.0	1,015.8	1.8	6.4	0.0
1903	1,354	9.7	956.9	1.4	20.7	0.6
1904	1,283	7.2	997.7	3.1	11.4	2.6
1905	1,256	9.3	1,134.1	0.9	7.5	0.2
1906	1,531	10.5	1,216.3	0.9	4.9	0.0
1907	1,767	6.9	1,164.6	0.5	10.9	0.0
1908	1,351	5.6	616.7	0.8	2.4	0.0
1909	1,037	6.7	706.6	0.7	12.2	0.0
1910	1,113	8.8	825.2	1.1	15.4	0.2
1911	1,428	7.4	1,339.0	3.3	17.3	2.8
1912	1,323	8.7	1,282.0	0.5	14.4	0.0

1913	1,291	8.2	1,526.9	0.5	21.4	0.0
1914	n/a					
1915	n/a					
Average p.a.	1,288	10.6	966.3	1.8	10.3	0.8
Ave. 1868–88	1,049	7.2	508.4	3.0	3.9	1.2
Ave. 1866–67	1,314	8.1	355.4	9.8	3.3	3.3
Ave. 1860–67	1,177		335.0		5.2	3.2
Ave. 1854–59	1,086		252.2		6.0	4.9

Notes: no. = number of vessels
n.t. = net tons

Sources: Mitchell and Deane (1962, pp. 220–22); Banbury (1971); Conways (1979 and 1985); Brassey (1909); Brassey and Leyland (1915); Palmer (1993); Board of Trade Annual Statements of Navigation and Shipping, 1889–1913.

On 16 February 1892, the Admiralty told their contractors that they would consider removing firms that did not comply from their lists of approved firms and in February 1893 they began to insert 'fair wages' clauses in their contracts. At first, apparently under the direction of Lord Spencer, the relevant clauses specified that the wages concerned should be those paid 'in the district where the work is carried on' but in 1895, at the instruction of Mr Goschen, by then the First Lord of the Admiralty, the wording was modified so as to require payment of the wages 'current in the trade' rather than those 'current in the district' (PRO Kew, ADM 116/389, f. 255).

Unfortunately, the resolution of the House of Commons had not been entirely explicit. The United Patternmakers Association, for example, agreed that the clause referring to 'district' was an 'amplification of the fair wages resolution of the House of Commons of February 1891', but argued that 'it was a necessary and essential amplification if the principle of the resolution was to have any force', as it was well-known that wages differed considerably in the same trade in different parts of the kingdom. In the particular context of the Admiralty contracts, they concluded that, if the words referring to district were left out, their

> omission will constitute an official intimation ... that the Admiralty will not expect [firms] to pay their workers on government jobs more than the lowest rate of wages 'current in the trade' ... [and] that it is intended as an intimation to those London firms (and others) that they cannot hope to secure Admiralty contracts unless they reduce the rates of wages which they at present pay. (*Times* 30 January 1896, p. 7)[3]

Although the wording of the clause could in principle affect workers in all but the cheapest district, the major effects were bound to be felt in the London area, where wages were thought to be about 15–20 per cent in excess of those in the provincial shipbuilding centres (TIQG Vol. 11, p. 5).

The main Thames yards

In the twenty years after the crisis of 1866, while the UK shipbuilding trade had grown by over 40 per cent, the share going to the London river fell by two-thirds, from 9.8 to 3 per cent. In particular, the Thames lost the ability to attract orders for medium and large-sized commercial vessels, which went mainly to Scotland and the north-east, and was left with a curiously bifurcated trade, consisting of highly sophisticated naval ships or very small and often very basic commercial and private boats.

Table 8 shows that these trends continued and intensified in 1889–1915. The region's share of UK shipbuilding tonnage fell from 3 to 1.8 per cent, although the proportion of the number of UK boats built on the river rose from 7.2 to 10.8 per cent. This indicates the extent to which the Thames was now making smaller boats; across this period, the average boat size in the UK was 750 tons (see Table 8, columns 1 and 3) but in London it was only 125 tons (see Table 9, columns 1 and 2). The local average annual tonnage of 17,400 was provided by the construction of 140 boats a year, comprising wooden vessels (6 per cent), iron and steel ships (37 per cent; average size 375 tons), foreign merchant work (5 per cent), foreign warships (4 per cent) and Admiralty orders (48 per cent; see Table 9). Most noteworthy of all was the fact that 52 per cent of the total Admiralty tonnage across the 25 year period consisted of just ten capital ships, eight of which were built by Thames Ironworks and two by Samuda Brothers.

In the evolution of iron shipbuilding on the Thames, eight yards had been of primary and four of secondary importance. Two had failed in 1866 (Millwall Ironworks and James Ash), two had not survived the death of

---

3. The specification of 'district' was consistent with the practice of the War Office, for example, although, interestingly, the London Society of Brushmakers voiced its concerns that the War Office contracts for brushes requiring contract firms to pay the 'wages generally paid in the district' *in the context of a London subdivided into districts* 'would benefit the workers but little', given that the East End was the poor end, and expressed a preference for the use of the word 'industry' instead of 'district' (*Times* 28 November 1891, p. 5).

their founders (J. & W. Dudgeon and Charles Lungley), while Wigram and Son had sold their yard in 1877 and Westwood and Baillie, at one time owned by the London Engineering and Iron Company, had turned to making bridges.

This left, in 1889, three firms whose output was modest and largely composed of small boats (Samuda, Rennie and Green) and three yards operating on a substantial scale and with a particular interest in naval work (Thames Ironworks, Thorneycroft and Yarrow). Within the latter group, Thorneycroft and Yarrow were specialised builders and produced highly technical, fast and moderate-sized ships whereas Thames tried to maintain the capability to produce the largest ships afloat but, in between occasional major naval contracts, generally constructed large numbers of very small boats.

Samuda Brothers Ltd. went into voluntary liquidation in 1892. R. & H. Green were incorporated in 1894 and concentrated on repair work, making their last ship in 1907. Thorneycroft and Yarrow moved to Woolston and Scotstoun in 1907 and 1908 respectively, Thames Ironworks failed in 1912 and J. & G. Rennie, who had been on the river since 1859, moved their shipbuilding business to Wivenhoe, on the River Colne, in 1915, bringing an end to shipbuilding on any serious scale on the Thames.[4]

Samuda (Yard 4: Samuda's Yard until 1892)

In 1891, the firm built two Admiralty second-class cruisers, HMS *Scylla* and *Sappho*, each of 3,400 displacement tons but the company was in difficulties and went into voluntary liquidation in December 1892, the various assets being sold off the following year, many of them to Yarrows (PRO Kew, BT31/3530/21537).

R. & H. Green (Yard 3: Blackwall Yard)

In 1892, Green was still building ships, a small steel tug, two passenger paddle-steamers for the Thames trade and nine steel barges, each of 100–150 tons deadweight (*Engineering* 6 January 1893), but, two years later, the business was incorporated as R. & H. Green Ltd and most of the

4. Specialist marine engine-building also waned: John Penn and Co. Ltd were taken over by Thames Ironworks in 1899 (their works being sold to a firm of general engineers in 1913), Maudslay went into liquidation in 1900 and the last firm of any size, Humphrys, Tennant and Dykes, closed in 1908.

Table 9. Ships built on the Thames, 1889–1915

	Total		Wood		Iron or steel		Foreign Merchant		Foreign War		Admiralty	
	(no.)	(n.t.)	(no.)	(n.t.)	(no.)	(n.t.)	(no.)	(n.t.)	(no.)	(n.t.)	(no.)	(n.t.)
1889	52	3,276	8	344	32	2,265	7	341	4	62	1	264
1890	91	22,071	20	1,234	33	3,226	23	1,931	14	582	1	15,098
1891	79	15,916	12	464	49	3,435	14	517	2	280	2	11,220
1892	49	26,039	6	319	32	1,337	7	108	2	20	2	24,255
1893	102	8,315	14	776	70	4,449	13	373	1	11	4	2,706
1894	118	8,843	10	326	95	4,364	3	343	1	2	9	3,808
1895	119	8,364	7	272	80	4,760	21	809	8	1,401	3	1,122
1896	167	17,162	23	1,279	104	7,679	24	737	12	5,421	4	2,046
1897	216	17,364	61	2,262	136	12,166	8	333	4	466	7	2,137
1898	290	39,669	35	2,381	228	12,275	7	130	13	628	7	24,255
1899	212	18,321	43	2,589	143	8,844	13	472	12	5,888	1	528
1900	282	17,459	43	3,168	179	12,256	26	1,337	34	698	0	0
1901	260	64,895	42	2,589	201	14,052	5	90	5	380	7	47,784
1902	273	18,047	24	1,509	236	15,912	12	476	1	150	0	0
1903	131	13,829	16	932	95	6,267	10	416	1	59	9	6,155
1904	93	31,000	14	611	45	3,429	22	1,049	7	451	5	25,460
1905	117	9,778	12	495	74	4,270	26	2,676	3	390	2	1,947
1906	160	11,135	17	704	68	5,354	65	4,449	10	628	0	0
1907	122	5,942	9	456	74	3,944	33	1,135	6	407	0	0
1908	75	4,719	7	367	38	2,669	28	1,661	2	22	0	0
1909	69	5,053	12	387	47	3,545	10	1,121	(a)	(a)	0	0
1910	98	9,270	3	132	79	6,500	15	1,079	(a)	(a)	1	1,559
1911	105	44,077	11	683	71	4,902	22	1,367	(a)	(a)	1	37,125
1912	115	6,152	16	401	87	5,493	12	258	(a)	(a)	0	0
1913	106	7,209	12	315	84	5,720	10	1,174	(a)	(a)	0	0
1914	n/a											
1915	n/a											
Av.1889–91	140	17,357	19	1,000	95	6,365	17	975	6	718	3	8,299
Av.1868–88	76	14,297	21	1,108	25	4,400	18	1,249	10	2,052	2	5,488

Notes: no. = number of vessels
n.t. = net tons
(a) = included in foreign merchant totals

Sources: Banbury (1971); Conways (1979 and 1985); Brassey (1909); Brassey and Leyland (1915); Palmer (1993); Board of Trade Annual Statements of Navigation and Shipping (1889–1913).

operations at Blackwall were turned over to repair work, 'which was becoming a more and more important business on the London river as bigger and bigger steamers were making it their terminal', although they did continue to build ships until 1907 (Bowen 1932, p. 4). In 1910, to further their core business of repair work, they merged with Messrs Silley Weir and Co., a relatively new firm in the industry, and took over a number of dry-docks, including those of Thames Ironworks when the latter went into liquidation.

Thorneycroft (Yard 7: Chiswick)

In the late 1880s, the Admiralty decided that the best way to counter the threat from torpedo boats was to commission larger and more robust gunboats, or destroyers, fast enough to catch and destroy them and in 1893 Thorneycroft built *Speedy* to Admiralty specifications. The boat could only achieve 20 knots, however, which was not fast enough and they (and Yarrow) were asked to build two destroyers to their own designs.

In 1893–94, Thorneycroft therefore built HMS *Daring* and *Decoy*, which achieved 28 and 27 knots respectively (partly because of the effectiveness of the firm's own design for water boilers) and this changed the nature of the firm's marine business. In future, Thorneycroft would focus increasingly on the construction of destroyers for the Admiralty and for several foreign navies, notably the Japanese (*Kentish Mercury* 12 January 1900), and would build some gunboats while continuing to fulfil commercial orders for launches and stern-wheelers. On the non-marine side, however, the firm began to diversify in 1896, when they started to make steam vans at the nearby Homefield works and then, as demand from industrial and municipal customers grew, at a new works in Basingstoke (Jeremy 1986, p. 516).

In 1899, however, the death of one of the partners, John Donaldson, aged only 58, precipitated a crisis, as John Thorneycroft personally did not have the money to buy out Donaldson's share of the business. A syndicate, consisting of the Scottish industrialist, William Beardmore, Rear Admiral Sir William Cecil Domville and Thorneycroft, was therefore formed to buy the business, pay off Donaldson's estate and sell the business on to a newly-formed public company. The new company was incorporated in May 1901, with a share capital of £260,000 consisting of £160,000 in 6 per cent preference shares, which were offered to the public, and £100,000 in £1 ordinary shares, which were taken up by the three directors and their associates. Beardmore, the chairman, bought 5,000 ordinary shares.

The company had built the *Livingstone* in 1900, the largest stern-wheeler made for missionary work on the Congo, and was now working on five torpedo boats for the Navy but business activities had been quite badly dislocated following Donaldson's death and the profits to May 1902 were very small.

A year later, orders were received for two 'river-class' destroyers and profits improved a little to £24,700, but the company was now experiencing major problems with the shallow depth of the region's measured mile off the Maplin sands, which made it more difficult to attain Admiralty speed targets – instead ships were sent to a measured mile at Skelmorlie in the Firth of Clyde. Moreover, the greater size and draught of destroyers, as compared with torpedo boats, was causing major problems at Hammersmith Bridge, which could only be passed en route to the sea at half-tide as, 'with more water the ships could not pass under the bridge and with less water they grounded on the bottom' (Barnaby 1964, p. 47). To get past the bridge even at half-tide, all superstructures, masts and funnels had to be removed and then refitted, a process that might have to be repeated several times if modifications were found to be necessary.

In June 1904, the shareholders accordingly approved a move to the Woolston yard near Southampton, which had been used as a barge and ship-building yard since 1876. The new yard was near to Portsmouth Naval Dockyard, to local docks owned by the London and South-Western Railway (which might require repair work on their steamer ferries) and to deep water, although it was still just as remote from sources of iron and steel. The move also required £210,000 in new capital: £50,000 in ordinary shares, £40,000 in preference shares and £120,000 in debentures. Later that year, there were the beginnings of a run-down of work at Chiswick, although Church Wharf was to remain in use for some time yet.

In 1905, the firm experienced 'exceptional difficulties' in establishing turbine construction capabilities, and incurred development costs of £50,000, a 'great deal higher' than expected, problems that delayed the construction of two new, turbine-driven Admiralty torpedo boats. They did, however, manage to build a yacht and tugboat using newly-developed gas-producers and a gas-engine and had also built a torpedo-boat destroyer for the Swedish government and increased their motor vehicle sales (which now included omnibuses), although not to a level that was really profitable, given the amount and cost of experimental work involved.

The firm had several contracts in hand, including one for five coastal and one ocean-going destroyer for the Admiralty and another for seven passenger steamers for the Indian government, and hoped to transfer the whole of the shipbuilding work to Southampton before the end of the year and thus avoid costly equipment duplication, but in order to do this (and to clear the existing bank overdraft of £40,000) they first had to raise a further £100,000 through preference shares.

Unfortunately, however, the report to the A.G.M. in 1905, at which William Beardmore presided, showed a trading profit of £35,302 which, after depreciation charges of £12,621, directors' fees, debenture interest and the preference dividends, did not provide any basis for the directors to recommend a dividend on ordinary shares. Great dissatisfaction was expressed at these results and there was even some suggestion that a committee of investigation should be appointed (*Times* 12 May 1906, p. 16; 23 May 1906, p. 4).

In 1906, the operating profits were even lower, at £23,687. The construction of the Admiralty's destroyers had cost more than expected, largely because of the new turbine technologies, although repeat orders had now been agreed at a higher price. The transition between Chiswick and Southampton continued to be costly, although the works at Southampton were now finished and would be cheaper for shipbuilding than Chiswick, and new Metropolitan police regulations had also adversely affected their sales of motor-buses in London. After depreciation charges of £12,772, directors' fees of £1,115 and debenture interest of £10,374 there were again no profits out of which to pay dividends on either the preference or the ordinary shares (*Times* 9 May 1907, p. 11; 12 May 1907, p. 14).

The following year, 1907, was little different. Operating profits improved a little to £27,052 but were absorbed by depreciation £12,531, directors' fees £1,016 and debenture interest £13,500, so that once again no dividends were possible. When the company was first set up, the prospectus had estimated future profits at about £54,000 a year, but over a seven-year period they had instead averaged nearer £16,000, partly because of unexpected technical problems but largely because the move from Chiswick had proved to be more difficult than expected. When the last of the coastal destroyers was delivered to the Admiralty in June 1907, shipbuilding work at Chiswick came to an end but the growth of marine-motor work had not yet increased sufficiently to make full use of the facilities that remained. Almost half the vessels built for the Admiralty had made losses, although work at Southampton had generally been carried on at a profit, apart from one contract for a paddle-steamer which 'owing to exceptional circumstances, had resulted in a considerable loss' (*Times* 9 May 1908, p. 18; 16 May 1908, p. 16).

By now, Beardmore had resigned as chairman. At first, he had probably seen Thorneycroft as a useful 'tied customer for the products (particularly light guns and angle iron) of his Parkhead foundry' and as a means of gaining experience of commercial vehicle production that could be transferred to Scotland, but he gradually lost interest, while the firm had no wish to be tied to only one (distant) supplier (Jeremy 1986, p. 517).

Although Woolston could handle an increased volume of work, the company's financial position was very difficult, as further capital was needed for buildings and for plant and equipment, and in 1908 the dividends were again passed over. The gradual expansion of activities and the absence of any new technologically based problems meant, however, that matters did gradually improve and profits of £40,700 in 1909 and £63,900 in 1910 at last enabled the company to clear the arrears of preference share dividends. Continued profitability in 1911 also meant that the ordinary shareholders received a 5 per cent dividend, the first since they had decided to move to Woolston, and a clear indication that a move from the River Thames had been no simple panacea.

Yarrow (Yard 8: Folly Shipyard, Poplar until 1908) – see also Appendix 3

Yarrow and Co. continued to make boats that performed well in shallow water. Their stern-wheelers, used on the Zambesi expedition and for river work in South America, were often made for sub-division into sections, which could be made so that they would float, to accelerate their reconstruction. The firm used similar technologies in the construction of its shallow-draught screw-propulsion gunboats, which were 145 feet long and 25 feet wide but needed a draught of only two feet and could be made with a hull that came in eleven sections that could be bolted together.

Yarrow continued to build their own engines and also made numerous torpedo boats; in the early 1890s, they often had seven boats under construction at once and also built a fleet of armed launches for the government. In 1893–94, they provided their own designs for fast, well-armed ships that could chase and destroy even the very speedy new French torpedo boats and duly constructed HMS *Havock* and *Hornet* for the Royal Navy, the latter (which incorporated Yarrow water-tube boilers) achieving a speed of 27 knots.

Alfred Yarrow was personally convinced, however, that even higher speeds could be achieved by using material of a higher tensile strength than mild steel for the construction of hulls and the development of a nickel metal called 'Yolla' enabled them to build the *Sokol* for the Russian government in 1895, the first ship to exceed 30 knots. The vessel was so satisfactory that it provided the pattern for a whole fleet of similar vessels, used with great success in the 1904 war between Russia and Japan. They were also purchased by the Argentine and Japanese governments.

The new destroyers were about 180 feet long and effectively superseded torpedo boats as far as major powers were concerned, although orders for torpedo boats (which were smaller and cheaper) continued to be received from some foreign navies, including the Austro-Hungarian and Chilean governments (*Engineering* 23 September 1898).

Yarrow maintained a reduced level of production during the Amalgamated Engineers strike that lasted from July 1897 to January 1898, and attempted to establish a standard day of eight hours. During the strike, the firm used non-union men and chartered the Royal Mail steamer, *Southampton*, mooring her off Blackwall Point as a 'safe hostel for "black labour"' and running launches to and from the landing piers (Banbury 1971, p. 301).

Yarrow and Co. became a private limited company, Yarrow and Co. Ltd, in 1897. They had been interested for some time in moving from their tight Folly Wall yard and, in 1899, a Japanese order for ten torpedo-boats and eight Sazanami class destroyers, that were 220 feet long, and had 6,000 hp engines that would achieve a speed of 32 knots, persuaded them to move to the former 'London Yard' of Westwood Baillie, about a mile away.

Yarrow continued to develop innovative, high-value designs, and in 1902 they built the 150-ton *Tarantula*, the first yacht to be fitted with steam-turbines, and also made an internal combustion-engine small yacht in 1906 which had a flat bottom, was very fast and 'figured prominently' on the Solent in Cowes week (*Engineer* 29 January 1932, p. 134).

The firm had never been a high tonnage shipbuilder but it was the next most important shipbuilder in the region to Thames Ironworks, and at times employed 1,300 people, so their decision to leave the area, consistent with Alfred Yarrow's concerns about local costs ('London rates were high and steel had to be brought in from the other end of the country, shipbuilding on the Thames was dying and the pool of labour was shrinking fast': quoted in Borthwick 1965, p. 30) was 'one of the most serious losses that the East End had ever suffered' (Editorial in *East London Advertiser* 4 February 1911). The contracts on the new yard at Scotstoun on the Clyde were signed in February 1906, and the first of their ships to be built in Scotland was launched in July 1908.

The London yard was closed in March 1908 and was then taken over by the Union Lighterage Co Ltd for barge-building and barge and tug repairs.

Thames Ironworks (Yard 2: Bow Creek Shipyard until 1912) – see also Appendix 3

Thames Ironworks had spent much of the period of the 'long slump' from 1868–88, 'bumping along the bottom', building quite inadequate volumes of small commercial and private boats and the occasional major British or foreign warship. During this period, the works became overly reliant upon naval orders and commercial business fell to only 15.8 per cent of total tonnage levels.

In the following period, 1889–1912, these trends intensified. Average annual tonnage levels rose 18 per cent (see Appendix 2), but commercial work virtually disappeared, comprising only 3.5 per cent of total tonnage. The Admiralty became almost a dominant single buyer, and took 75.3 per cent of the firm's output, with foreign warships taking the remainder.

Such a degree of reliance on the British government was strategically unwise, particularly when it consisted almost entirely of eight major contracts, for HMS *Blenheim*, *Grafton*, *Theseus*, *Albion*, *Duncan*, *Cornwallis*, *Black Prince* and *Thunderer*, work which was eagerly pursued by some of the most powerful companies in the land. The Thames Ironworks' chairman told a shareholders' meeting that naval contracts were worth more than their ostensible value because they 'put a company in the front rank and enabled them to secure foreign contracts'[5] although, during the whole of this period, their foreign tonnage consisted almost entirely of two Japanese orders for the battleships *Fuji* (an improved version of the British Admiral class) and *Shikishima*.

The awarding of the various naval contracts was obviously a matter of great relief and local celebration and the company maintained the long-standing tradition of running up a flag to show the local population that an important government order had been obtained (Pollard 1950, p. 83).[6] When the contract for HMS *Grafton* and *Theseus* was received on 5 October 1889, the company's flag was soon at the flag-staff head, as 'a cheery sign for the neighbourhood' (TIQG Vol. 10, p. 165).[7] Similarly, when the order for the *Shikishima* was received on 25 July 1896, only four months after the launching of the *Fuji*, there was 'general rejoicing' in the area.[8]

Thames Ironworks was clearly a competent organisation with a tradition of producing high-quality ships, but they had lost most of their commercial work of any size because their prices consistently proved to be higher than those of their competitors. Their survival and success were now dependent upon Admiralty orders, and the period from 1889–1912 increasingly came to concern the operation of the 'fair wage' clauses in naval contracts and its relationship with their own labour and other cost levels.

The wording of the 'fair wage' clauses was, in principle, a matter of general application but in reality the dispute concerned the London area, where wages were thought to be about 15–20 per cent in excess of those in the provincial shipbuilding centres, and therefore Thames Ironworks in particular, as the only potential high-volume producer in the area (TIQG Vol. 11, p. 5).

---

5. Annual General Meeting 1 July 1899 (*Iron and Coal Trades Review* 4 May 1900)
6. Church bells were apparently rung to mark the end of a strike.
7. The British cruisers were of a type new to the service, however, and the company lost a large amount of money on their construction, in common with Messrs. Earle and Co. of Hull and Napiers of Glasgow who built other ships of the same class (TIQG Vol. 3, p. 2).
8. Later that same year, Captain Yendo was presented with a 1/8 inch scale model of the *Fuji*, 'with which he was delighted' (TIQG Vol. 12, p. 149).

The changes made to the wording of naval contracts in 1895 led to the calling of a conference of local authorities at Limehouse Town Hall and the Stepney Board of Guardians duly wrote to the Admiralty to complain that no orders for government work were now being given to the shipyards of East London, that this was in large measure due to the fair wages clauses and that this potential effect was one 'that the Admiralty were well aware of at the time of making the change' (*Economic Journal* vol. VI, 1896, pp. 153–4; PRO Kew, ADM 116/429, f. 295). The clear insinuation was that the Admiralty's policies were effectively being determined by the major shipbuilders of northern England and Scotland.

Soon afterwards, in February 1896, the Chairman of Thames Ironworks, Arnold Hills wrote to the *Times* to complain about the failure of the Admiralty to take into account the differences in the cost of the labour part of contract bids from different shipbuilding areas, which he blamed for the fact that no Admiralty orders for warships had gone to the Thames area since 1889. It appeared from the details provided of tenders made by Thames Ironworks for eleven vessels and of those accepted by the Admiralty that the London prices concerned were, on average, 9.4 per cent above the successful bids although the margin was not consistent; in five cases it was over 18 per cent, in four cases it was close to 8 per cent and in the other two the margins were 1.9 per cent and 3.5 per cent respectively (*Times* 2, 5, 7 February, 14 March 1896).

The controversy was such that a Select Committee was set up in 1897 to consider the workings of this resolution. In evidence thereto, Hills maintained that:

a) when the government passes a resolution it is duty bound to observe the spirit of its own resolution (P.P. 1897, p. 204).
b) when the Resolution was passed it was Admiralty practice to specify that contractors should pay the rates of wages prevailing in their districts but that they had now removed the words 'in their districts' from their contracts (pp. 199–201).
c) the effect of their so doing would be to diminish the present rates of wages in London (which had not increased in 15 years), and then elsewhere, or to drive labour away or to lead to strikes (p. 203).
d) it had driven work from the Thames; in the six years since the resolution was passed, only £294,000 out of over £7,000,000 of Admiralty contracts had come to the Thames (p. 202).
e) London wages were very much affected by the rates used in contracts by the London County Council, which had long since passed similar rules on local wages (p. 203).
f) the Admiralty in awarding contracts should allow for the differences in the district wage rates as they were 'acting for the nation and upon the authority given by the nation in the House of Commons, which fixes the rates to be paid' (p. 201).[9]

9. Similar points were also made to the Committee into Arrears of Shipbuilding (P.P. 1902, pp. 129–34).

The Committee for their part observed that:

a) sweating existed largely in disorganised trades, whereas those concerned with shipbuilding were perhaps the best-organised in the country (p. 205).
b) London County Council did not fix shipbuilding rates, although they did determine engineers rates (even if both Penn and Maudslay did not in fact pay the LCC rates for engineers).

No substantive changes were made as a result of the committee's deliberations.

Labour costs at Thames Ironworks were partly a function of factors general to the London area and partly of the particular wage and labour policies that the company adopted.

The firm was very much under the control of the managing director, Arnold Hills, whose approach was far from conventional. He was a man of unusually strong principles, had founded the London Vegetarian Society and a number of temperance societies and was sufficiently interested in local social problems as to have lived for five years in East India Dock Road, close by his works.

His values were, however, essentially patrician and were not often consistent with those of his employees, while his support for the firm's right to engage non-union men was deeply unpopular. After the great dock strike, 'strike fever was in the air and West Ham took the infection badly. The Thames Ironworks were the worst sufferers' (TIQG Vol. 13, p. 4). The boilermakers were on strike from 9 July 1889 until 20 October, the labourers went on strike in August and were followed by the joiners (from 1 March until 23 June 1890), the engineers (for three weeks in August 1891) and the shipwrights, who were seeking 7s a day for a 48-hour week, and who went on strike for 18 months from 24 November 1892.

During this time, 'groaners' went round the streets, the bands played the 'Dead March' outside the works and Hills was 'hissed by his own workmen' as he came into the yard. The yard gates were picketed and some of the replacement hands were maltreated when they left the works. It was a time, 'if not of terror, at all events of the most unhappy feelings', but the company survived the disputes, partly by lodging and boarding new, 'black-leg' workmen on a cruiser which 'happened to be lying in their mud dock' (TIQG Vol. 3, p. 2).

After this, Hills decided that radical changes were needed to their labour-relations practices and he proposed a profit-sharing scheme whereby 10 per cent of the firm's profits in any given year be put in a fund to be distributed among the 'staff and workmen in proportion to the wages they respectively received'. This was criticised as 'absurd' by other members of the Board and, after seven days' reflection, Hills resigned but his resignation was refused and his proposal was put to the workers. The unions were, however, 'perhaps rather sore from their recent reverses' and they balloted their members and the proposals were rejected by a majority of two to one.

Hills was, however, determined to end the 'almost incessant conflict' with workmen and in 1892 he successfully introduced a 'Good Fellowship scheme' of group incentive bonuses allied to standard wage rates. Two years later a standard working day of eight rather than nine hours was introduced throughout the Works, in order to 'create a more friendly order of things in these works' (TIQG Vol. 9, pp. 99–101).

The scheme paid out the following sums, with the wage bill for that year shown in parenthesis; 1892 £4,804 (£199,858), 1893 £2,503 (£112,590), 1894 £1,112 (£106,243), 1895 £5,852 (£152,916), 1896 £5,081 (£165,637), 1897 £7,774 (£231,415), 1898 £15,399 (£265,209), 1899 £13,135 (£279,115), 1900 £11,976 (£301,472), 1901 £9,579 (£324,049), 1902 £4,984 (£239,647).

In this period the Good Fellowship Scheme cost the company £82,195, but it also brought a number of advantages. Hills saw the principle of Good Fellowship as being as

> simple in abstract theory as it is complicated in actual practice ... all work, wherever possible is given out into the yard shops at fixed prices; every workman is paid a standard rate of wages and if by increased care or exertion, he is able (alone or with his mates) to produce a given piece of work at less cost than the price already fixed, then the difference is paid over once a month to those who have executed the work.

Hills also claimed that it had been the 'keynote of our administration of the Thames Iron Works during the last twenty years ... to prove that the interests of Capital and Labour are not antagonistic but identical ... and we have convinced ourselves that the secret of industrial success is to be found in the concentration of united forces' (TIQG Vol. 6, p. 4).

It could be seen as a 'scientific form of payment by result', or as piece-work on a gigantic scale, although it was group-based and thus differed from the usual individualised version of piece-work, which 'makes each man independent of his neighbour'. It was a relatively elaborate system that could not be applied universally (it never included more than 50 per cent of the workforce, generally not more than 30 per cent and in the engineering department had completely broken down by 1900: McGrath 1983, p. 21), and the uncertainty of the results could lead to frustrations, as for example when the men might 'exert themselves to the uttermost' but find their bonus small or non-existent, or that 'their' gains had been cancelled out by the less productive work of their colleagues (Howarth and Wilson 1977, pp. 162–3).

As a policy, as Pollard has suggested (1950, p. 87), despite the frustrations, it undoubtedly helped to 'neutralise the unions' and increased the plausibility of the company's appeals against strike action, on the grounds that everyone could now be 'inspired with a common desire to make the best profits [they could] out of the work we have in hand' (TIQG Vol. 6, p. 4).

Its key benefit to the firm, however, was probably informational; as Hills said on one occasion, 'so scientifically developed a system' secured for the first time perfect knowledge of the prime cost of all contracts, providing an accurate overall view of the financial results of the month's working, of the position of each job, and even of what 'profit or loss each individual worker – man or boy – under each separate contract, in each department has made' (TIQG Vol. 1, p. 24).

Even the reduced working hours consequent upon the introduction of the eight-hour day were not as costly as they appeared for

> in the old days, when the workmen came in at half-past six in the morning, we were always plagued through the winter with loss of time, while the early darkness had to be relieved at a constant expenditure of gas and candles. Now that we begin work at half-past seven, we have no longer complaints of work being stopped because some members of a gang have not come in to time. We have therefore gained increased regularity in our hours of work but, further than that, we have dispensed with one of the old breaks in the day, which used to be made for breakfast. Now we only break off for dinner in the middle of the day. (A. F. Hills in 1899 in TIQG Vol. 6, p. 4)

Hills also spent a lot of time and money on the formation of works clubs of every kind, and including a temperance league, cycling club, cricket club, literary club, dramatic society, a choral society and the noted Thames Ironworks Band. He was proud when the football team 'carried off the West Ham Charity Cup' and hoped it would 'maintain its present position at the head of the London League' (TIQG Vol. 3, p. 3) although, when further progress could only be achieved by becoming a professional not works team, he broke off links between the company and the football club.[10] Above all, the clubs were there to 'modify the social conditions of the yard' and even the *Thames Ironworks Gazette* was intended to serve the same function and operate as a 'means of friendly communication between our shareholders, our staff, our workmen and myself' (Hills TIQG Vol. 13, p. 3). He was aware, however, that it was an uphill struggle; many of the clubs merely 'flourish for a season and then dissolve' and it could become like

> building ropes of sand – lectures, debates, concerts, gymnastics, temperance leagues, cricket clubs, football clubs – all the appurtenances of energetic and capable citizenship were tried in turn, all passed through an ephemeral prosperity and then began to decline. There seemed no permanent vitality in any of these institutions. I found myself, like Mr Maskellyne, spinning plates which continually required to be touched up to prevent them falling. (TIQG vol. 3, p. 1)

By 1894, the firm's activities covered nearly 30 acres on the Essex side of Bow Creek (as against less than 10 acres in 1856) with Orchard Place used

---

10. Which then became West Ham United (see Korr 1978).

for offices and storage rather than shipbuilding (Survey of London 1994, p. 675). The shipyards, together with the iron and brass foundries, plate and angle-iron bending and angle-smiths' furnaces and shops, five smithies (containing eighty hearths), punching and drilling sheds covered nearly 27,000 square yards of building space and had a frontage onto the creek of nearly 1200 feet. The machinery included 'six steam hammers, twenty punching presses, sixteen shearing presses, two bar-straightening machines, three plate rolls and two plate levellers' while the eight building slips were from 2–400 feet long. Throughout the shipyard, rails had been laid on which five steam cranes ran continuously, moving materials from place to place (*Engineer* 13 December 1894, p. 573). The yards were also used from time to time for building iron bridges, notably for the London County Council during the 1890s. In 1895, Thames set up their own boat-building yard, in which they were eventually to make 206 shore-based lifeboats for the RNLI, each costing between £700 and £1,200.

The Ironworks facilities were, however, still rather cramped and an unfortunate event took place on 21 June 1898 which served to emphasise this in a very public way. An unexpectedly large crowd of at least 20,000 people had turned up for the launching of HMS *Albion* and were quite beyond the control of the available police. They crowded along the banks of the creeks adjacent to the slip-ways of Thames Ironworks, swarmed all over Bow Creek itself and entered a number of prohibited areas, dangerously close to the actual launching area. When the ship went down the slip-way and hit the water, the wash shattered a flimsy workman's bridge on an adjacent slip-way, throwing two hundred people into the water, some forty of whom drowned.

In May 1899, Thames took over the business and works of the famous London engine-makers and engineers, John Penn and Co. Ltd and formed a public company, the Thames Ironworks Shipbuilding and Engineering Co. Ltd, to take over the assets of both businesses. The new business maintained an ordinary share capital of £300,000 and sought to raise an additional £500,000 on the London market by way of fixed return, non-voting 5 per cent preference and 4 per cent debenture capital.

The takeover gave Thames an 'in-house' ability to 'construct the machinery as well as the hulls of the largest vessels of all descriptions' but, as a form of vertical integration, it did not even begin to compete with the mergers that were taking place in the north of England and in Scotland. The absorption of John Penn, although welcome, did not give the company the armaments capability that the leading shipbuilding firms in the country now had and the volume of business on the Thames did not warrant the infusion of capital on a scale that would match Vickers' acquisition of the shipyards at Barrow or John Brown's takeover of Clydebank Shipbuilding. Indeed the intention was merely to seek capital that would not threaten the existing control of the Hills family, who continued to own almost all the ordinary shares.[11]

The prospectus dated 19 July 1899 showed that the new company did not acquire Penn's business direct but bought it from the old Thames Ironworks company, that had acquired it one week earlier.[12] This arrangement meant that the sub-division of the purchase price between the two former businesses did not need to be published, and operated so as to provide the Hills family with a substantial short-term gain that had not been earned and that would merely serve to raise the future burden of overhead costs. Private correspondence between Hills and C. J. Hambro, who advised on and handled the share issue, reveals that the merchant bankers were unhappy at the asset valuation for the old Ironworks business because it would 'water' the capital. Hambro advised in letters written on 31 May and 12 June 1899 that the suggested capital of £600,000 was too high 'because your old capital was £300,000 and you are adding to it Penn's works for £100,000' and because anticipated (operating) profits of around £50,000 a year would provide an inadequate return, after the payment of prior capital charges, on equity share capital.[13]

These were to prove prophetic words but, at the time, the preference issue was partially successful, even if £100,000 of the shares had to be taken up by A. F. Hills, with the ownership of the remainder being quite widely dispersed. The issue prospectus had, however, been rather misleading in giving the profits of the old Ironworks company as: 1895 £27,407; 1896 £29,677; 1897 £41,462 and 1898 £47,518, as these were operating profits that did not take into account the (fairly substantial) interest charges on loans, directors' fees and managing director's remuneration, rather than net profits available for dividend.

The acquisition of John Penn's business in 1899 led to 'extensive remodelling' of the works at Greenwich and Deptford, some integration of shipbuilding and engine supply activities and the addition of large amounts of modern electrical machinery, although the acquisition did little to reduce the dependence of the company on naval demand, for it was 'Admiralty orders for machinery that were expected to keep our new shops full of profitable work' for next two or three years.[14]

---

11. In May 1893 all but three of the 6,000 £50 shares in Thames Ironworks had been owned by the Hills family, A. F. Hills owning over 50 per cent. In June 1898, his share increased to 5,796 out of 6,000: PRO Kew, BT31/1722/6293.
12. See company files in the PRO Kew, BT31/16240/62972 and the Prospectus dated 19 July 1997, Guildhall Manuscripts Department, MS19096.
13. Guildhall Manuscripts Department, MS19096.
14. Annual Report to AGM on 30 October 1899; Greater London Record Office, O/45/1.

Despite this concentration, matters seemed to be improving when, in April 1900, the company had four first-class battleships for British and foreign governments in course of construction for the first time ever. Hills saw Admiralty work as putting the company 'in the front rank' and helping with foreign contracts, although he claimed not to be 'one of those builders who was particularly enamoured of Admiralty work as it meant a tremendous lot of labour ... and it seemed to him that every year the conditions under which such work had to be carried out became more exacting'. Net profits were £40,000 and a dividend of 5 per cent p.a. on the preference shares was proposed, after payments of £25,431 to the old company, equivalent to a dividend of about 8.5 per cent on the ordinary shares (*Times* 12 April 1900, p. 13).

A year later the company claimed that 'each of its large departments had made a substantial profit' and therefore, quite misleadingly, that its business was 'established not upon the shifting sands of naval politics but upon the bedrock of manufacturing supremacy' but profits available to ordinary shareholders fell to £19,000 and then to only £8,000 in 1901.[15] In 1902, however, the lack of Admiralty orders was a matter of concern, although the following year matters improved when they obtained the order for the *Black Prince*, an armoured cruiser of 13,550 tons, and heard that the Admiralty had decided to allow private firms to carry out naval repairs, which brought them work worth over £100,000, paid for on a 'cost plus a percentage' basis. This apart, they were building only barges, tugs and lifeboats, although their engineering department had orders for machinery for government ships and was making good progress on caissons for the docks at Keyham and Gibraltar. The company paid the 5 per cent preference dividend but this left no profits available to equity shareholders and the setting aside of £5,000 towards the redemption fund for second mortgage debentures merely reduced the retained profits to £4,300. Some shareholders were now openly critical of the low market price of the company's shares (*Times* 9 April 1903, p. 13).

In 1903, the directors, drawing and office staff finally moved from Blackwall across Bow Creek to the 30-acre site on the West Ham or Essex side. The portion of the original Orchard Shipyard which they had retained, after the expiry of the original long lease in 1867, was used under the terms of an annual tenancy from the London and India Docks, who had sold the freehold to the Limmer Asphalt Company,[16] who wanted the area themselves

15. Annual Report to AGM on 3 April 1901; Greater London Record Office, O/45/1

16. The take-over of the site by a cement-making firm merely returned the site to its usage prior to the days of Ditchburn and Mare, when it was used by a Mr Montague to make Roman cement, grinding his materials with an old 'Sun and Planet' engine made by Watt in the early days of steam-powered machinery.

and duly gave the requisite six months' notice. This ended a 65 year occupancy, but put an end to the arrangement whereby a chain ferry transferred men and materials across the creek (which was 50 feet wide even at low tide and in bad or rainy weather could be impassable: TIQG Vol. 9, p. 52). In the previous five years, the company had spent £90,000 on new machinery and £67,000 on maintaining its plant and they intended to investigate the production of machinery for the better handling of coal at land and sea and to start making steam lorries and tractors. But their core business was little different: the *Black Prince* was under construction but the other building work was modest, consisting of a 50-ton floating crane for the London and India Docks Co., small boats for the Admiralty and the Thames Conservancy, several barges and 13 lifeboats, although the repair work in the dry-docks was proving profitable. The year's operating profit of £34,015 covered the debenture interest, the preference dividend and directors' salaries but left profits available to equity shareholders of £3,000 and only £2,778 to carry forward. It was now three years since a dividend had been paid on the ordinary shares (*Times* 12 April 1904, p. 12) and, in the four years from January 1900 to December 1903, annual returns to equity shareholders averaged less than 2.5 per cent, well below the cost of debt.

In 1904, the general economic depression fell comparatively lightly on the company and their operating profits improved to £52,633, which again covered the debenture interest, directors' fees and preference dividends, leaving £5,000 for debenture redemption, providing for a 5 per cent dividend on the ordinary shares and leaving £8,000 to carry forward (*Times* 8 April 1905, p. 11; 13 April 1905, p. 14). The profits represented a more promising return on equity shareholders' funds of 8 per cent. In that same year, the London County Council belatedly added fuel to the 'fair wages' debate when they decided to run a river service to replace that discontinued by the Thames Steamboat Company. It wanted a fleet of 30 steam-boats, each of about 120 gross tons and costing £6,000 but aroused controversy by stating that 'the lowest tender will not necessarily be accepted as full consideration will be given to the suitability, quality and attractiveness of the steamers' and that, 'if the contractor shall employ any workmen in any trade not included in the Council's list, the rates of pay shall be not less, nor the hours of labour more, than those recognised by the association of employers and trade unions and in practice obtained in London'. The latter stipulation provoked a 'violent criticism which raged through the provincial Press' (TIQG Vol. 11, p. 3) and the orders were eventually subdivided between three London firms, Thorneycroft, Napiers and Miller, and Thames Iron Works (although some of the building was sub-contracted in order to meet the deadlines concerned: Burtt 1949, pp. 140–41).[17]

17. When Thames Ironworks built ten of the steamboats, they made the rather

The improvement continued the following year, 1905, and operating profits rose to £64,498, the largest to date. The profits represented the highest return, 11 per cent, on equity shareholders' funds for some years and enabled £5,000 to be put aside for debenture redemption and £10,000 for general purposes, a 5 per cent ordinary dividend to be paid and £15,287 to be carried forward. Thames had built an experimental 1,000-ton coal-bagging lighter for coaling vessels in harbour, with some future prospects, and had obtained Romanian government orders for eight torpedo vedette boats for service on the Danube but the engineering department had been 'somewhat short of work', the *Black Prince* had been completed, the company had not obtained any of the contracts for the newest cruisers and the First Lord of the Admiralty had announced that once again repair work would only be carried out by the Royal Dockyards (*Times* 7 April 1906, p. 8; 12 April 1906, p. 14).

In 1906, profits held up well and represented a return of nearly 9 per cent on equity shareholders' funds. After transfers of £5,000 to debenture redemption and £10,000 to general reserve the company did not, however, pay an ordinary dividend (preferring to increase the carry-forward to £30,930), perhaps because the company had not obtained new Admiralty contracts of any size and was 'now in want of fresh work'. Ominously, it was now apparent that none of the existing docks on the Thames were wide enough to cope with completion work on the new Dreadnoughts (*Times* 6 April 1907, p. 9).

In 1907, there was a marked deterioration in financial performance. Net profits were only £8,232, and the payment of the preference dividend of £15,000 reduced the reserves and left no scope for an ordinary dividend. The torpedo vedette boats for Romania had been built, as had two Turkish steam-boats and the caissons for Keyham and Gibraltar but new work was looking thin and the Admiralty still objected to Dreadnoughts being finished off at Tilbury or Dagenham, which effectively barred Thames Ironworks from that class of work (*Times* 10 April 1908, p. 6). The lack of work had reduced employment at the yard from 3180 in 1902 to 1020 in the first half of 1907 (University of London 1966, p. 15) and Hills' ill-health was now too severe to enable him to attend even the annual general meetings.

In 1908, there was a marked expansion in naval contracts placed in the private sector and the board looked forward to obtaining their 'fair share of

smug statement that 'even if the prices of the Thames are higher than those of lower-paid districts, the superiority of the article produced is well worth the difference in price' (Annual Report to AGM on 3 April 1905; Greater London Record Office, 0/45/1). The entire initiative by London County Council also turned out to be badly misconceived; by October 1907, it was clear that the service could only be run at a heavy loss and the Council decided in February 1908 to sell off all the boats (Jordan 1925, p. 29).

this work' but this did not happen and, with 'their costs 10 per cent higher than on the Clyde' (Bowen 1945, p. 376), work was hard to obtain and losses were made of £29,000 in 1908 and £19,000 in 1909, converting modest retained profits to accumulated losses of £15,800.

In 1909, Hills finally persuaded the Admiralty that their slip-ways were long and strong enough and the river itself suitable for the new Dreadnoughts (although there were still no docks wide enough for fitting-out) and on 13 February 1910 they were awarded the contract for the largest warship (with a full-load displacement tonnage of 22,500 tons) ever to be built on the Thames, HMS *Thunderer*.

Although Hills claimed that this was a turning point (stating that Thames Ironworks was going 'from strength to strength', that enquiries and orders had 'poured in from all parts of the globe' [TIQG Vol. 13, p. 6] and that one further battleship order would place Thames Ironworks 'in the full tide of prosperity')[18], although the yard did exceptionally well to launch the vessel within a year from the receipt of the Admiralty order and only nine months after the keel was laid, the underlying situation was far more problematic.[19]

The keel of HMS *Thunderer* was laid by Mrs Arnold Hills on 16 April 1910 on the same building slip as HMS *Warrior*, some 50 years earlier. As flags waved over the yard, 'Mrs Hills pulled a lever and the crane brought the keel-plate (some thirty feet long) slowly into position. Workmen then picked up the red-hot rivets and drove them into their place, Mrs Hills helping to fasten them by a few taps given with a silver hammer [and] Mr Johns, the Admiralty overseer declared the work well and truly done' and a band struck up 'O weel may the keel row'. Mr Hills was there in a specially designed ambulance chair and, despite his considerable physical afflictions, took some delight in commenting on 'foolish canards' in the Metropolitan press which made out he was 'wholly paralysed and almost suggested that he was conducting the affairs of the Thames Ironworks out of a padded room in a lunatic asylum' (TIQG Vol. 13, pp. 11–12).

Although HMS *Thunderer* was using the same building slips as HMS *Warrior*, the slips had to be lengthened and greatly strengthened and a further £100,000 was needed for new plant (including a powerful 150-ton floating crane) and for fitting out the new deep-water finishing berth at Dagenham, where Thames were making use of use of a modern depot for coaling and dredging which included a massive jetty at Dagenham Lake, although the Admiralty did not really find this satisfactory (*East End News* 14 April

18. Annual Report to AGMs for 1906–11; Greater London Record Office, O/45/1.
19. By 1910 the company had withdrawn from the Federation of Shipbuilders and the construction of the *Thunderer* went forward even during the strike and lock-out of 1910, when work at many firms stopped.

Admiralty did not really find this satisfactory (*East End News* 14 April 1908; TIQG Vol. 13, pp. 19–22; Howarth and Wilson 1907, p. 150). HMS *Thunderer* was much wider than previous battleships and the firm's launching ways had to be widened, which entailed cutting and driving some 600 pitch-pine piles into place (TIQG Vol. 13, p. 57). The firm was required to provide a guarantee of £80,000 to the Admiralty, who now paid out little in the way of instalments until the work was finished.

As a result, a further issue of £150,000 of debentures was needed and in order to obtain the support of the existing providers of capital, it was agreed that no dividends would be paid on ordinary capital until £100,000 of the second debentures had been redeemed. It was also noted that the preference shares were cumulative, that no dividend had been paid since the middle of 1908 and that any arrears would need to be made good before any ordinary dividends could be paid (*Times* 4 January 1910, p. 18).

Although the company was working on HMS *Thunderer*, HMS *Nautilus* (a 27-knot torpedo-boat destroyer) and sundry other contracts, the financial losses for 1910 were a threatening £55,000. These were much the worst results since the new company was formed in 1899 and meant that the average annual returns on the equity capital over the twelve years was only 1.4 per cent per annum![20]

Hills had long been concerned about two aspects of Admiralty contracting: the operation of the government's fair wage legislation and the nature of the competition by the members of the 'armaments ring'.[21]

Concerning the first, he claimed that, as 'London rates of wages are from 15 to 20 per cent higher than those of the provincial out-ports, it follows that London contractors are disadvantageously handicapped to the extent

20. These figures are based upon the annual reports and accounts: Greater London Record Office, O/45/1. The low returns were masked to some extent by the tendency of the directors to refer to profit figures that were prior to the charging of debenture interest and by the company's practice of carrying forward expenditures on 'patents, trade and other investments, interests in parliamentary promotions and advertising' as assets, despite the reservations of the auditors. The major part of the losses for 1910 were also set off against capital reserves and not shown in the profit and loss account.

21. The leading producers of armour plate formed a notorious cartel, the 'armaments ring', which held up prices and profits and also made it very difficult for outsiders to compete; see Pollard and Robertson (1979, p. 214). This also provides an interesting case of history repeating itself; in the latter part of the eighteenth century a select group of shipbuilders on the London river were described as the 'shipbuilder's ring' because they had obtained a monopoly on building first-class ships to be chartered to the East India Company and a near-monopoly on Admiralty contracts for 'anything but the smallest men-of-war' (Bowen 1948, p. 289).

of this difference of wage rates' when tendering to build warships (Hills 1912, p. 1). In this assertion, he could refer to the 1908 Fair Wages Committee, that had returned to the issues raised by the Fair Wages Resolution of February 1891 and recommended the retention of fair wages clauses which 'oblige the contractor to pay the current rates of wages for competent workmen in the district where the work is carried out', as best reflecting the intention of the Act (P.P. 1908, p. 25).

Hills accordingly argued that the difference in wage rates involved an average handicap of some 5 per cent upon the cost of all government contracts, the margin of profit for which government contractors had generally been willing to work and that the issue had been significant in its effects upon contract allocations. His arguments provoked objections from northern shipbuilders to the insinuations that workmen were 'sweated' at Barrow and on the Clyde and that Hills was the only shipbuilder who had the good of his workmen at heart. They argued instead that their prices were lower because they had invested in more efficient machinery (*Times* 4 February 1896).

On the second matter, Hills maintained that his firm suffered from the 'pernicious monopolies in armour and armament' which the Admiralty had allowed to develop and which subjected 'shipbuilding firms like our own, Messrs Earle of Hull, Laird of Birkenhead, Palmers on the Tyne and Thompson and Napiers on the Clyde ... to an entirely illegitimate and disastrous competition', amounting to an effective restraint of trade, whereby the members of the 'armaments ring' undercharged for hull and machinery construction and recouped the money 'out of their monopoly profits on the supply of armour and guns' (TIQG Vol. 12, pp. 51–2). Thus, during the previous ten years, £75m of Admiralty monies had gone to the gun and armour ring, £25m to 'the Royal Dockyards and other shipbuilding firms of the country while less than £2m of orders have found their way to the Thames' (*Thames Ironworks* v *Admiralty* 1911, p. 27). The *Economist* thought that the Admiralty made no real answers to the charges (*Economist* 6 January 1912, p. 16).[22]

Matters came to a head in 1911, as the financial pressures at Thames intensified.[23] They bid £312,000 apiece to build two Admiralty cruisers, firms outside 'the Ring' (for example, Palmers, Fairfields, London and Glasgow, Scotts, Swan Hunter and Hawthorn Leslie) bid £291–300,000 (consistent with the Thames bid save only for the London wage differentials of £12–15,000) but other tenders were as low as £269–280,000, which Hills

22. The Liberal government was thought to have had political reasons for supporting the northern yards (see Editorial, *East London Observer* 12 March 1927).

23. Thames Ironworks had to seek further debenture finance in June 1911.

thought could only be attributed to the determination of 'the Ring ... to make no mistake this time' (Hills 1911, pp. 3–4).

The First Lord of the Admiralty, Churchill, was unconvinced by these arguments, confirmed that 'the outlook for the Thames was not promising' (*East London Advertiser* 18 November 1911), since their quotes for the two cruisers were so much higher than many of the bids, and indicated that a loss to the public of over £80,000 on these two vessels would have meant a 'complete departure from the principles approved by Parliament in regard to public contracts' and could not be reconciled with the 'fair and thrifty administration of public funds' (letter to *Receiver* 2 January 1912).

The Admiralty was also known to have serious reservations about the desirability of maintaining, 'at considerable expense to the taxpayer, a repairing war base on the Thames' (*East End News* 17 November 1911) and a deputation of London mayors and MPs also lobbied the First Lord, in what Marder has seen as a continuation of the firm's recent past; whenever a bad season coincided with a lack of Admiralty orders, as in 1893–95 and 1902, 'Thames Ironworks would organise mass meetings of working men and persistent appeals by East End MPs in order to pressurise the Admiralty into providing work despite their higher costs', tactics which produced the naval orders of 1896, 1899 and 1902 (Marder 1964, p. 36).

On 1 January 1912, 10,000 people, mostly from the East End, marched in procession through London to a 'great demonstration' in Trafalgar Square to 'demand the right of East London to participate in the building of the British Navy'. The Mayor of Poplar questioned the reasonableness of the government looking to London merely as a base for taxation revenues (it contributed one-seventh of British taxes) and providing few benefits (*East London Advertiser* 18 November 1911) and, later that month, the employees of Thames Ironworks met in the Public Hall, Canning Town to consider the 'Admiralty Ultimatum'.

Since mid-November 1911, Thames Ironworks bankers had 'declined to honour the company's cheques' and the firm was being run by a receiver-manager, Mr F. B. Smart. Since the great lock-out of 1897, the northern shipbuilders had been strongly opposed, to the eight-hour day and it was widely suggested that the Admiralty orders could still be secured if the men returned to working a 53-hour week (which Mr Smart later confirmed 'most probably would have enabled him to make the necessary reduction in the tender': *Times* 30 January 1912, p. 8) but 'it was evident from the whole-hearted expression of disapproval that the men viewed with entire displeasure a return to the longer hours' (*Times* 6 January 1912, p. 8). A later meeting of 600 men from the Ironworks did, however, agree to forego the rise in wages they had obtained the previous November of 2s a week on old contracts and 3s a week on new (although they had had no rise in wages for 19 years before that), as long as their sacrifice secured the Admiralty contracts, but this was unavailing (*Times* 29 January 1912, p. 7).

There were rumours of Palmers Shipbuilding taking over the works but it then became clearer that the Admiralty were instead encouraging Vickers towards that outcome, apparently offering the contracts for the two cruisers at £280,000 apiece (with two torpedo-boat destroyers to follow the following year), on condition that 'the firm was reconstructed and satisfactory guarantees given as to good management and finance'. This would have meant a takeover, thereby ending the role of the receiver, and the introduction of additional working capital of about £250,000, but there were no signs of the men giving up the eight-hour day and Vickers did not go ahead.

The Admiralty remained unwilling to award warship contracts to any company that was under receivership and, by 15 March 1912, no other buyers had come forward so the government duly allocated the contracts for the two cruisers to the Royal Dockyards.

On 21 December 1912, the receiver-manager closed the works, giving the clerical staff 14 days' notice and making redundant the remaining 800 employees.

Hills kept trying: in January 1913 he tried to establish a reconstruction fund of £100,000 to restart the works (*Times* 3 January 1913, p. 3) and in June suggested that Poplar Council contribute £10,000 towards the £300,000 required to repurchase the Ironworks and start them up again, but the Council 'regretted that it was unable to accede to Mr Hills request' and indicated that the sum concerned would represent a 3.5 pence in the pound rate (*Times* 10 June 1913, p. 8).

The site at Canning Town was sold in May 1913 to the Great Eastern Railway Company for £145,000, the former Penn works at Greenwich were taken over and reopened by Messrs Defries, engineers of Deptford, who bought them for £28,000 and a good deal of excellent shipbuilding machinery at Orchard Place was sold at only 'old iron prices' (*East London Observer* 21 June 1913; Jordan 1925, p. 17). As the business was closed down, Hills was left to remind observers of the one tradition of which he was 'inordinately proud', that 'no Thames Ironworks-built ship has ever yet gone down at sea'.

Rennie (Yard 5: Norman Road, Greenwich until 1915)

In 1892, Rennies turned out three screw tugs (of 95, 95 and 250 tons), a steel paddle-steamer of 350 tons, a floating dock of 1,000 tons and 19 steel lighters, oil barges and river barges totalling 2,835 tons (*Engineering* 6 January 1893).

Although Rennies continued to build screw-steamers, the great majority of their craft (58 out of 60 in 1899) were steel lighters and other small vessels, including tugs, motor-boats, barges and dredgers. In 1905 they built four LCC paddle-steamers, by sub-contract with Thorneycroft.

J. & G. Rennie left their yard at Greenwich in 1915 and joined up with Forrestt and Co., who had left the Thames in the late 1880s, and moved to Wivenhoe on the Colne, where there was a dry-dock, covered slip-ways and plenty of room to expand their production, particularly of larger ships, away from the 'severe handicap of London rates and wages' (Bowen 1948, p. 618).

CHAPTER EIGHT

Conclusions

When ships were built mostly from wood, the Thames was the leading shipbuilding area in Britain. In the early part of the nineteenth century, iron began to replace wood as the main construction material and transformed a traditional, skilled craft into an innovative, heavy industry.

In time, the economic growth that the new technology engendered was to benefit the Clyde, Belfast and the north-east of England in particular but, at first, London pioneered many of the new developments and became even more the focus of the UK trade. As Pollard has said, London did not simply decline as the dominant technology changed; instead, with the 'introduction of iron as a shipbuilding material and of steam as the propelling power, that supremacy became still more pronounced' (1950, p. 72).

Later in the nineteenth century, however, shipbuilding on the London river declined very rapidly and by 1915 there was no ship construction on any serious scale on the Thames. The reasons for the initial growth of iron shipbuilding on the river, and then for its rapid decline, have never been fully explained, although Pollard (1950), Banbury (1971) and Palmer (1993) have shed some light thereon, leading Walker to describe the decline as due to 'mysterious reasons which continue to attract historians and economists to this day' (1984, p. 43).

The intention of this book has been to investigate these 'mysterious reasons' and to identify the factors that were causal as well as examine the effects the growth and then the decline of the iron shipbuilding industry had on its locality.

The London region possessed its own particular advantages (for example, a skilled labour force, access to local sources of capital) and disadvantages (for example, the cost of labour, the distance from raw materials, etc.) for shipbuilding and the latter undoubtedly contributed to, but do not fully explain, the decline of the local trade.

Whereas the wooden shipbuilding trade had been carried on in a large number of small yards, the fundamental economics of iron shipbuilding required production to take place on a larger scale and, even when London was dominant, there were never all that many iron shipbuilding yards of any importance on the river, so that the mistakes and misfortunes of individual entrepreneurs could be as important in their effects on local output levels as more gradual changes in broad economic factors.

Some explanations of the decline have been based upon rather incomplete data sources and considerable effort has therefore been put into improving the available data series so as to provide the basis for a more rigorous analysis of events. The aggregate tonnage figures of Mitchell and Deane (1962) have been extended beyond their existing base of 'ships built in the UK for British Citizens or Companies' (Mitchell and Deane 1962, p. 220), so as to include tonnage built for foreign citizens and companies, foreign navies and the British Admiralty. Tonnage figures have also been obtained for the most important iron shipbuilding yard on the Thames, the Orchard Shipyard-Bow Creek operation of, at first, Ditchburn and Mare, and latterly Thames Ironworks, from 1837 to 1912, which provide important insights into how business conditions changed during this period.

Iron shipbuilding initially flourished on the Thames because of the proximity of expertise in related technologies, because the Isle of Dogs was still largely undeveloped even along its waterside and because the local shipyards contained highly skilled men who could see how the new material could improve ship design. Iron hulls provided a better vessel for propulsion by steam and the leading marine engineers and engine-makers were on the Thames; it was no accident that the first iron ship constructed in the south of England was built by the noted marine engine-maker, Maudslay. Pioneers in iron construction, such as William Fairbairn and David Napier were attracted from Manchester and Glasgow respectively by locations in Millwall, while the work that Thomas Ditchburn did, as manager to the noted wooden shipbuilders, Fletcher and Fearnall, to increase the speed of wooden-hulled steam vessels soon led him to a realisation of the possibilities of the new material. Thus, in the period from 1832–46, the London shipbuilding yards were an important centre of technical innovation and development and helped to establish the UK iron shipbuilding trade.

In the following period, from 1847–53, business innovation combined with continued technical development to strengthen the region's position. Ditchburn, who had been in partnership with C. J. Mare since 1838, left the partnership over Mare's plans for expansion and the latter went ahead on his own, buying land across Bow Creek from Orchard Yard and piling the marshy land until it could become the site for a pioneering, vertically-integrated, single-site approach to iron production and shipbuilding that provided far more efficient ways to build larger ships. Some important firms failed, such as Fairbairn (through business over-extension) and Napier (through under-use of his yard) but their yards were taken over by the distinguished naval architect, John Scott Russell, as a base that would eventually be used for the construction of a 'gigantic ship' (subsequently to become the *Great Eastern*) on a scale that had never previously been attempted.

The first crisis for the local shipbuilding industry came in the second half of the 1850s. The conflict in the Crimea brought a huge number of naval contracts for gunboats and other relatively small vessels to firms on the Thames (contracts for 101 out of 156 gunboats were placed with private builders on the river) but rapid cost-inflation on fixed-price contracts brought ruin to a number of important firms, including Mare who went bankrupt in September 1855. Brunel's managerial inflexibilities and a fundamental under-pricing of the tender for building the *Great Eastern* then forced Russell into bankruptcy and eventually out of ship construction.

After the Crimean War, shipbuilding volumes fell back, but from 1859 trade recovered and there was a feverish boom in 1863–66, encouraged by the newly liberalised arrangements for forming limited liability companies. There were only ever two really large iron shipyards on the Thames, both with their own iron-works for converting 'best London scrap-iron' into panels and armour plates, and for a time Mare's family controlled both of them. When Mare was bankrupted, his father-in-law, Peter Rolt took over the Orchard Yard-Bow Creek operation, re-formed it as Thames Ironworks, obtaining the contract for the revolutionary HMS *Warrior* in 1859 (partly because of the work's reputation for making 'hammered iron of proven quality') and developing a working relationship with the Admiralty that was to survive until 1912. Mare obtained new financial backing and took over Russell's extensive former works, initially under his own name and then as Millwall Ironworks, but was bought out by Overend Gurney in 1862.

Iron shipbuilding was a business that could bring good returns but it was also a highly risky trade and mistakes could have consequences on a scale that would mean simple ruin. Shipyards were prone to destruction by fire but the most serious problems seemed to occur over launching, particularly when the ships concerned were unusually heavy and beyond the remit of past experience. Launching failure had helped to ruin Scott Russell and, in March 1866, Millwall Ironwork's inability to launch HMS *Northumberland* (the heaviest ship to be launched from an excavated slip-way) in front of a 'brilliant and numerous assembly' that included the Prince of Wales brought public embarrassment, the firm's failure the following month and also helped to precipitate the failure of her backers, Overend Gurney, in May 1866.

This caused an economy-wide credit crisis and other businesses on the river failed (although most survived with difficulty), the decline in the local shipbuilding trade causing social problems in the East End which were to make it a byword for suffering and pauperism.

Shipbuilders on the Thames had been leaders in their industry until

1866 but, in the next twenty years, while the UK industry overcame a series of cyclical down-turns to advance its volumes by 50 per cent, the London region instead went into a long slump from which it would never recover its former position. In 1866–67, London built nearly 10 per cent of UK tonnage, but in 1883–88 constructed less than 2.5 per cent of UK tonnage, and suffered an spectacular decline in the medium-sized, 'bread-and-butter' commercial tonnage that helped to provide proper volumes of throughput for shipyards with costly facilities, largely because economic factors made it extremely difficult for London shipbuilders to compete on price. Wigrams stopped building and Dudgeon's business failed after the largest ship they had ever built, the Brazilian Navy's *Independencia*, was almost wrecked by its attempted launching. At the same time, however, two smaller but technologically advanced firms of shipbuilders, Thorneycroft and Yarrows, began to successfully expand their business, particularly with the Admiralty and a number of foreign navies.

By 1888, of the eight major and four secondary yards on the river, two had failed for financial reasons, two had not survived the death of their owners and two had continued but as firms that did not build ships. In the final period, 1889–1915, of the three remaining firms that built mainly small boats, Samuda went into liquidation in 1892, Greens decided to repair rather than build ships and J. & G. Rennie, who had been building ships on the river since 1859, moved in 1915 to Wivenhoe on the Colne where there was more space and costs were lower.

Of the other three firms, two (Thorneycroft and Yarrows) were specialist builders of light, fast, commercial and naval vessels. Both left the London river in 1907–08, one for Woolston near Southampton (partly to escape a location upriver of Hammersmith Bridge that was becoming almost impossible as a site for building destroyers) and the other for the Clyde, where costs were lower and there was better access to support facilities.

The remaining yard was that of Thames Ironworks, the major volume producer on the river since the demise of Millwall Ironworks. The firm had virtually lost its commercial business and its collection of barge, tug and other small-boat constructions was latterly providing only 3.5 per cent of its total tonnage. Instead, the Admiralty had become a dominating single buyer, taking 75 per cent of tonnage, with the remainder going to overseas navies. The discrepancy between the firm's commercial and naval work was the more acute because the naval contracts were for the largest ships that could be built, so that Thames Ironworks was effectively building either Dreadnoughts or barges. The problem was, of course that the major contracts required very substantial and sophisticated facilities but the throughput and usage of these facilities for commercial orders was almost non-existent.

Thames Ironworks was in a difficult position because London labour costs were high and because it had watered its own capital in 1899 and, when the major armaments producers in the north of England and Scotland in the late 1890s brought in structural business innovations that changed the nature of the working relationships between shipyards, steel producers and armaments manufacturers, there was no longer to be any future in making ships of any size on the River Thames.

APPENDIX 1

Admiralty ships built in London private yards, 1832–1915

Year	Name	Builder	tons		Details
1832	Snake	Fletcher & Fearnall	418		Brig
1832	Serpent	Fletcher & Fearnall	418		Brig
			836		
1835	Ranger	Bottomley, Rotherhithe	358		Packet brig
1835	Alert	Bottomley, Rotherhithe	358		Packet brig
1835	Swift	Colson, Deptford	358		Packet brig
1835	Express	Colson, Deptford	358		Packet brig
			1,432		
1841	Memnon	Fletcher & Fearnall	1,516	bm	
			1,516		
1842	Rocket	Fairbairn, Millwall	93	bm	Steamer for dockyards
			93		
1843	Princess Alice	Ditchburn and Mare	359	bm	
			359		
1845	Harpy	Ditchburn and Mare	458	bm	
1845	Onyx	Ditchburn and Mare	388	bm	
1845	Trident	Ditchburn and Mare	1,131	bm	
1845	Torch	Ditchburn and Mare	452	bm	
1845	Myrmidon	Ditchburn and Mare	462	bm	
1845	Violet	Ditchburn and Mare	388	bm	
1845	Grappler	Fairbairn, Millwall	743	bm	
1845	Megaera	Fairbairn, Millwall	1,850	bm	
			5,872		
1846	Garland	Fletcher & Fearnall	392	bm	
1846	Recruit	Ditchburn and Mare	470		Iron brig
1846	Minx	Miller & Ravenhill	403	bm	
			1,265		
1847	Llewellyn	Miller & Ravenhill	865	bm	
1847	Terpsichore	Wigram, Blackwall	801	bm	Corvett
			1,665		
1848	Enterprise	Wigram, Blackwall	626	bm	Storeship
			626		
1849	Vulcan	Mare, C. J.	2,396	bm	Iron screw frigate
			2,396		

1851	Argus	Green, Blackwall	423	bm	
			423		
1854	Wrangler	Green, Blackwall	634	bm	
1854	Viper	Green, Blackwall	634	bm	
1854	Mortar floats	Green, Blackwall	255	bm	Mortar floats
1854	Pincher	Pitcher, Northfleet	287	bm	Gunboat (Gleaner)
1854	Badger	Pitcher, Northfleet	287	bm	Gunboat (Gleaner)
1854	Pelter	Pitcher, Northfleet	287	bm	Gunboat (Gleaner)
1854	Snapper	Pitcher, Northfleet	287	bm	Gunboat (Gleaner)
1854	Esk	Scott Russell	1,555	bm	Steam corvette
1854	Mortar floats	Mare, C. J.	340	bm	Mortar floats
1854	Urgent	Mare, C. J.	2,420	bm	Despatch vessel
1854	Perseverance	Mare, C. J.	2,420	bm	Despatch vessel
1854	Transit	Mare, C. J.	2,775	bm	Transport
1854	Arrow	Mare, C. J.	1,420	bm	Despatch vessel
1854	Beagle	Mare, C. J.	1,420	bm	Despatch vessel
1854	Lynx	Mare, C. J.	1,420	bm	Despatch vessel
1854	Snake	Mare, C. J.	1,420	bm	Despatch vessel
1854	Mortar floats	Thompson, Rotherhithe	170	bm	Mortar floats
1854	Mortar floats	Wigram, Blackwall	935	bm	Mortar floats
			18,968		
1855	Louisa	Fletcher & Fearnall	309	bm	Gunboat (Dapper)
1855	Julia	Fletcher & Fearnall	309	bm	Gunboat (Dapper)
1855	Wanderer	Green, Blackwall	898	bm	
1855	Griper	Green, Blackwall	309	bm	Gunboat (Dapper)
1855	Fancy	Green, Blackwall	309	bm	Gunboat (Dapper)
1855	Dapper	Green, Blackwall	309	bm	Gunboat (Dapper)
1855	Glatton	Green, Blackwall	2,042	bm	
1855	Trusty	Green, Blackwall	2,047	bm	
1855	Jasper	Green, Blackwall	309	bm	Gunboat (Dapper)
1855	Mortar floats	Lungley Deptford	510	bm	Mortar floats
1855	Nightingale	Mare, C. J.	309	bm	Gunboat (Dapper)
1855	Meteor	Mare, C. J.	700	bm	Floating battery
1855	Thunder	Mare, C. J.	700	bm	Floating battery
1855	Victor	Mare, C. J.	1,042	bm	
1855	Stork	Pitcher, Northfleet	309	bm	Gunboat (Dapper)
1855	Charger	Pitcher, Northfleet	309	bm	Gunboat (Dapper)
1855	Bustard	Pitcher, Northfleet	309	bm	Gunboat (Dapper)
1855	Sandfly	Pitcher, Northfleet	309	bm	Gunboat (Dapper)
1855	Dove	Pitcher, Northfleet	309	bm	Gunboat (Dapper)
1855	Weazel	Pitcher, Northfleet	309	bm	Gunboat (Dapper)
1855	Seagull	Pitcher, Northfleet	309	bm	Gunboat (Dapper)
1855	Cracker	Pitcher, Northfleet	309	bm	Gunboat (Dapper)
1855	Tickler	Pitcher, Northfleet	309	bm	Gunboat (Dapper)
1855	Biter	Pitcher, Northfleet	309	bm	Gunboat (Dapper)
1855	Redwing	Pitcher, Northfleet	309	bm	Gunboat (Dapper)

1855	Boxer	Pitcher, Northfleet	309	bm	Gunboat (Dapper)
1855	Swinger	Pitcher, Northfleet	309	bm	Gunboat (Dapper)
1855	Banterer	Pitcher, Northfleet	309	bm	Gunboat (Dapper)
1855	Plover	Pitcher, Northfleet	309	bm	Gunboat (Dapper)
1855	Skylark	Pitcher, Northfleet	309	bm	Gunboat (Dapper)
1855	Clinker	Pitcher, Northfleet	309	bm	Gunboat (Dapper)
1855	Grasshopper	Pitcher, Northfleet	309	bm	Gunboat (Dapper)
1855	Skipjack	Pitcher, Northfleet	309	bm	Gunboat (Dapper)
1855	Forward	Pitcher, Northfleet	309	bm	Gunboat (Dapper)
1855	Bullfrog	Pitcher, Northfleet	309	bm	Gunboat (Dapper)
1855	Sheldrake	Pitcher, Northfleet	309	bm	Gunboat (Dapper)
1855	Snap	Pitcher, Northfleet	309	bm	Gunboat (Dapper)
1855	Thistle	Pitcher, Northfleet	309	bm	Gunboat (Dapper)
1855	Cockchafer	Pitcher, Northfleet	309	bm	Gunboat (Dapper)
1855	Carnation	Pitcher, Northfleet	309	bm	Gunboat (Dapper)
1855	Starling	Pitcher, Northfleet	309	bm	Gunboat (Dapper)
1855	Aetna	Scott Russell	1,954	bm	Floating battery
1855	Hind	Thompson, Rotherhithe	309	bm	Gunboat (Dapper)
1855	Jackdaw	Thompson, Rotherhithe	309	bm	Gunboat (Dapper)
1855	Mortar floats	Thompson, Rotherhithe	425	bm	Mortar floats
1855	Intrepid	Wigram, Blackwall	826	bm	Gunboat
1855	Beaver	Wigram, Blackwall	309	bm	Gunboat (Dapper)
1855	Carron	Wigram, Blackwall	160	bm	Mortar vessel
1855	Surly	Wigram, Blackwall	117	bm	Mortar vessel
1855	Beacon	Wigram, Blackwall	117	bm	Mortar vessel
1855	Magnet	Wigram, Blackwall	160	bm	Mortar vessel
			23,114		
1856	Pert	Cox & Curling	282	bm	Gunboat (Cheerful)
1856	Mohawk	Cox & Curling	903	bm	
1856	Midge	Cox & Curling	282	bm	Gunboat (Cheerful)
1856	Sparrowhawk	Cox & Curling	899	bm	
1856	Tiny	Cox & Curling	282	bm	Gunboat (Cheerful)
1856	Onyx	Cox & Curling	282	bm	Gunboat (Cheerful)
1856	Flamer	Fletcher & Fearnall	309	bm	Gunboat (Dapper)
1856	Cormorant	Fletcher & Fearnall	898	bm	Gun vessel
1856	Fly	Fletcher & Fearnall	309	bm	Gunboat (Dapper)
1856	Firm	Fletcher & Fearnall	309	bm	Gunboat (Dapper)
1856	Osprey	Fletcher & Fearnall	907	bm	Gun vessel
1856	Traveller	Green, Blackwall	309	bm	Gunboat (Dapper)
1856	Forester	Green, Blackwall	309	bm	Gunboat (Dapper)
1856	Rocket	Green, Blackwall	207	bm	Gunboat
1856	Thrasher	Green, Blackwall	309	bm	Gunboat (Dapper)
1856	Camel	Green, Blackwall	309	bm	Gunboat (Dapper)
1856	Caroline	Green, Blackwall	309	bm	Gunboat (Dapper)
1856	Crocus	Green, Blackwall	309	bm	Gunboat (Dapper)
1856	Assurance	Green, Blackwall	906	bm	
1856	Confounder	Green, Blackwall	309	bm	Gunboat (Dapper)

1856	Cherokee	Green, Blackwall	309	bm	Gunboat (Dapper)
1856	Spanker	Green, Blackwall	309	bm	Gunboat (Dapper)
1856	Cochin	Green, Blackwall	309	bm	Gunboat (Dapper)
1856	Fervent	Green, Blackwall	309	bm	Gunboat (Dapper)
1856	Fidgit	Joyce, Greenwich	282	bm	Gunboat (Cheerful)
1856	Flirt	Joyce, Greenwich	282	bm	Gunboat (Cheerful)
1856	Bouncer	Mare, C. J.	309	bm	Gunboat (Dapper)
1856	Hyaena	Mare, C. J.	309	bm	Gunboat (Dapper)
1856	Violet	Mare, C. J.	309	bm	Gunboat (Dapper)
1856	Wolf	Mare, C. J.	309	bm	Gunboat (Dapper)
1856	Savage	Mare, C. J.	309	bm	Gunboat (Dapper)
1856	Pheasant	Pitcher, Northfleet	309	bm	Gunboat (Dapper)
1856	Pickle	Pitcher, Northfleet	309	bm	Gunboat (Dapper)
1856	Garret	Pitcher, Northfleet	310	bm	Gunboat (Clown)
1856	Haughty	Pitcher, Northfleet	309	bm	Gunboat (Dapper)
1856	Mackerel	Pitcher, Northfleet	309	bm	Gunboat (Dapper)
1856	Hasty	Pitcher, Northfleet	309	bm	Gunboat (Dapper)
1856	Hunter	Pitcher, Northfleet	310	bm	Gunboat (Clown)
1856	Handy	Pitcher, Northfleet	310	bm	Gunboat (Clown)
1856	Porpoise	Pitcher, Northfleet	309	bm	Gunboat (Dapper)
1856	Mayflower	Pitcher, Northfleet	309	bm	Gunboat (Dapper)
1856	Insolent	Pitcher, Northfleet	309	bm	Gunboat (Dapper)
1856	Herring	Pitcher, Northfleet	309	bm	Gunboat (Dapper)
1856	Peacock	Pitcher, Northfleet	309	bm	Gunboat (Dapper)
1856	Shamrock	Pitcher, Northfleet	309	bm	Gunboat (Dapper)
1856	Staunch	Pitcher, Northfleet	309	bm	Gunboat (Dapper)
1856	Leveret	Pitcher, Northfleet	309	bm	Gunboat (Dapper)
1856	Fenella	Pitcher, Northfleet	310	bm	Gunboat (Clown)
1856	Tilbury	Pitcher, Northfleet	309	bm	Gunboat (Dapper)
1856	Procris	Pitcher, Northfleet	309	bm	Gunboat (Dapper)
1856	Charon	Pitcher, Northfleet	309	bm	Gunboat (Dapper)
1856	Prompt	Pitcher, Northfleet	309	bm	Gunboat (Dapper)
1856	Primrose	Pitcher, Northfleet	309	bm	Gunboat (Dapper)
1856	Spey	Pitcher, Northfleet	309	bm	Gunboat (Dapper)
1856	Thunderbolt	Samuda, Poplar	1,954		
1856	Brune	Scott Russell	355	bm	Gunboat
1856	Bann	Scott Russell	355	bm	Gunboat
1856	Nimrod	Scott Russell	1,142	bm	Wooden gun vessel
1856	Roebuck	Scott Russell	1,150	bm	Wooden gun vessel
1856	Daisy	Westbrook, Blackwall	282	bm	Gunboat (Cheerful)
1856	Dwarf	Westbrook, Blackwall	282	bm	Gunboat (Cheerful)
1856	Whiting	Wigram, Blackwall	309	bm	Gunboat (Dapper)
1856	Foam	Wigram, Blackwall	309	bm	Gunboat (Dapper)
1856	Parthian	Wigram, Blackwall	309	bm	Gunboat (Dapper)
1856	Wave	Wigram, Blackwall	309	bm	Gunboat (Dapper)
1856	Delight	Wigram, Blackwall	309	bm	Gunboat (Dapper)
1856	Growler	Wigram, Blackwall	309	bm	Gunboat (Dapper)

1856	Ripple	Wigram, Blackwall	309	bm	Gunboat (Dapper)
1856	Quail	Wigram, Blackwall	309	bm	Gunboat (Dapper)
1856	Surprise	Wigram, Blackwall	680		
1856	Goshawk	Wigram, Blackwall	309	bm	Gunboat (Dapper)
1856	Goldfinch	Wigram, Blackwall	309	bm	Gunboat (Dapper)
1856	Grappler	Wigram, Blackwall	309	bm	Gunboat (Dapper)
1856	Possum	Wigram, Blackwall	309	bm	Gunboat (Dapper)
1856	Hardy	Wigram, Blackwall	309	bm	Gunboat (Dapper)
1856	Partridge	Wigram, Blackwall	309	bm	Gunboat (Dapper)
1856	Tiny	Young, Limehouse	282	bm	Gunboat (Cheerful)
1856	Midge	Young, Limehouse	282	bm	Gunboat (Cheerful)
1856	Onyx	Young, Limehouse	282	bm	Gunboat (Cheerful)
1856	Pert	Young, Limehouse	282	bm	Gunboat (Cheerful)
			31,026		
1857	Jaseur	Green, Blackwall	400	bm	
1857	Leven	Pitcher, Northfleet	300		
1857	Slaney	Pitcher, Northfleet	300		
1857	Lee	Pitcher, Northfleet	301		
1857	Algerine	Pitcher, Northfleet	299		
			1,600		
1860	Warrior	Thames Ironworks	9,137		Ironclad broadside
			9,137		
1861	Resistance	Westwood Baillie	6,070		Ironclad broadside
			6,070		
1862	Plover	Green, Blackwall	570		Wooden gunvessels
1862	Torch	Green, Blackwall	570		Wooden gunvessels
1862	Mullett	Lungley, Deptford	570		Wooden gunvessels
1862	Dart	Mare, C. J.	570		Wooden gunvessels
1862	Griffon	Pitcher, Northfleet	570		Wooden gunvessels
1862	Dromedary	Samuda, Poplar	657		
1862	Snipe	Scott Russell	570		Wooden gunvessels
1862	Sparrow	Scott Russell	570		Wooden gunvessels
1862	Lee	Wigram, Blackwall	570		Wooden gunvessels
1862	Cygnet	Wigram, Blackwall	570		Wooden gunvessels
			5,787		
1863	Tamar	Samuda, Poplar	2,812		
1863	Minotaur	Thames Ironworks	10,690		Ironclad broadside
1863	Valiant	Westwood Baillie	6,710		Ironclad broadside
			20,212		
1864	Prince Albert	Samuda, Poplar	3,687		Coast defence
			3,687		
1865	Viper	Dudgeon, Limehouse	1,230		Armoured gunboat
1865	Vixen	Lungley, Deptford	1,230		Armoured gunboat
1865	Serpent	Mare, C. J.	877		Wooden gunvessels
1865	Lily	Scott Russell	877		Wooden gunvessels
1865	Eclipse	Scott Russell	877		Wooden gunvessels
1865	Racehorse	Wigram, Blackwall	877		Wooden gunvessels

1865	Cormorant	Wigram, Blackwall	877	Wooden gunvessels
			6,845	
1866	Northumberland	Millwall Ironworks	10,784	Ironclad broadside
1866	Waterwitch	Thames Ironworks	1,280	Armoured gunboat
1866	Serapis	Thames Ironworks	6,210	Torpedo Boat
			18,274	
1867	Crocodile	Wigram, Blackwall	4,173	Torpedo Boat
			4,173	
1868	Rocket	London Eng Co, Millwall	6,03	Composite gunvessel
1868	Hornet	Penn	603	Composite gunvessel
			1,206	
1869	Active	Thames Ironworks	3,080	Iron screw corvette
1869	Volage	Thames Ironworks	3,080	Iron screw corvette
			6,160	
1870	Abyssinia	Dudgeon, Poplar	2,901	Coast defence
1870	Magdala	Thames Ironworks	3,344	Coast defence
			6,245	
1871	Hecate	Dudgeon, Poplar	3,480	Coast defence
1871	Cyclops	Thames Ironworks	3,480	Coast defence
			6,960	
1872	Bonnetta	Rennie, J. & G.	254	Flat-iron gunboat
1872	Arrow	Rennie, J. & G.	254	Flat-iron gunboat
			508	
1873	Sappho	Wigram, Blackwall	940	Composite screw sloop
			940	
1874	Neptune	Dudgeon, Poplar	9,130	Masted turret ship
1874	Rover	Thames Ironworks	3,460	Iron screw corvette
1874	Daring	Wigram, Blackwall	940	Composite screw sloop
			13,530	
1875	Assistance	Green, Blackwall	2,515	Torpedo Boat
1875	Superb	Thames Ironworks	9,710	Ironclad battery
			12.225	
1876	Bellisle	Samuda, Poplar	4,870	Armoured ram
			4,870	
1877	TB1	Thorneycroft, Chiswick	32	Torpedo boat
			32	
1878	TB13	Maudslay	28	Torpedo boat
1878	TB17–18	Yarrow, Poplar	66	Torpedo boat
			94	
1879	Orion	Samuda, Poplar	4,870	Armoured ram
1879	TB51–62	Thorneycroft, Chiswick	132	Torpedo boat
1879	TB2–12	Thorneycroft, Chiswick	308	Torpedo boat
1879	TB14	Yarrow, Poplar	33	Torpedo boat
			5,343	
1880	TB20	Rennie, J & G	28	Torpedo boat
1880	Swift	Thames Ironworks	788	Composite gunvessel
1880	Linnet	Thames Ironworks	788	Composite gunvessel

			1,604	
1881	Stork	Samuda, Poplar	465	Composite gunboat
1881	Raven	Samuda, Poplar	465	Composite gunboat
1881	Starling	Samuda, Poplar	465	Composite gunboat
1881	TB64–73	Thorneycroft, Chiswick	130	Torpedo boat
			1,525	
1882	Troton	Samuda, Poplar	410	Torpedo Boat
1882	Alecto	Westwood, Baillie	620	Torpedo Boat
			1,030	
1883	Sphinx	Green, Blackwall	1,130	Special
1883	TB98	Thorneycroft, Chiswick	15	Torpedo boat
1883	TB76–95	Thorneycroft, Chiswick	125	Torpedo boat
1883	TB74–75; 96–7	Yarrow, Poplar	48	Torpedo boat
			1,318	
1884	TB82–87	Yarrow, Poplar	510	Torpedo boat
			510	
1885	TB21–22	Thorneycroft, Chiswick	128	Torpedo boat
1885	Benbow	Thames Ironworks	10,600	Barbette ship
1885	TB39–40	Yarrow, Poplar	80	Torpedo boat
			10,808	
1886	TB25	Thorneycroft, Chiswick	60	Torpedo boat
1886	TB26–29; 41–60	Thorneycroft, Chiswick	1,440	Torpedo boat
1886	TB99–100	Thorneycroft, Chiswick	24	Torpedo boat
1886	TB23–24	Yarrow, Poplar	134	Torpedo boat
1886	TB79	Yarrow, Poplar	75	Torpedo boat
			1,733	
1887	Sans Pareil	Thames Ironworks	10,470	Turret ship
1887	TB30–33; 61–78	Yarrow, Poplar	1,320	Torpedo boat
1887	TB80	Yarrow, Poplar	105	Torpedo boat
			11,895	
1888	TB100; 102–103	Thorneycroft, Chiswick	288	Torpedo boat
1888	TB49–50	Yarrow, Poplar	30	Torpedo boat
			318	
1889	TB39–48	Yarrow, Poplar	160	Torpedo boat
			160	
1890	Blenheim	Thames Ironworks	9,150	Cruiser 1st class
			9,150	
1891	Sappho	Samuda, Poplar	3,400	Cruiser 2nd class
1891	Scylla	Samuda, Poplar	3,400	Cruiser 2nd class
			6,800	
1892	Grafton	Thames Ironworks	7,350	Cruiser 1st class
1892	Theseus	Thames Ironworks	7,350	Cruiser 1st class
			14,700	
1893	Daring	Thorneycroft, Chiswick	280	Destroyer
1893	Speedy	Thorneycroft, Chiswick	810	Torpedo gunboat
1893	Hornet	Yarrow, Poplar	275	Destroyer
1893	Havock	Yarrow, Poplar	275	Destroyer

			1,640	
1894	Decoy	Thorneycroft, Chiswick	280	Destroyer
1894	TB91–92	Thorneycroft, Chiswick	282	Torpedo boat
1894	Boxer	Thorneycroft, Chiswick	265	Destroyer
1894	TB93	Thorneycroft, Chiswick	136	Torpedo boat
1894	Ardent	Thorneycroft, Chiswick	265	Destroyer
1894	TB88–89	Yarrow, Poplar	315	Torpedo boat
1894	Hasty	Yarrow ,Poplar	255	Destroyer
1894	Dasher	Yarrow, Poplar	255	Destroyer
1894	Charger	Yarrow, Poplar	255	Destroyer
			2,308	
1895	Zebra	Thames Ironworks	310	Destroyer
1895	Bruiser	Thorneycroft, Chiswick	265	Destroyer
1895	TB90	Yarrow, Poplar	105	Torpedo boat
			680	
1896	Mallard	Thorneycroft, Chiswick	310	Destroyer
1896	Desperate	Thorneycroft, Chiswick	310	Destroyer
1896	Fame	Thorneycroft, Chiswick	310	Destroyer
1896	Foam	Thorneycroft, Chiswick	310	Destroyer
			1,240	
1897	Coquette	Thorneycroft, Chiswick	335	Destroyer
1897	Ariel	Thorneycroft, Chiswick	310	Destroyer
1897	Angler	Thorneycroft, Chiswick	310	Destroyer
1897	Nightingale	Yarrow, Poplar	85	Shallow draught steamer
1897	Robin	Yarrow, Poplar	85	Shallow draught steamer
1897	Sandpiper	Yarrow, Poplar	85	Shallow draught steamer
1897	Snipe	Yarrow, Poplar	85	Shallow draught steamer
			1,295	
1898	Albion	Thames Ironworks	13,150	Battleship 1st class
1898	Woodlark	Thorneycroft, Chiswick	150	Shallow draught steamer
1898	Cygnet	Thorneycroft, Chiswick	335	Destroyer
1898	Melik	Thorneycroft, Chiswick	150	Torpedo Boat
1898	Albatross	Thorneycroft, Chiswick	430	Destroyer
1898	Woodcock	Thorneycroft, Chiswick	150	Shallow draught steamer
1898	Cynthia	Thorneycroft, Chiswick	335	Destroyer
			14,700	
1899	Stag	Thorneycroft, Chiswick	320	Destroyer
			320	
1901	Duncan	Thames Ironworks	13,745	Battleship 1st class
1901	Cornwallis	Thames Ironworks	13,745	Battleship 1st class
1901	TB107	Thorneycroft, Chiswick	185	Torpedo boat
1901	TB108	Thorneycroft, Chiswick	185	Torpedo boat
1901	TB98–99; 107–8	Thorneycroft, Chiswick	740	Torpedo boat
1901	Teal	Yarrow, Poplar	180	Shallow draught steamer
1901	Moorhen	Yarrow, Poplar	180	Shallow draught steamer
			28,960	
1903	TB111	Thorneycroft, Chiswick	200	Torpedo boat

1903	TB113	Thorneycroft, Chiswick	200	Torpedo boat
1903	Kennet	Thorneycroft, Chiswick	550	Destroyer (River class)
1903	TB109–13	Thorneycroft, Chiswick	1000	Torpedo boat
1903	TB110	Thorneycroft, Chiswick	200	Torpedo boat
1903	TB109	Thorneycroft, Chiswick	200	Torpedo boat
1903	TB112	Thorneycroft, Chiswick	200	Torpedo boat
1903	Teviot	Yarrow, Poplar	590	Destroyer (River class)
1903	Usk	Yarrow, Poplar	590	Destroyer (River class)
			3,730	
1904	Black Prince	Thames Ironworks	13,550	Cruiser 1st class
1904	Jed	Thorneycroft, Chiswick	550	Destroyer (River class)
1904	Ribble	Yarrow, Poplar	590	Destroyer (River class)
1904	Widgeon	Yarrow, Poplar	195	Shallow draught steamer
1904	Welland	Yarrow, Poplar	545	Destroyer (River class)
			15,430	
1905	Garry	Yarrow, Poplar	590	Destroyer (River class)
1905	Gala	Yarrow, Poplar	590	Destroyer (River class)
			1,180	
1910	Nautilus	Thames Ironworks	945	Torpedo boat
			945	
1911	Thunderer	Thames Ironworks	22,500	Battleship
			22,500	
			379,968	

Notes: For some early naval ships, the known tonnages in 'builders measurements' have been converted to displacement tonnage by multiplying by a factor of 1.33. This reflects the average relationship between the two measures in those cases where both were known.
The tonnage of 11 boats (1.05 per cent ot the total set) has been estimated.

Sources: Analysis based on data in:
Banbury (1971); Brassey (1883, pp. 550–61); Brassey (1909, pp. 154–68); Brassey and Leyland (1915, pp. 98–112); Conway (1979); Conway (1985); Dockyard Expense Accounts 1914–16, pp. 133–46; Hythe and Leyland (1914, pp. 420–35); Lyon (1993); Osbon (1965, pp. 103–15); Osbon (1965, pp. 211–20); Preston and Major (1967); P.P. Navy Gunboats (1861); private listings for the period 1825–60, kindly made available by David Lyon.

Tonnage built by Ditchburn, Mare and Thames Ironworks, 1837–1912

	(1) Commercial (d.t.)	(2) UK gov (d.t.)	(3) Foreign gov (d.t.)	(4) Total (d.t.)	(5) Commercial (% of total)
1837					
1838	665			665	100.0
1839	300			300	100.0
1840	1,220			1,220	100.0
1841	1,025			1,025	100.0
1842	634			634	100.0
1843	878	359		1,237	71.0
1844	1,310			1,310	100.0
1845	2,669	3,314		5,983	44.6
1846	5,983	462		6,445	92.8
1847	3,300		997	4,297	76.9
1848	2,625		1,680	4,305	61.0
1849	4,251	2,396		6,647	64.0
1850	10,041		5,636	15,677	64.0
1851	847		2,929	3,776	22.4
1852	218			218	100.0
1853	35,920			35,920	100.0
1854	18,732	26,930		45,662	41.0
1855	9,094	8,021		17,115	53.1
1856	4,253	1,295		5,548	76.7
1857	1,203			1,203	100.0
1958	12,017			12,017	100.0
1959	4,594	8,828		13,422	34.2
1860	3,376			3,376	100.0
1861	883			883	100.0
1862	3,659	9,870		13,529	27.0
1863	1,045		17,846	18,891	5.5
1864	11,446		3,395	14,841	77.1
1965	3,221			3221	100.0
1866	560	7,441		8001	7.0

1867	101	375	11,377	11,853	0.9
1868	90			90	100.0
1869	366	6,666	2,314	9,346	3.9
1870	54	6,567	2,720	9,341	0.6
1871	2,199			2,199	100.0
1872		3,364		3,364	0.0
1873	1,080			1,080	100.0
1874				0	
1875				0	
1876	167	17,988	8,994	27,149	0.6
1877	359			395	100.0
1878	296	31	5,731	6,058	4.9
1879	350	1,565	661	2,576	13.6
1880	285		84	369	77.2
1881	98	144	3,500	3,742	2.6
1882	4,826	10,011	633	15,470	31.0
1883	454		1,112	1,566	29.0
1884	63		1,141	1,204	5.2
1885	87	10,538		10,625	0.0
1886	93			93	100.0
1887	4,304		285	4,589	93.0
1888	663		345	1,008	65.0
1889	823			823	100.0
1890	124	9,150	289	9,563	1.3
1891	60			60	100.0
1892	637	14,700		15,337	4.2
1893				0	
1894		303	13,495	13,798	0.0
1895				0	
1896		29		29	0.0
1897	267		14,850	15,117	1.8
1898		13,150	26	13,176	0.0
1899				0	
1900				0	
1901		27,490		27,490	0.0
1902	147	174		321	45.0
1903	50			50	100.0
1904	1,757	13,550		15,307	11.5
1905				0	
1906			51	51	0.0
1907	330			330	100.0
1908	50	1,060		1,110	4.5
1909				0	

1910	65			65	100.0
1911	500	22,500		23,000	2.2
1912					
Totals	165,785	228,271	100,091	494,147	33.5
Averages:					
1837–46	1,468	414	6	1,882	78.0
1847–53	9,172	342	1,606	10,120	80.7
1854–59	8,316	7,512	0	15,828	52.5
1860–67	3,036	2,211	4,077	9,324	32.6
1868–88	756	2,708	1,310	4,774	15.8
1889–1912	200	4,254	1,196	5,651	3.5

Notes: d.t. = displacement tons
Tonnages are given for the year of launching

Sources: Based on data in Thames Ironworks Catalogue (1911).

APPENDIX 3

Ship lists for the main iron shipbuilding yards

The main iron ship-producing firms also typically produced wooden and composite ships and other iron products, such as bridges.

These lists attempt to identify, within the limits imposed by the available data, the ships built (whether or not constructed of iron) at the main yards in each of the periods identified in the preceding chapters.

The listings exclude Admiralty vessels, which are shown in Appendix 1.

The lists cover those periods in which the firms concerned were producing iron ships.

The tonnage figures should be regarded as indicative, not definitive. They are marked as follows: (*) estimated, (b) builder's measurements, (g) gross (d) draught.

Where several similar ships are included as one item, the tonnage figure given is the total for the ships concerned.

1832–46 (Chapter 2)

William Fairbairn (Yard 1: Millwall Shipyard, 1835–46)

Quality of data: Poor, highly incomplete

Year	Ship name	Tons	Brief details
1836	Ludwig	175	First ship, for Lake Constance
1837	Sirius	250	Paddler for Rhone
1838	Nevka		Iron steam yacht, Czar of Russia
	Prevesiche Adler	100	Paddler for the Elbe
	Ladoga	215	Packet and despatch vessel
1839	Rose		
	Thistle		Hunter River SN Co
	Woronzow		Shallow draught paddler for Black Sea
	Pradpriatie		Shallow draught paddler for Black Sea
	Unknown (12)	4,008	Shallow draught paddlers, East India Co
1841	Juno	135	Iron steamer, London to Hull
1846	Pottinger	1,401g	P&O
Unknown	Little Dreadnought	14	For own use on river

Unknown		Iron steam yacht for King of Denmark
Concordia	118	Shallow draught paddler, German rivers
Dolphin	106	Shallow draught paddler, German rivers
Telegraph	206	Shallow draught paddler, German rivers
Shell	110	for Thames
Iron Duke	110	for Demerara

Main sources: Pole (1970); Banbury (1971).

Ditchburn and Mare (Yard 2: Orchard Shipyard, 1838–46)

Quality of data: Good, relatively complete

The listing includes ships, marked (a), built at Dudman's Dock, Deptford, prior to the firm's move to Orchard Shipyard.

Year	Ship name	Tons	Brief details
1838 (a)	Inkerman	365	Russian government
	Starlight	75*	Iron Steamboat Co
	Daylight	75*	Iron Steamboat Co
	Moonlight	75*	Iron Steamboat Co
	Twilight	75*	Iron Steamboat Co
1839	Bride	100	Iron Steamboat Co
	Bridegroom	100	Iron Steamboat Co
	Bridesmaid	100	Iron Steamboat Co
1840	Father Thames	120d	Passenger
	Mermaid	123d	Passenger
	Queen Elizabeth	317d	Cargo
	Propeller		
	Locomotive		
	Cardinal Wolsey		
	Triton	358	GSN Co
1841	Brunswick	126d	Passenger
	Blackwall	126d	Passenger
	Satellite	101d	Passenger
	Eagle	195d	Passenger
	Railway	126d	Passenger
	Waterman (1–4)	116d	Passenger
	Cairo	26d	Passenger
	Sapphire	184d	Cargo
	Mystery	25	Iron racing yacht, Lord Paget
1842	Flirt	43d	Passenger
	Waterman (5 & 8)	72d	Passenger
	Coquette	43d	Passenger
	Mystery	21d	Yacht

	Tugs (1–3)	56d	Tugs for Rome
	Locomotive	66d	Passenger
	Magician	176d	Cargo
	Blue Belle	20d	Yacht
	Echo	37d	Passenger
	Matrimony	50	
	Queen		Greenwich SP Co
1843	South Western	180d	London and SW Railway Co.
	Waterman (1 new)	45d	Passenger
	Wittikind	60d	Tug
	Wartzburg	52d	Tug
	Paddle Tug	59d	Tug
	Heron	205d	Cargo
	City of Rome	69d	Passenger
	Manheim	208d	Passenger/cargo
1844	Waterman (10)	49d	Passenger
	Waterman (12)	47d	Passenger
	Princess Royal	48d	Passenger
	Georgian	165d	Cargo
	Waterman (11)	47d	Passenger
	Princess Mary	294d	Passenger, South Eastern Railway Co.
	Princess Maude	294d	Passenger, South Eastern Railway Co
	Wonder	222d	Passenger
	Water Lily	94d	Passenger
	Wedding Ring	50	
1845	Manheim (2)	210d	Passenger
	Waterman (13)	48d	Passenger
	Queen of Belgians	212d	Cargo, South Eastern Railway Co.
	Belvidere	19d	Yacht
	Wedding Ring	59d	Tug
	Fairy	210d	Screw-propelled Queen's Yacht
	Bremen	60d	Passenger
	Levantine	400d	Cargo
	Wezer	60d	Passenger
	Ariel	709d	Cargo, P&O
	Triton	477d	Cargo
	Queen of French	205d	Cargo, South Eastern Railway Co.
1846	Citizen A–G	240d	Passenger
	New Starlight	30d	Passenger
	Bee	32d	Passenger
	Ant	32d	Passenger
	Lady of Lake	30d	Passenger
	Starlight	30d	Passenger
	Lalla Rooke	31d	Passenger
	Childe Harold	31d	Passenger
	Waverly	31d	Passenger
	Rose	160d	Cargo

	Pearl	160d	Cargo
	Volcano	500d	Cargo
	City of Rotterdam	304d	Cargo/passenger
	City of London	304d	Cargo/passenger
	Times	193d	Cargo
	Sharpshooter	585d	Cargo
	Capri	609d	Cargo
	Dredger	113d	Dredger
	Cricket	47d	Passenger
	Vesuvio	609d	Cargo
	Erin	1,065d	Cargo, P&O
	Antelope	857d	Cargo

Main sources: Thames Ironworks Historical Catalogue, Crystal Palace (1911); Banbury (1971).

Money Wigram (Yard 3: Blackwall Yard, 1843–46)

Quality of data: Fairly good

The listing is of ships built by Money Wigram from 1843, when the Blackwall Yard was divided between Money Wigram, who built iron ships and Richard Green, who did not.

Year	Ship name	Tons	Brief details
1844	Royal Albert	663	
1845	Minerva	829	
1846	Ripon	1509g	Iron paddle steamer, P&O
1847	Indus	1386g	Iron paddle steamer, P&O

Main sources: Listings by C. J. Cotton, THLHL 901.2; Banbury (1971).

1847–53 (Chapter 3)

C. J. Mare (Yard 2: Orchard and Bow Creek Shipyard)

Quality of data: Good, relatively complete

Year	Ship name	Tons	Brief details
1847	Norfolk	200d	Cargo
	Zuluetas Wood Boat	514d	Cargo
	Waterman No. 7	33d	Passenger
	Zuluetas Iron Boat	112d	Cargo
	Lord John Russell	396d	Cargo

	Sir Robert Peel	396d	Cargo
	Prince Metternich	440d	Cargo
	Prussian Eagle	997d	Iron despatch, Prussian Navy
	Manheim No. 3	207d	Passenger/Cargo
	Sardinian Vessel	436d	Cargo
	Citizen H-J	93d	Passenger
	Albion	473d	Cargo, GSN
1848	Vladimir	1,680d	Paddle Sloop, Russian govt.
	Caradoc	591d	Cargo
	Express	275d	Cargo/Passenger, LSW Rway
	Despatch	306d	Cargo/Passenger, LSW Rway
	Courier	306d	Cargo/Passenger, LSW Rway
	Danube	110d	Cargo/Passenger
	Citizen K	32d	Passenger
	Sardinian Tug	157d	Tug for Sardinia
	Admiralty Tug	97d	Tug
	Enicole	600d	Cargo
	Mosquito	60d	Sailing yacht
	Russian Tug	96d	Tug for Russia
1849	Hellespont	643d	Cargo iron steamer, GSN
	Bosphorus	643d	Cargo iron steamer, GSN
	Uncle Sam		Tug, Wm Watkins
	Rhine	584d	Cargo/Passenger, GSN
	Propontis	643d	Cargo iron steamer, GSN
	Highflyer	1,738d	Cargo
1850	Francisco d'Asisi	2,818d	Wood Paddle Sloop, Span. govt.
	Isabel Secunda	2,818d	Wood Paddle Sloop, Span. govt.
	Russian Tug	73d	Tug for Russia
	Peterhoff	218d	Cargo
	Harbinger	1,486d	Cargo
	Panther	500d	Cargo, GSN
	Queen of South	2,588d	Cargo, GSN
	Lady Jocelyn	2,588d	Cargo, GSN
	Indiana	2,588d	Cargo, GSN
1851	Faid Gihaad	2,929d	Paddle yacht, Viceroy of Egypt
	Queenstown	58d	Passenger
	Ravensbourne	789d	Cargo
1852	Alexandroff	218d	Cargo
1853	Himalaya	3,947d	Cargo/Passenger, P&O
	Sea Mew	302d	Cargo/Passenger
	Calcutta	2,563d	Cargo, GSN
	Hydaspes	2,563d	Cargo, GSN
	San Giovanni	81d	Tug
	Tiber	68d	Tug
	Victoria	84d	Tug
	Moselle	646d	Cargo, GSN
	Mauritias	2,563d	Cargo, GSN

Argo	2,563d	Cargo, GSN
Dragon Fly	43d	Tug
Nagler	564d	Cargo
Valetta	944d	Cargo/Passenger, P&O
Guadalquivir	169d	Passenger
Guadalope	169d	Passenger
Craesus	3,335d	Cargo, GSN
Jason	3,335d	Cargo, GSN
Golden Fleece	3,335d	Cargo, GSN
Prince	3,576d	Cargo
Rajah	878d	Cargo, P&O
Freyer	185d	Cargo

Main source: Thames Ironworks Historical Catalogue, Crystal Palace (1911).

John Scott Russell (Yard 1 : Millwall Shipyard)

Quality of data: Poor, highly incomplete

Year	Ship name	Tons	Brief details
1847	Benares		
1848	Taman		Iron ship for Russian govt.
1849	Manchester		
	Argonaut		Iron ship for Russian govt.
1850	Her Majesty	90g	Packet
	Titania (1)	100b	Sailing yacht
1851	Nix	468d	Gunboat for Prussia
	Salamander	468d	Gunboat for Prussia
	Danzig	1,280b	Gunboat for Prussia
1852	Wave Queen	196g	Packet
	Victoria	1,350g	Australian Royal Mail Co
	Adelaide	1,350g	Australian Royal Mail Co
1853	Cleopatra		Egyptian Royal Yacht
	Rouen	357g	Packet
	Pacific	1,469g	Mail steamer
	Titania (2)	184b	Yacht

Main source: Banbury (1971).

Money Wigram (Yard 3: Blackwall Yard)

Quality of data: Fairly good

Year	Ship name	Tons	Brief details
1847	Scotia	479	Iron paddler, Chester & Holyhead Railway
	Indus	1,386	Iron paddler, P&O
1848	Devonshire	831	Sheathed wood
1849	Cornwall	580	Sheathed wood
1850	Flying Dutchman	268	Iron 3 masted schooner
	Prince of Wales		
	Boulac	272	Iron paddler, P&O
1851	Ysabel Catolica	1,567	Iron paddler, Spanish Navy
	Parana	2,934	Wooden paddler for RMSP to Brazil
	Hampshire		
1852	Mystery	105	Wooden tug, RD Ross of London
	Surprise		
	Kent	998	Wooden, passengers to Melbourne
	Amazon	2,256g	Wooden paddler, RMSP
1853	Victoria		
	Sussex		

Main source: Listings by C. J. Cotton, THLHL 901.2.

1854–59 (Chapter 4)

John Scott Russell (Yard 1: Millwall Shipyard)

Quality of data: Poor, highly incomplete

Year	Ship name	Tons	Brief details
1855	Kiev	692	
	Baron Osy	607g	Belgian packet
1856	Orleans	279g	Packet
	Lyons	279g	Packet
1858	Great Eastern	18,914g	
	El Rey Jaime II		Iron steam yacht, Sultan of Turkey
	Cleopatra		Iron steam yacht, Hama El Pasha
1859	Thunderer		Paddle-steamer
	Prince Consort		Steam sloop
	Donna Maria Anna	400	Wooden screw gunboat, Portugal

Main source: Banbury (1971).

C. J. Mare (Yard 2: Orchard and Bow Creek Shipyard until 1855)

Quality of data: Good, relatively complete

Year	Ship name	Tons	Brief details
1854	Candia	2,548d	Cargo/Passenger, P&O
	Guillaume Tell	73d	Passenger
	Natal	679d	Cargo
	Cape of Good Hope	679d	Cargo
	Fairy	36d	Yacht
	Manilla	998d	Cargo, P&O
	Woronzoff	74d	Passenger
	For New Zealand	56d	Passenger
	For New Zealand	56d	Passenger
	Illawarra	189d	Cargo/Passenger
	Haarlingen	610d	Cargo
	Industry	998d	Cargo
	Supply	998d	Cargo
	Flying Venus	2,258d	Cargo
	Albert	84d	Passenger
	Venus	161d	Passenger
	Victor Emanuel	2,097d	Cargo
	Conte di Cavour	2,097d	Cargo
	Standard	610d	Cargo
	Queen	220d	Channel steamer
	Empress	220d	Channel steamer
	Pilot	877d	Cargo, GSN
	Europa	1,675d	Cargo
	Mutlah	439d	Sailing brig
1855	Pera	2,862d	Cargo/Passenger, P&O
	C. J. Mare	412d	Cargo
	South Wales	1,031d	Cargo
	Ferry Boat	242d	Ferry boat for India
	Ferry Boat	242d	Ferry boat for India
	General Victoria	829d	Cargo
	General Morelos	829d	Cargo
	Hadgier Barbier	40d	Yacht
	Teir Neil		Launch
	Torino	2,607d	Cargo boat for Italy

Main source: Thames Ironworks Historical Catalogue, Crystal Palace (1911).

Thames Iron Works Ltd (Yard 2: Orchard and Bow Creek Shipyard from 1856)

Quality of data: Good, relatively complete

Year	Ship name	Tons	Brief details
1856	Genova	2,607d	Cargo boat for Italy
	Dolphin	936d	Cargo, GSN
	Fire float	60d	Fire float
	Havre	650d	Cargo
1857	Prince F. William	249d	Dover Mail Steamer
	Wolf	702d	Cargo
	Fantasie	252d	Passenger
1858	Nepaul	1,335d	Steamer, P&O
	St Paul	67d	Tug
	St Peter	79d	Tug
	Paramatta	5,060d	Steamer, RMSP
	Seine	5,060d	Steamer, RMSP
	Vulcan	166d	Tug
	Emeralde	250d	Cargo
1859	Immac. Conception	652d	Yacht for Pope
	Delta	2,336d	Steamer, P&O
	Sextant	288d	Tug
	Ly-ee-Moon	1,318d	Opium clipper

Main source: Thames Ironworks Historical Catalogue, Crystal Palace (1911).

Money Wigram (Yard 3: Blackwall Yard)

Quality of data: Moderate

Year	Ship name	Tons	Brief details
1854	Northam		
	Phoenix		
	Elizabeth		
	Radetzky	2,234	Screw frigate, Austrian govt.
1855	Aid	112	Tug, Ramsgate harbour
	Southern Cross	70	Schooner
	Dorsetshire		
1856	Harrier		
	Argus	331	Iron paddler, Trinity House
1857	Bloomer		
	Suffolk		
	Norfolk	953	Sheathed wood

1858	Nursery Packet	257	Wooden brig, Scrutton Steam Co.
	Lincolnshire	1,024	Sheathed wooden barque
1859	Unknown		Corvette for Turkish govt.
	Beyrnt		
	Yorkshire	1,057	Wooden

Main source: Listings by C. J. Cotton, THLHL 901.2.

1860–67 (Chapter 5)

Millwall Ironworks Ltd (Yard 1: Millwall Shipyard, 1863 to 1866)

Quality of data: Poor

Year	Ship name	Tons	Brief details
1863	Golconda	1,909g	Cargo/Passenger, P & O
	Affondatore	3,000	Italian government
	Collier	900	Collier
	Sundry (six)	1,500	Sailing ships
	Unknown		Iron ships for Russian govt.
1864	Baroda	1,874g	Cargo/Passenger, P&O
	Centaur		Sail
	Meteor		Sail
1865	Rhone	2,738g	Cargo/Passenger, RMSP
	Danube	2,000g	Cargo/Passenger, RMSP
1866	Mataura	1,786g	NZ & Australia Royal Mail Co.

Main source: Banbury (1971).

Thames Iron Works Ltd (Yard 2: Orchard and Bow Creek Shipyard)

Quality of data: Good, relatively complete

Year	Ship name	Tons	Brief details
1860	John Penn	259d	Channel steamer
	Mooltan	3,091d	Steamer
	Unknown	10d	Yacht
	Oberon	16d	Yacht
1861	Lord of the Isles	117d	Passenger
	Sunbeam	125d	Yacht
	Lady of the Lake	121d	Passenger

	Paraguari	520d	Cargo paddler, Paraguay
1862	Coonanbara	579d	Cargo paddler
	Poonah	3,080d	Cargo/passenger
1863	Morning Star 4	64d	Yacht
	Princess Alaxandra	581d	Paddle yacht
	Unknown (2)	115d	Gunboats, Peruvian govt.
	Absolon	527d	Armoured gunboat, Danish govt.
	Esbernsnare	527d	Armoured gunboat, Danish govt.
	Pervenetz	3,277d	Armoured warship, Russian govt.
	Vittoria	7,000d	Armour-clad, Spanish govt.
	Sultan Mahmoud	6,400d	Warship, Turkish govt.
	Izzedin	1,218d	Cruiser yacht, Sultan of Turkey
1864	Charkieh	2,177d	Cruiser, Egyptian gov
	Golconda	2,843d	Cargo/passenger
	Nyanza	2,844d	Steamer, P&O
	Napoleon III	5,759d	Mail steamer, France
1865	Tanjore	3,069d	Steamer, P&O
	Unknown (2)	152d	Tugs
1866	Anglia	560d	Tug
1867	Konig Wilhelm	9,602d	Armour-clad, Prussian govt.
	King George	1,775d	Armour-clad, Greek govt.
	La Poste	101d	Tug
	Unknown		Iron tank vessel

Main source: Thames Ironworks Historical Catalogue, Crystal Palace (1911).

Money Wigram (Yard 3: Blackwall Yard)

Quality of data: Fairly good

Year	Ship name	Tons	Brief details
1861	True Briton	1,046	Wood
1862	City of London	150	Iron river paddler
	Beacon	262	Iron paddler, Trinity House
	Essex	1,042	Wooden sailing barque
	Gerente	375	Iron paddler for Brazil
	Southern Cross	92	Schooner
	Samphire	366g	Steel paddler, L, C and Dover Rway
	Petrel	503g	Steel paddler, L, C and Dover Rway
1863	Beyazit	140	Wooden paddler, Bosphorus Ferries
	Buyukada	140	Wooden paddler, Bosphorus Ferries
	Exploratore	981d	Paddle despatch, Italian Navy
	Breeze	344g	Steel paddler, L, C and Dover Rway
	Wave	344g	Steel paddler, L, C and Dover Rway

1864	Delhi	1899	Iron screw, P&O
	Canopus	765	Iron barque, Lynch Bros
	London	1,752g	Iron screw steamer
1865	Dakahlieh	1,553	Iron screw, Khedive Steam Ships
	Bahariye	140	Wooden paddler, Bosphorus Ferries
	Asayis	140	Wooden paddler, Bosphorus Ferries
1867	Mystery		
	Somersetshire	2,342	Iron barque

Main source: Listings by C. J. Cotton, THLHL 901.2.

1868–88 (Chapter 6)

Thames Iron Works Ltd (Yard 2 : Bow Creek Shipyard)

Quality of data: Good, relatively complete

Year	Ship name	Tons	Brief details
1868	Anchor Hoy	90d	
1869	Avni Illah	2,314d	Armour clad, Turkish govt.
	John Penn	366d	Cargo
1870	Fethi-Bulend	2,720d	Armour clad, Turkish govt.
	Unknown	54d	Boat for Nile
1871	Kouban	733d	Cargo, Russia
	Terek	733d	Cargo, Russia
	Kodor	733d	Cargo, Russia
1872	Unknown		Boat for Nile
1873	Castilia	1,080d	Twin passenger vessel
1876	Mesoudiye	8,994d	Armour clad, Turkish govt.
	Memdouhiye	8,994d	Armour clad, Turkish govt.
	Dom Augusto	167d	Paddle steamer, Portugal
1877	Fox	89d	Tug
	Cleopatra		Special
	Ajax	51d	Tug
	Trojan	51d	Tug
	Somtseu	115d	Cargo
1878	Purus	1,355d	Troopship, Brazilian govt.
	Vasco da Gama	2,479d	Armour clad, Portuguese govt.
	Zieten	951d	Torpedo cruiser, German govt.
	Principe Don Carlos	435d	Transport ship, Portuguese govt.
	Sphinx	33d	Torpedo boat, Greek gov
	Guadiana	99d	Customs vessel, Portuguese govt.
	Faro	150d	Customs vessel, Portuguese govt.
	Tejo	229d	Customs vessel, Portuguese govt.
	Unknown	31d	Experimental brass torpedo boat

	Hawk	53d	Tug
	Stour	107d	Paddle steamer, G.E. Railway
	Enterprise	50d	Tug
	Imperial	86d	Paddle steamer, G.E. Railway
1879	Middlesex	112d	Paddle steamer, G.E. Railway
	Queen	61d	Tug
	Canada	116d	Tug
	Duke	61d	Tug
	Eonia	31d	
	P. de Grao Para	431d	Brazilian
	Guadiana	230d	Customs vessel, Portuguese govt., 1880
	Fulminante	84d	Mine layer, Portuguese govt.
	Albion	61d	Tug
	D'Affonso	146d	Paddle steamer, Portugal
	Retort	78d	Tug
1881	Hydra	485d	Gunboat, Greek gov
	Spetzia	485d	Gunboat, Greek govt.
	Aghilea	84d	Mine layer, Greek govt.
	Napoloen	84d	Mine layer, Greek govt.
	Monemvassiea	84d	Mine layer, Greek govt.
	Gravina	1,139d	Cruiser, Spanish govt.
	Velasco	1,139d	Cruiser, Spanish govt.
	Vilhena	144d	Gunboat
	Thames	22d	Thames Conservancy yacht
	Unknown		Water boat
	Unknown	54d	Tug
1882	Mircea	390d	Training brig, Romanian govt.
	Rahova	53d	Romania
	Smardan	53d	Romania
	Opanez	53d	Romania
	Alexandru cel Bun	84d	Mine layer, Romanian govt.
	Invicta	1,282d	Channel steamer
	Norfolk	109d	Paddle steamer, G.E. Railway
	Paddle steamers (4)	496d	Paddle steamer, Brahmapootra river
	Unknown (3)	2,514d	Cargo flats
	Lion	238d	Cargo
	Dolphin	86d	Tender
	Diana	58d	Tug
	Unknown	43d	Single screw launch
1883	A. de Alberquerque	1,112d	Corvette, Portuguese govt.
	Anchor Hoy	90d	Iron screw launch
	Unknown	68d	Iron screw launch
	Unknown	81d	Water boat
	Rotifer	87d	Tug
	Romulus	64d	Tug
	Remus	64d	Tug
1884	Thrush	99d	Customs vessel, Greek govt.

	Nightingale	99d	Customs vessel, Greek govt.
	Magpie	99d	Customs vessel, Greek govt.
	Alpheois	422d	Cruiser, Greek govt.
	Acheloos	422d	Cruiser, Greek govt.
	Emperor	63d	Tug
1885	Benbow	87d	Tug
1886	Unknown	93d	Screw water boat, Indian govt.
1887	Oltul	95d	Customs vessel, Romanian govt.
	Siretul	95d	Customs vessel, Romanian govt.
	Bistrita	95d	Customs vessel, Romanian govt.
	Regina	82d	Tug
	Rodney	82d	Tug
	Angel	637d	Sailing light
	Casilda	637d	Sailing light
	Genara	637d	Sailing light
	Carlos	637d	Sailing light
	Jose	637d	Sailing light
	Ramona	637d	Sailing light
	Dona Ramona	315d	Paddle tug
1888	M. Machahon	345d	Transport, Portuguese govt.
	Unknown	26d	Launch, Portugal
	Carlos	637d	Sailing light

Main source: Thames Ironworks Historical Catalogue, Crystal Palace (1911).

Money Wigram (Yard 3: Blackwall Yard until 1877)

Quality of data: Fairly good

Year	Ship name	Tons	Brief details
1869	Seygur	109	Wooden paddler, Bosphorus SN Co
	Terrakki	109	Wooden paddler, Bosphorus SN Co
	Surat	109	Wooden paddler, Bosphorus SN Co
	Taygar	109	Wooden paddler, Bosphorus SN Co
	Duke of Edinburgh	95	Iron paddler, Ryde Steam Packet Co
	Princess Alice	95	Iron paddler, Ryde Steam Packet Co
1870	Hampshire	1,214	Composite
1871	Serendib	408	Composite screw steamer
	Northumberland	2,178	Iron screw steamer
1874	Durham	2284g	Iron passenger ship
1876	Kent	2484g	Iron passenger ship

Main source: Listings by C. J. Cotton THLHL 901.2.

Yarrow (Yard 8: Folly Shipyard, Poplar)

Quality of data: Moderate

Year	Ship name	Tons	Brief details
1869	Seygur	109	Wooden paddler, Bosphorus SN Co.
1874	Le Stanley		Mission steamer
	Faraday		
1875	Italy		
	Itala		Steamer, Nyassa mission
	Unknown		Torpedo boats, Argentine govt.
1876	Unknown		Steamer, King of Burma
	Stephenson Clarke		Sternwheeler
1877	Unknown		Stern-wheeler, Columbia USA
1878	Pollux		Torpedo boat, Spanish govt.
1879	Inez Clarke		Sternwheeler
	General Troquilla		Sternwheeler
	Batoom		Torpedo boat, Russian govt.
1880	Unknown		Torpedo boat, Japanese govt.
1881	Cyprus		Torpedo boat, Greek govt.
	Unknown (6)		Boats, Greece
	Anita		Sternwheeler
1882	Alert		Torpedo boat, Argentine govt.
	Centella		Torpedo boat, Argentine govt.
	Etna		Torpedo boat, Dutch govt.
	Hekla		Torpedo boat, Dutch govt.
	Colonel Urseanu		Torpedo boat, Romanian govt.
	Unknown		Torpedo boat, Romanian govt.
	Marscal Sucre		Sternwheeler
1883	Le Congo		Steamer, King of the Belgians
	Urmita		Sternwheeler
	Nirmala		Sternwheeler
	Carthagena		Sternwheeler
1884	Riachuelo		Torpedo boat, Brazilian govt.
	Unknown		Torpedo boat, German govt.
	Cauca		Sternwheeler
1885	Lotus		River gunboat
	Waterlily		River gunboat
	Katoka		Torpedo boat, Japanese govt.
	Retamosa		Torpedo boat, Spanish govt.
	America		River gunboat
	Sabia		River gunboat
	Colibri		River gunboat
	Butuhy		River gunboat
	Shushan		River gunboat
	Abu Klea		River gunboat

	Kirbikan	River gunboat
	Matemnah	River gunboat
1886	Adler	Torpedo boat, Austrian govt.
	Falke	Torpedo boat, Austrian govt.
	Sargento Aldea	Torpedo boat, Chilean govt.
	Ardjoeno	Torpedo boat, Dutch govt.
	Primera	Sternwheeler
	Kendat	Sternwheeler, Irawaddy Co.
	Pedro Velez	Sternwheeler
	Holland	Sternwheeler
	Ibera	Sternwheeler, Argentine Railways
1887	Segunda	Sternwheeler
	Halcon	Torpedo boat, Spanish govt.
	Azor	Torpedo boat, Spanish govt.
	Unknown	Torpedo boat, Chinese govt.
1888	Empong	Torpedo boat, Dutch govt.

Main source: Borthwick (1965).

1889–1915 (Chapter 7)

Thames Iron Works Ltd (Yard 2: Bow Creek Shipyard until 1912)

Quality of data: Good, relatively complete

Year	Ship name	Tons	Brief details
1889	D'Amelia	150d	Paddle ship, Portugal
	Satmiento	105d	Paddle tug
	Unknown (2)	568d	Saloon steamers, Turkey
1890	Limpopo	289d	Transport, Portuguese govt.
	Woolwich	124d	Ferry, G.E. Railway
1892	Beatrice	39d	Launch, Thames Conservancy
	Hilda	95d	Tug
	Coaltar	503d	Sailing tank vessel
1894	Fuji	12,512d	Battleship, Japanese govt.
	Samoyed	983d	Survey vessel, Russian govt.
1896	Unknown	29d	British Ambassador's launch
1897	Shikishima	14,850d	Battleship, Japanese govt.
	Alexandra	89d	Paddler, Thames Steamboat Co.
	Boadicea	89d	Paddler, Thames Steamboat Co.
	Cleopatra	89d	Paddler, Thames Steamboat Co.
1898	Unknown	26d	Russian Ambassador's launch
1902	Sir F Walker	174d	War Office
	Unknown	75d	Tug, Portugal
	Roding	72d	Launch, Thames Conservancy

1903	Unknown	50d	Tug, War Office
1904	Unknown (10)	1,260d	Paddler Steamers, L.C.C.
	Unknown		Houseboat, Queens College Oxford
	Unknown	1,571d	Coaling lighter
	Unknown (4)		Barges
	Unknown (11)		Lifeboats
1905	Unknown (2)		Coaling lighters
1906	Unknown (8)	405d	Vedette boats, Romanian govt.
1907	L26 A & B	330d	Passenger boats, Turkey
1908	Unknown (5)		Horse boats
1910	Unknown	65d	Grab dredging barge
1911	Unknown (3)	1,500d	Passenger boats, Turkey

Main source: Thames Ironworks Historical Catalogue, Crystal Palace (1911).

Yarrow (Yard 8: Folly Shipyard, Poplar until 1908)

Quality of data: Moderate

Year	Ship name	Tons	Brief details
1889	Chirim		Gunboat, Portuguese govt.
	Cuama		Gunboat, Portuguese govt.
	Matta Machado		Sternwheeler, Fry Miers and Co.
1890	Thorne		Torpedo boat, Argentine govt.
	Pinedo		Torpedo boat, Argentine govt.
	Buchardo		Torpedo boat, Argentine govt.
	King		Torpedo boat, Argentine govt.
	Bathurst		Torpedo boat, Argentine govt.
	Jorge		Torpedo boat, Argentine govt.
	Antoinette		Sternwheeler, Nieuwe Afrikaansche
1891	Branlio Garrillo		Torpedo boat, Costa Rican govt.
	Argonaut		Sternwheeler, African Flotilla Co.
	John Stephenson		Sternwheeler, Crossley and Co.
1892	La Foudre		Torpedo boat, French govt.
	Opale		Gunboat, French govt.
	Gossomer		Sternwheeler, Kilburn Brown and Co.
	Manuwai		Sternwheeler, Hatrick and Co.
1893	Michipam		Sternwheeler, A Chazaro
	Catemaco		Sternwheeler, A Chazaro
	Tuxtepec		Sternwheeler, A Chazaro
	Kalewa		Sternwheeler, Indian Office
	Libertador		Sternwheeler, Jose Bonnet
1894	Unknown		Torpedo boat, US govt.
1895	Lacerda		Gunboat, Portuguese govt.
	Serpa Pinto		Gunboat, Portuguese govt.

	Capella	Gunboat, Portuguese govt.
	Iveno	Gunboat, Portuguese govt.
	Sokol	Destroyer, Russian govt.
	John Cameron	Sternwheeler, African Flotilla Co.
	Boyaca	Sternwheeler, Ramon Reel
	Sitalla	Sternwheeler, Hoare, Miller and Co.
	Henriette	Sternwheeler, Nieuwe Afrikaansche
1896	Santa Fe	Destroyer, Argentine govt.
	Entre Rios	Destroyer, Argentine govt.
	Misiones	Destroyer, Argentine govt.
	Corrientes	Destroyer, Argentine govt.
	Viper	Torpedo boat, Austrian govt.
	Cirujano Videla	Torpedo boat, Chilean govt.
	Xahka	Sternwheeler, Russian Railway Co.
	Alostville	Sternwheeler, Central African Co.
	Sultan	River gunboat
1897	Ingeniero Hyatt	Torpedo boat, Chilean govt.
	Capt. M. Thomson	Torpedo boat, Chilean govt.
	Teniente Rodriguez	Torpedo boat, Chilean govt.
	Guardia Marina	Torpedo boat, Chilean govt.
	Cartreras	Torpedo boat, Chilean govt.
	Martinez Bossio	Sternwheeler, Bossio and Co.
	Manuela Aycarda	Sternwheeler, Bossio and Co.
	Sheikh	River gunboat
	Injeniero Hyatt	River steamer
1898	Boa	Torpedo boat, Austrian govt.
	Cobra	Torpedo boat, Austrian govt.
	Ikadsuchi	Destroyer, Japanese govt.
	Playa Vicente	Sternwheeler, Perez and Co
1899	Kigyo	Torpedo boat, Austrian govt.
	Python	Torpedo boat, Austrian govt.
	Inadsuma	Destroyer, Japanese govt.
	Sazanami	Destroyer, Japanese govt.
	Akebono	Destroyer, Japanese govt.
	Niji	Destroyer, Japanese govt.
	Unknown (10)	Torpedo boats, Japanese govt.
	Redemptor	Sternwheeler, Ms Roveggio
	Zambeze	Sternwheeler, Co da Zambezia
	Chire	Sternwheeler, Co da Zambezia
1900	Hydra	Torpedo boat, Dutch govt.
	Scylla	Torpedo boat, Dutch govt.
	Negara	Sternwheeler, Dutch Steam Packet
1901	Ophir	Torpedo boat, Dutch govt.
	Pangrango	Torpedo boat, Dutch govt.
	Rindjani	Torpedo boat, Dutch govt.
	Akatsuki	Destroyer, Japanese govt.
	Santa Rosa	Sternwheeler, Smith Wood and Co.

1902	Kasumi	Destroyer, Japanese govt.
	Mode	Destroyer, Swedish govt.
	Tarantula	Steam turbine yacht
1903	El Sucre	Sternwheeler, Aubert and Co.
	Inca	Sternwheeler, Amazon Steam Navig.
1904	Fushimi	Gunboat, Japanese govt.
	Caroline	Steam yacht
1905	Huszar	Destroyer, Austrian govt.
	Kaiman	Torpedo boat, Austrian govt.
	Acre	Gunboats, Brazilian govt.
1906	Amapa	Gunboats, Brazilian govt.
	Jurua	Gunboats, Brazilian govt.
	Missoes	Gunboats, Brazilian govt.

Main source: Borthwick (1965).

Bibliography

Primary sources

Guildhall Manuscripts Department (MS 19096)

Prospectus, Millwall Freehold Land and Docks Co., 1865.
Prospectus, Millwall Iron Co. Ltd.
Prospectus, Millwall Iron Works Ship Building and Graving Docks Co. Ltd, 1864.
Prospectus, Thames Iron Works, Ship Building, Engineering and Dry Dock Co. Ltd 1864.
Prospectus, Thames Ship Building, Graving Docks and Iron Works Co. Ltd, 1871.
Directors' report 1898, correspondence, prospectuses and papers relating to share issue of Thames Ironworks, Shipbuilding and Engineering Co. Ltd in 1899.

Greater London Record Office (O/45/1)

Minute book and annual reports and accounts, Thames Ironworks, Shipbuilding and Engineering Co. Ltd 1899–1911

PRO, Kew

Admiralty files in ADM 116 series.
Dissolved company files of Board of Trade.
Dudgeon and Co. Ltd BT31/2400/11995.
(T & W) Forrestt and Son Ltd BT31/5418/37373.
(T & W) Forrestt and Co. Ltd BT31/10665/80755.
London Engineering and Iron Ship Building Co. Ltd BT31/988/1489c.
Millwall Ironworks and Shipbuilding Co. Ltd BT31/725/151c.
Millwall Ironworks, Shipbuilding and Graving Docks Co. Ltd BT31/946/1252c.
Overend Gurney and Co. Ltd BT31/1128/2280c.
Northumberland Graving Docks and Engineering Co. Ltd BT31/1905/7734.
Samuda Bros. Ltd BT31/3530/21537.
Thames Ironworks and Shipbuilding Co. Ltd BT31/219/686.
Thames Ironworks, Shipbuilding, Engineering and Dry Dock Co. Ltd. BT31/913/1080c.
Thames Shipbuilding, Graving Docks and Ironworks Co. Ltd BT31/1597/5338.
Thames Ironworks and Shipbuilding Co. Ltd BT31/1722/6293.
Thames Ironworks, Shipbuilding and Engineering Co. Ltd BT31/16240/62972.
(J I) Thorneycroft and Co. Ltd BT31/70274.
Yarrow and Co. Ltd BT31/15744/51710.

Sundry

Cotton C. J., Ships built at Blackwall by Money Wigram and Sons Collection (Tower Hamlets Local History Library, 901.2).
Lyon, David, Private listing of ships built in the period 1825–60.

Official publications

P.P.

Committee into Arrears of Shipbuilding, (Report of) Cmnd 1055, P.P. 1902
Board of Trade Annual Statements of the Navigation and Shipping of the UK, vols:

LXVI	(1867)
LXVII	(1867–68)
LVIII	(1868–69)
LXIII	(1870)
LXIII	(1871)
LVI	(1872)
LXIII	(1873)
LXIV	(1874)
LXXIII	(1875)
LXXII	(1876)
LXXX	(1877)
LXXI	(1878)
LXVIII	(1878–79)
LXXI	(1880)
LXXXVII	(1881)
LXVIII	(1882)
LXX	(1883)
LXXVII	(1884)
LXXIV	(1884–85)
LXIV	(1886)
LXXX	(1887)
XCVII	(1888)
LXXV	(1889)
LXXII	(1890)
LXXXII	(1890–91)
LXXVII	(1892)
LXXXVIII	(1893–94)
LXXXIV	(1894)
XCV	(1895)
LXXXIII	(1896)
LXXXVII	(1897)

XCI	(1898)
XCVI	(1899)
LXXXVIII	(1900)
LXXV	(1901)
C	(1902)
LXXXI	(1903)
XCI	(1904)
LXXX	(1905)
LXXXIV	(1907)
CIV	(1908)
LXXXIV	(1909)
LXXXVII	(1910)
LXXXV	(1912–13)
LXI	(1913)

Dockyard Expense Accounts; Annual Accounts of Shipbuilding and Dockyard Transactions etc. including Manufacture; Cmd. 330, Vol. XLVIII (1884–85); Cmnd 219, Vol. LII (1890–91); Cmnd 268, Vol. XL (1914–16).

Dockyards and Ironworks of Great Britain and France (Report by J. W. King to the US House of Representatives) 1864 (Admiralty Library Da258).

Fair Wages Committee (Report of), Cmnd 4422, P.P. 1908.

Inspector of Factories Return on Factories and Workshops, Cmnd 440, P.P. 1871, Vol. LXII.

Navy Appropriations and Expenditures, Return on Shipping, Cmnd XLI, P.P. 1847–48.

Navy Gunboats, Cmnd 206, P.P. 1861, Vol. XXXVIII.

Royal Commission on Trade Unions, 1867–68, Ninth Report, P.P. 1867–68, Vol. XXXIX

Select Committee on Government Contracts (Fair Wages Resolution), (Report of), Cmnd 334, P.P. 1897.

Secondary sources

Archibald E. H. H., *The Metal Fighting Ships in the Royal Navy, 1860–1970* (Blandford Press, London 1971).

Armstrong J., 'Hooley and the Bovril Company', *Business History*, Vol. 28 (1986), pp. 18–34.

Ballard G. A., 'The Fighting Ship from 1860 to 1890', *Mariners Mirror*, Vol. 38 (1952), pp. 23–33.

Banbury P., 'Vanished Slipways', *Sea Breezes* (1962), pp. 190–209.

Banbury P., *Shipbuilders of the Thames and Medway* (David and Charles, Newton Abbot 1971).

Banfield F., 'Mr A. F. Yarrow at Poplar', *Cassells Family Magazine* (1897), pp. 470–5.

Bankers Magazine.

Banking Almanac.

Barnaby K. C., *100 Years of Specialised Shipbuilding and Engineering* (J. Thorneycroft Centenary) (Hutchinson, London 1964).

Barnes E. C., *Alfred Yarrow: his Life and Work* (Edward Arnold, London 1924).

Barry P., *Dockyard Economy and Naval Power* (T. Danks, London 1863).

Baxter C. F., 'The Duke of Somerset and the creation of the British Ironclad Navy, 1959–66', *Mariners Mirror,* Vol. 63 (1977), pp. 279–84.

Beck E. J., *A History of the Parish of St. Mary, Rotherhithe* (Cambridge University Press, Cambridge 1907).

Borthwick A., *Yarrow and Co. Ltd: the First Hundred Years* (Yarrow, Glasgow 1965).

Bowen F. C., 'The Green's and the London River', *Journal of Commerce and Shipping Telegraph* (13 October 1932).

Bowen F. C., 'When Ships were built by the Thames', *Port of London Authority Monthly* (December 1938), pp. 51–3.

Bowen F. C., 'Pitchers of Northfleet', *Port of London Authority Monthly* (February 1943), pp. 173–4.

Bowen F. C., 'Shipbuilders of other days: Ditchburn and Mare and C. J. Mare and Co', *Shipbuilding and Shipping Record*, Vol. 64 (1944), p. 500.

Bowen F. C., 'Shipbuilders of other days: The Thames Ironworks', *Shipbuilding and Shipping Record*, Vol. 22 (1945), pp. 375–6.

Bowen F. C., 'Shipbuilders of other days: Charles Lungley of Deptford', *Shipbuilding and Shipping Record* (30 October 1947), pp. 510–12.

Bowen F. C., 'Shipbuilders of other days: Pitcher's Dockyard at Northfleet', *Shipbuilding and Shipping Record* (4 March 1948), pp. 289–90.

Bowen F. C., 'Shipbuilders of other days: Rennie of London', *Shipbuilding and Shipping Record* (20 May 1948), pp. 616–18.

Bowen F. C., 'Shipbuilders of other days: J. & W. Dudgeon of London', *Shipbuilding and Shipping Record* (13 July 1950), pp. 53–4.

Bowen F. C., 'Shipbuilders of other days: Fletcher, Son and Fearnall', *Shipbuilding and Shipping Record* (10 July 1952), pp. 56–7.

Bowen F. C., 'Shipbuilders of other days: Sir William Fairbairn of Manchester and Millwall', *Shipbuilding and Shipping Record* (21 August 1952), pp. 245–7.

Bowen F. C., 'Shipbuilders of other days: Money Wigram and Sons', *Shipbuilding and Shipping Record* (24 December 1953,) pp. 855–6.

Bowley A. L. and G. H. Wood, 'The Statistics of Wages in the United Kingdom during the Nineteenth Century: Part IV Engineering and Shipbuilding', *Journal of the Royal Statistical Society,* Vol. LXIX (1906), pp. 148–96.

Brassey Sir T., *The British Navy*, Vols 1 and 2 (Longman, London 1883).

Brassey Sir T., *The Navy Annual 1909* (J. Griffin, London 1909).

Brassey Earl T. and J. Leyland, *Brassey's Naval Annual 1915* (William Clowes, London 1915).

Brownlee W., *Warrior: the First Modern Battleship* (Cambridge University Press, Cambridge, 1985).

Burtt F., *Steamers of the Thames and Medway* (Tilling, London 1949).

Bushell T. A., *Royal Mail 1839–1939* (Trade and Travel, London 1939).

Cable B., *A Hundred Year History of the P&O* (Ivor Nicholson and Watson, London 1937).

Campbell C., *Shipbuilding and Working Class Organisation in Govan* (Communist Party Pamphlet, Sheffield 1986).

Campbell R. H., *The Rise and Fall of Scottish Industry 1707–1939* (Donald, Edinburgh 1980).

Checkland S. G., *Rise in Industrial Society in England 1815–85* (Longman, Harlow 1971).

Clapham J. H., *An Economic History of Modern Britain: the Early Railway Age, 1820–*

1850, (Second Edition, Cambridge University Press, Cambridge 1964).
Conway's All the Worlds Fighting Ships, 1860–1905 (Conway, London 1979).
Conway's All the Worlds Fighting Ships, 1906–1921 (Conway, London 1985).
Cornford L. C., *A Century of Sea Trading 1824–1924: the General Steam Navigation Co.Ltd.* (Black, London 1924).
Cottrell P. L., *Industrial Finance 1830–1914* (Methuen, London 1980).
Cowper B. H., *A Descriptive and Statistical Account of Millwall* (Robert Gladding, London 1853).
Crighton J. (Jnr.), Contributions to the Maritime History of Great Britain (Tower Hamlets Local History Collections, 901.2).
Crory W. G., *East London Industries* (Longman Green, London 1876).
Daily Mail.
Devine T. M., *The Tobacco Lords* (Edinburgh University Press, Edinburgh 1990).
Dodd G., *Days at the Factories* (Charles Knight, London 1843).
Dougan D., *The History of Northeast Shipbuilding* (George, Allen Unwin, London 1968).
Dowden P., *Ships of the Royal Mail Lines* (Coles, London 1953).
Dumpleton B. and M. Miller, *Brunel's Three Ships* (Colin Venton, Melksham 1974).
East End News.
East London Advertiser.
East London Observer.
Economic Journal.
Economist.
Elmers C. and A. Werner, *Blackwall Yard* (Reuters, London 1989).
Emmerson G. S., *J. Scott Russell: a Great Victorian Engineer and Naval Architect* (John Murphy, London 1977).
Engineer.
Engineering.
Finch H., *The Tower Hamlets Connection* (Stepney Books, London 1996).
Gardiner R., *Steam, Steel and Shellfire: the Steam Warship 1815–1905* (Conway, London 1992).
Glover G., 'The Decline of Shipbuilding on the Thames', *Journal of the Royal Statistical Society,* Vol. 32 (1869), pp. 288–92.
Graham G. S., 'The Transition from Paddle-wheel to Screw Propellor', *Mariners Mirror,* Vol. 64 (1958), pp. 35–48.
Green H. and R. Wigram, *Chronicles of Blackwall Yard* (Whitehead Morris and Lowe, London 1881).
Guillery P., 'Building the Millwall Docks', *Construction History,* Vol. 6 (1990), pp. 3–21.
Hawes D., *Merchant Fleets: Union, Castle and Union-Castle Lines* (TCL, Hereford, 1990)
Hicks C. S., 'Shipbuilding on the Thames – part III', *Port of London Authority Monthly,* (January 1928), pp. 79–88.
Hills A. F., *Causes of the Thames Iron Works Collapse* (Siegle and Sons, London 1912)
Hollett D., *Men of Iron: the Story of Cammell Laird Shipbuilders 1828–1991* (Countyrise, Birkenhead 1992).
Hostettler E., *An Outline History of the Isle of Dogs* (Island History Trust, London 1990).
Howe G. W., 'Down River to the Sea', *Port of London Authority Monthly,* Vol. 41 (1966), pp. 216–22.

Howarth E. G. and M. Wilson, *West Ham: a study in social and industrial problems*, (J. M. Dent, London 1907).

Hume J. R., and M. S. Moss, *Beardmore* (Heinemann, London 1979).

Hunt B C, *The Development of the Business Corporation in England 1800–67* (Harvard University Press, Cambridge Mass. 1936).

Hythe Viscount and J. Leyland (eds), *The Navy Annual 1914* (William Clowes, London 1914).

Illustrated London News.

Illustrated News of the World.

Illustrated Times.

Jones G. S., *Outcast London* (Penguin, London 1976).

Jones L., *Shipbuilding in Britain, mainly between the two World Wars* (University of Wales Press, Cardiff 1957).

Jordan C. H., *Some Historical Records and Reminiscences relating to the British Navy and Mercantile Shipping* (Lloyds, London 1925).

Kentish Mercury.

Keys D. and K. Smith, *Down Elswick Shipways: Armstrong's Ships and People, 1884–1918* (Newcastle 1996).

King J. W., *Report on the Dockyards and Ironworks of Great Britain and France* (to the US House of Representatives: Admiralty Library Da258).

King W. T. C., *History of the London Discount Market*, (Routledge, London 1936).

Korr C., 'West Ham Football Club and the Beginning of Professional Football in East London 1895–1914', *Journal of Contemporary History*, Vol. 13, No. 2 (1978), pp. 211–32.

Kynaston D., *The City of London, Volume 1: a World of its Own 1815–1890* (Pimlico, London 1995).

Lambert A., Warrior: *Restoring the World's First Ironclad*, (Conway, London 1987).

Lambert A. D., *The Crimean War* (Manchester University Press, Manchester 1990).

Lammins C., 'The Old Orchard House', *East London Papers*, Vol. 4, No. 1 (April 1961), pp. 33–37.

Levi L., 'On Joint-stock Companies', *Journal of the Royal Statistical Society* (1870), pp. 1–27.

Listener.

Lyon D., *The Ship: Steam, Steel and Torpedoes* (HMSO, London 1980).

Lyon D., *The Sailing Navy List, 1688–1860* (Conway, London 1993).

McClelland K., and A. Reid, 'Wood, iron and steel: technology, labour and trade union organisation in the shipbuilding industry, 1840–1914', in (eds) R. Harrison and J. Zeitlin, *Divisions of Labour* (Harvester Press, Brighton 1985), pp. 151–84

Marder A. J., *The Anatomy of British Sea Power* (Frank Cass, London 1964).

Maywald K, 'The Construction Costs and the Value of the British Merchant Fleet, 1850–1938', *Scottish Journal of Political Economy*, Vol. 3 (1956), pp. 44–66.

McGrath S. J., *The Thames Ironworks, 1880–1912* (MA Thesis, NE London Polytechnic 1983).

Memoir of the late T. J. Ditchburn (Tower Hamlets Local History Collection 902).

Middlemiss N. L., *British Shipbuilding Yards*, Vol. 3 (Shield Publications, Newcastle 1995).

More C., 'Armaments and Profits: the case of Fairfield', *Business History*, Vol. 24 (1982), pp. 175–85.

Mitchell B. R. and P. Deane, *Abstract of British Historical Statistics*, (Cambridge University Press, Cambridge 1962).

Moss M., *The Clyde: a Portrait of a River* (Canongate, Edinburgh 1997).

Murphy H., L., Johnman and A. Ritchie, 'De-accessioning and British Shipbuilding Records', in (ed.) L. M. Richmond *Proceedings of the Annual Conference 1997 of the Business Archives Council* (Business Archives Council, London 1998), pp. 159–185.

Napier D., *David Napier, Engineer 1790–1869* (James Maclehose, Glasgow 1912).

Neal F., 'Shipbuilding in the Northwest of England in the Nineteenth Century', *Research in Maritime History*, No 4 (1993), pp. 111–52.

Osbon G. A., 'The Crimean Gunboats Part I', *Mariners Mirror*, Vol. 51 (May 1965), pp. 103–15.

Osbon G. A., 'The Crimean Gunboats Part II', *Mariners Mirror*, Vol. 51 (August 1965), pp. 211–20.

Palmer S., '"The Most Indefatigable Activity": the General Steam Navigation Company, 1824–50" *Journal of Transport History* (Third series), Vol. 3, No. 2 (September 1982), pp.1–22.

Palmer S., 'Ship-building in South-east England, 1800–1913', *Research in Maritime History*, No. 4 (June 1993), pp. 45–74.

Peebles H. B., *Warship Building on the Clyde: Naval Orders and the Prosperity of the Clyde Shipbuilding Industry, 1889–1959* (Edinburgh 1987).

Peebles H. B., 'A Study in Failure: J. & G. Thomson and Shipbuilding at Clydebank, 1871–1890', *Scottish Historical Review*, Vol. 69, No. 1 (April 1990), pp. 22–48.

Petree J. Foster, 'Maudslay, Sons and Field as General Engineers', *Excerpts of the Transactions of the Newcomen Society*, Vol. 15 (1934–35).

Pewsey S., *Stratford, West Ham and the Royal Docks* (Sutton Publishing, Stroud, Gloucester, 1996).

Picture Times.

Pole W. (ed.), *The Life of Sir William Fairbairn, Bart* (David and Charles, Newton Abbott 1970).

Pollard S., 'The decline of shipbuilding on the Thames', *Economic History Review*, Second Series, Vol. 3 (1950), pp. 72–89.

Pollard S, 'Laissez-faire and shipbuilding', *Economic History Review*, Second series, Vol. 5, No. 1 (1952), pp. 98–115.

Pollard S., and P. Robertson, *The British Shipbuilding Industry, 1870–1914* (Harvard University Press, Cambridge, Mass. 1979).

Pool B., 'Navy Contracts after 1832', *Mariners Mirror*, Vol. 54, No. 3 (August 1968), pp. 209–26.

Port of London Authority Monthly.

Preston A., and J. Major, *Send a Gunboat* (Longmans, London 1967).

Rabson S., and K. O'Donoghue, *P&O: a Fleet History* (World Ship Society, Kendal Cumbria 1988).

Ritchie L. A., *The Shipbuilding Industry: a Guide to Historical Records* (Manchester University Press, Manchester 1992).

Ritchie-Noakes N., *Old Docks* (Shire Publications, Aylesbury 1987).

Rolt L. T. C., *Isambard Kingdom Brunel: a Biography* (Longmans, London 1964).

Rose M., *The East End of London* (Bath 1973).

Royal Commission on the Historical Monuments of England, *Survey of London, Vols 43 and 44 Poplar, Blackwall and the Isle of Dogs* (Athlone, London, 1994).

Russell, J. Scott, *The Modern System of Naval Architecture* (3 vols: Strangeways and Walden, London 1865).

Shannon H. A., 'The Limited Companies of 1866–83', *Economic History Review*, o.s. 4 (1933), pp. 290–316.

Sheppard F., *London 1808–1870; The Infernal Wen* (Secker and Warburg, London 1971).

Simmons J., and G. Biddle, *The Oxford Companion to British Railway History* (Oxford University Press, Oxford 1997).

Singleton J, 'Full steam ahead? The British arms industry and the market for warships, 1850–1914' in (eds) J. Brown and M. B. Rose, *Entrepreneurship, Networks and Modern Business* (Manchester University Press, Manchester 1992), pp. 229–58.

Slaven A., *The Development of the West of Scotland, 1750–1960* (London 1975).

Slaven A., 'The Shipbuilding Industry', in (ed.) R. Church, *The Dynamics of Victorian Business*, (Allen and Unwin, London 1980), pp. 107–25.

Slaven A., 'British Shipbuilders: Market Trends and Order Book Patterns between the Wars', *Journal of Transport History* Vol. 3, No. 2 (1982), pp. 37–61.

Slaven A., 'Modern British Shipbuilding 1800–1990', in (ed.) L. A. Ritchie, *The Shipbuilding Industry: a Guide to Historical Records*, (Manchester University Press, Manchester 1992), pp. 1–24.

Slaven A., 'Shipbuilding in Nineteenth-Century Scotland', *Research in Maritime History*, No. 4 (June 1993), pp. 153–76.

Smith E. C., 'Thames Steam Pioneers; Rise and Decline of a Great Industry', *Lloyds List* (13 February 1924).

Smith E. C., 'Thames Steam Pioneers; The Iron Shipbuilders', *Lloyds List* (26 March 1924).

Stern W. M., 'The First London Dock Boom and the Growth of the West India Docks', *Economica*, Vol. XIX (February 1952), pp. 59–77.

Sumida J. T., *In Defence of Naval Supremacy: Finance, Technology and British Naval Policy, 1889–1914,* (Unwin, Hyman, Boston, Mass. 1989).

Temple Bar.

Thames Ironworks Historical Catalogue, Souvenir for Festival of Empire, Crystal Palace 1911.

Thames Ironworks Quarterly Gazette, Vols 1–12 (1895–1906) and Vol. 13 (1911).

Thames Iron Works and Shipbuilding Co, Souvenir of the International Congress of Naval Architects and Marine Engineers (1897).

Thames Ironworks v *Admiralty*, (London, 1911).

Thomas S. E., Extracts from the Biography of Joseph D'Aguilar Samuda (Tower Hamlets Local History Library Collection 902).

Thomas W. A., *The Provincial Stock Exchanges* (London 1973).

Thorne W. B., *Poplar, Past and Present* (London 1937).

Times.

Times Weekly Edition.

Todd G., 'Joint Stock Companies, 1844–1900', *Economic History Review*, o.s. 4 (1932).

University of London Institute of Historical Research, *The Victoria History of the County of Essex*, Vol. 5 (Oxford University Press, Oxford 1966).

Walker F. M., *Song of the Clyde: a history of Clyde Shipbuilding* (Cambridge 1984).

Westminster Budget.

Wheatley K., *National Maritime Museum Guide to Maritime Britain* (Webb and Bower, Exeter 1990).

Working Man, The.

Yarrow A. F., 'Fast Torpedo Boats', *Cassier's Magazine* (1897), pp. 292–318.

Index

For Product Safety Concerns and Information please contact our EU representative GPSR@taylorandfrancis.com Taylor & Francis Verlag GmbH, Kaufingerstraße 24, 80331 München, Germany

T - #0118 - 160425 - C0 - 216/150/11 - PB - 9781138728165 - Gloss Lamination